AF711647

Mastering Prolog Programming

From Basics to Expert Proficiency

Copyright © 2024 by HiTeX Press
All rights reserved. No part of this publication may be reproduced, distributed, or transmitted in any form or by any means, including photocopying, recording, or other electronic or mechanical methods, without the prior written permission of the publisher, except in the case of brief quotations embodied in critical reviews and certain other noncommercial uses permitted by copyright law.

Contents

Introduction

Prolog, a programming language rooted in formal logic, offers a distinctive approach to problem-solving that emphasizes declarative programming over procedural paradigms. Developed in the early 1970s by Alain Colmerauer and Robert Kowalski, Prolog stands for "Programming in Logic." It has since become a potent tool for tasks requiring complex pattern matching, symbolic computation, and advanced problem solving. Unlike conventional programming languages, which focus on defining explicit sequences of operations, Prolog allows developers to specify what they want to achieve, leaving the determination of how to accomplish it to the language's logical inference engine.

Prolog operates on the premise of facts and rules, forming a knowledge base that can be queried to derive conclusions. Its underlying mechanism, termed "backtracking," enables efficient navigation through the search space of possible solutions, retrying alternative paths when necessary to reach a solution. This inherent ability to handle ambiguous and incomplete information makes Prolog especially suitable for applications like natural language processing, artificial intelligence, and expert systems.

The elegant simplicity of Prolog's syntax and semantics belies a powerful computational model. Variables in Prolog are logical variables, representing unknown values that can be unified with other variables or constants to satisfy conditions. Through a process known as unification, Prolog matches patterns and propagates constraints, facilitating the emergence of solutions from declarative specifications.

The objective of this book is to lead you from foundational principles to expert proficiency in Prolog programming. Each chapter builds progressively on core concepts, integrating theoretical insights with practical examples to ensure a comprehensive understanding. Starting with an introduction to Prolog's fundamental constructs, we will explore the broad landscape of logic programming, from basic syntax and data structures to advanced features like meta-programming and constraint logic programming.

Effective use of Prolog requires a shift in thinking for many programmers accustomed to procedural or object-oriented paradigms. Embracing a declarative mindset, where the focus is on what needs to be achieved rather than how, is crucial. Through detailed explanations and thoughtfully crafted exercises, this book aims to make this paradigm shift as seamless as possible.

Prolog's application potential extends across various domains. In artificial intelligence, it offers robust tools for knowledge representation and automated reasoning. In natural language processing, Prolog's pattern matching capabilities make it ideal for parsing and interpreting human languages. The ability to model complex logical relationships lends itself to creating sophisticated expert systems, capable of emulating decision-making processes of human experts.

Throughout this book, you will be encouraged to experiment with Prolog programs, reinforcing your learning through hands-on implementation. The chapters are structured to offer both breadth and depth, ensuring that you develop a well-rounded proficiency in Prolog programming.

The journey through Prolog starts here, with an exploration of its history and core concepts, setting the stage for deeper dives into its versatile programming capabilities. Whether you are a novice eager to learn a new programming language or a seasoned developer looking to expand your toolkit, this book is designed to equip you with the knowledge and skills to master Prolog programming.

Chapter 1

Introduction to Prolog

The introductory chapter provides a foundational understanding of Prolog, detailing its historical development, core principles of logic programming, and basic syntax. It guides readers through installing Prolog, writing initial programs, and familiarizes them with key concepts such as facts, rules, queries, unification, and Prolog's execution model. This foundation supports more comprehensive exploration in subsequent chapters.

1.1 The History and Evolution of Prolog

The Prolog programming language, short for *Programming in Logic*, was developed in the early 1970s by Alain Colmerauer and Philippe Roussel at the University of Marseille, France. Prolog represents one of the first forays into logic programming, a paradigm operated on the principle of declaring a set of rules and facts from which implications can be inferred. This diverges significantly from imperative programming languages that focus on explicit step-by-step instructions for computation.

Prolog's development was driven by the need for a formal language that could operationalize automated reasoning. Its foundation lies in formal logic, primarily predicate logic, which was adapted into a programmable structure. The developers drew heavily on the work of Robert Kowalski, who formalized the connection between logic and algorithms. Kowalski's contributions on the procedural interpretation of logic formed a cornerstone for Prolog's design.

The initial implementation of Prolog leveraged the concepts of resolution and unification. Resolution, a rule of inference leading to the proof of theorems, and unification, a process to make different logical expressions identical, allowed Prolog engines to efficiently query and infer solutions from given rules and facts. This was a radical departure from then-prevailing computational paradigms, moving away from algorithm-based programming to a system where relationships and constraints defined the behavior.

The first practical Prolog implementation was carried out on a DEC-10 computer and reflected fundamental operations relevant to automated theorem proving and natural language processing. These initial applications underscored Prolog's strengths in areas requiring complex logic operations and reasoning, establishing it as a robust tool for artificial intelligence research.

In 1977, David H. D. Warren produced the DEC-10 Prolog, which significantly enhanced the language's performance using the Warren Abstract Machine (WAM). The WAM represented an abstract architecture designed explicitly for efficiently executing Prolog code. It formalized the operational semantics of Prolog into a virtual machine, optimizing the language's execution through improved handling of memory and control flow. The introduction of WAM marked a pivotal evolution point, standardizing performance models and fostering broader adoption.

The 1980s witnessed Prolog's increased integration into AI research and applications, most notably through Japan's Fifth Generation Computer Systems project. This ambitious project aimed to leap-frog existing computer technologies by developing highly parallel computing architectures emphasizing declarative programming and knowledge processing. Prolog's reliance on logic-based representations and inferencing was central to these goals. Despite the project's limited long-term success, it underscored the potential of Prolog in pioneering intelligent systems and influenced subsequent research and development within the field.

During the same period, several dialects and variations of Prolog emerged to cater to specific needs or to enhance certain aspects of the language. Notable versions include Turbo Prolog (later known as PDC Prolog), which introduced strong typing to the language, and micro-Prolog, designed for microcomputers and educational settings. These variations indicated the language's flexibility and adaptability to diverse computing environments and needs.

The advancements in Prolog continued into the 1990s and beyond, with the development of ISO Prolog standardization efforts initiated around 1990, culminating in the publication of the ISO/IEC 13211-1 standard in 1995. This standardization provided a cohesive framework for Prolog's syntax and semantics, facilitating cross-implementation compatibility and fostering a more unified developer community.

Modern implementations of Prolog have continued to innovate, integrating more sophisticated optimization techniques, seamless interoperability with other programming languages, and robust development tools. Prolog environments like SWI-Prolog, GNU Prolog, and YAP have added features to improve usability, such as graphical user interfaces, debugging tools, and interfaces to external databases and networking functionalities. These advancements have ensured Prolog remains relevant, dynamically interacting with contemporary software ecosystems.

Prolog's evolution underscores its adaptability and enduring relevance. Its logic-based nature has found a persistent niche in applications requiring structured inference and deep logic processing, such as natural language understanding, machine learning, and complex problem-solving domains. Prolog's history reflects a rich journey shaped by theoretical advancements and pragmatic necessities, continuing to inform and inspire developments within logic programming and beyond.

1.2 Understanding Logic Programming

Logic programming is a programming paradigm that is fundamentally different from procedural and object-oriented programming. At its core, logic programming involves expressing facts and rules about some problem domain using logical formulas. Execution is performed by querying these facts and rules to infer new information or to find specific solutions.

Prolog (short for "Programming in Logic") is the most well-known logic programming language. To effectively understand logic programming, we need to delve into several key concepts: symbolic reasoning, declarative problem-solving, and the principles of inference engines.

Symbolic Reasoning

Symbolic reasoning entails manipulating symbols rather than numeric values, which places it in stark contrast with arithmetic-based languages like C or Java. In Prolog, symbols represent objects or relations between objects, and they are used to denote both static concepts (facts) and dynamic concepts (rules).

```
% Example of symbolic reasoning in Prolog
parent(john, doe).
parent(mary, doe).
```

In this example, parent is a symbol representing the relationship between two individuals. The interpretation of these facts can be queried to infer relationships within a family.

Declarative Problem-Solving

Declarative problem-solving is another fundamental aspect of logic programming. Instead of outlining step-by-step instructions to solve a problem (as in procedural programming), you describe the problem's properties and the logical relationships between different entities. Prolog's strength lies in its ability to define what needs to be solved rather than how to solve it.

Consider the problem of finding a child's siblings. In Prolog, we describe the problem as follows:

```
% Defining sibling relationship
sibling(X, Y) :- parent(P, X), parent(P, Y), X \= Y.
```

Here, the rule sibling(X, Y) is defined by finding a common parent P for both X and Y and ensuring that X is not equal to Y. We declare what conditions must be met for two individuals to be considered siblings, abstracting away the specific steps required to search for such pairs in a dataset.

Inference Engines

Inference engines form the operational core of logic programming languages. They resolve queries by applying inference rules to the known facts and rules. Prolog's inference engine uses a technique called backtracking combined with unification to explore possible solutions.

Backtracking

Backtracking is a method for finding all possible solutions by systematically exploring, undoing, and re-exploring decisions. Specifically, the Prolog engine will:

- Attempt to satisfy a given query using the first applicable rule.
- If the attempt fails, the engine will backtrack to try the next appli-

cable rule.

- This process continues until either a solution is found or all possibilities are exhausted.

Unification

Unification is the process through which Prolog attempts to make different logical terms conform to one another. It is central to pattern matching in Prolog. Two terms are unified if there is a substitution that makes the terms identical.

Consider the following example:

```
% Defining a simple rule
likes(john, pizza).
```

To query if john likes pizza, Prolog will unify the query likes(john, pizza) with the fact defined. If a match is found, Prolog confirms the truth of the query.

```
% Querying the fact
?- likes(john, pizza).
% Output
true.
```

If the query term does not directly match any fact, Prolog will attempt to apply any relevant rules until it either finds a match or exhausts all possibilities.

Recursion in Logic Programming

Recursion is another important concept in logic programming. Recursive rules allow Prolog to solve problems by breaking them down into smaller subproblems. For instance, consider the computation of the Fibonacci series:

```
% Defining the Fibonacci series using recursion
fib(0, 0).
fib(1, 1).
fib(N, F) :-
    N > 1,
    N1 is N - 1,
    N2 is N - 2,
    fib(N1, F1),
    fib(N2, F2),
    F is F1 + F2.
```

In this example, the $\text{fib}/2$ predicate describes both the base cases and the recursive case for computing Fibonacci numbers. $N > 1$ ensures that the recursive case is only applied for indices greater than 1, avoiding infinite recursion.

Queries and Solutions

To use Prolog effectively, one must understand how to compose and interpret queries. Queries are expressed as goals that the Prolog engine attempts to achieve through unification and backtracking.

Given our definition of the Fibonacci series, querying fib(5, F) will initiate backtracking and recursive invocations until the solution is found.

```
% Querying for the 5th Fibonacci number
?- fib(5, F).
% Output
F = 5.
```

The Prolog engine eventually computes the value for N=5 by recursively evaluating and summing smaller Fibonacci numbers, showcasing the power of logic programming in handling complex mathematical sequences using succinct declarations.

In understanding logic programming, it becomes clear that the expressiveness of Prolog stems from its foundation in symbolic reasoning, declarative problem-solving, and the power of its inference engine. This paradigm enables developers to frame solutions in terms of logical relationships and rules, abstracting away the procedural details involved in traditional programming approaches.

1.3 Basic Syntax and Structure of Prolog

Prolog, a logic programming language, is based on predicate calculus and exhibits a distinct syntax and structure compared to other programming languages. Understanding the syntax and structure of Prolog is critical for effectively writing and debugging Prolog programs. Key components include atoms, variables, facts, rules, and queries.

Atoms

Atoms are the simplest form of data in Prolog and can be constants or symbolic names. They are analogous to strings in other programming languages. Atoms can be composed of lowercase letters, digits, and underscores, and they can include special characters if enclosed in single quotes.

```
% Example of an atom
apple
'the quick brown fox'
```

Variables

Variables in Prolog start with an uppercase letter or an underscore and are placeholders for terms. Unlike atoms, variables do not have a fixed value. Here are some examples of variables in Prolog:

```
% Example of variables
X
Person
_Var
```

Facts

Facts are used to state information about objects and their relationships. A fact comprises an atom or a functor, a name followed by a list of arguments enclosed in parentheses. The arguments can be constants, variables, or complex terms. Facts always end with a period.

```
% Example of facts
parent(john, mary).
likes(mary, pizza).
```

Rules

Rules are used to express more complex relationships by defining conditions under which a statement is true. A rule consists of a head and a body, separated by the ':-' symbol. The head is a single term, while the body is a conjunction of one or more terms.

```
% Example of a rule
sibling(X, Y) :- parent(Z, X), parent(Z, Y).
```

This rule states that two individuals X and Y are siblings if they share at least one common parent Z.

Queries

Queries are used to ask questions about information defined by facts and rules. They are written in the same way as facts and rules but are used interactively in the Prolog interpreter to retrieve information.

```
% Example of a query
?- sibling(mary, john).
```

Here, Prolog will attempt to determine whether *mary* and *john* are siblings based on the defined facts and rules.

Lists

In Prolog, a list is a fundamental data structure used to store sequences of terms. A list is enclosed in square brackets, and terms within the list are separated by commas. Lists can contain any Prolog terms.

```
% Example of a list
[apple, banana, cherry]
[1, 2, 3, 4, 5]
[X, Y, Z]
```

The empty list is represented by [].

Comments

Comments are essential for explaining and documenting the code. In Prolog, comments can be either single-line or multi-line. Single-line comments start with a % symbol, while multi-line comments are enclosed within /* and */.

```
% This is a single-line comment

/*
This is a
multi-line
comment
*/
```

Operators

Prolog includes several predefined operators that facilitate various operations and comparisons. Some commonly used operators are:

- Arithmetic Operators: +, -, *, /, mod
- Comparison Operators: =, \=, <, >, =<, >=
- Logical Operators: , (AND), ; (OR), \+ (NOT)

Operators play a crucial role in defining the conditions within rules and queries.

Example: Defining and Querying Relationships

To illustrate the integration of these elements, consider the following example. We will define a family relationship and use queries to retrieve information.

```
% Facts
parent(john, mary).
parent(john, mike).
parent(mary, susan).

% Rule
grandparent(X, Y) :- parent(X, Z), parent(Z, Y).

% Query
?- grandparent(john, susan).
```

The provided query checks whether *john* is a grandparent of *susan*. Prolog evaluates the query using defined facts and rules, determining the relationships and returning the result accordingly, represented as follows:

```
true
```

This execution implies that according to the defined facts and rules, *john* is indeed a grandparent of *susan*. Mastery of Prolog's syntax and structure is essential for progressing to more advanced topics and developing complex logic programs.

1.4 Installing and Setting Up Prolog

Prolog is a robust and versatile programming language widely used in artificial intelligence, computational linguistics, and problem-solving tasks. Before diving into Prolog programming, ensuring a proper installation and setup of the Prolog environment is crucial. This section will guide you through the steps required to install and configure Prolog on various operating systems.

- Windows
- macOS
- Linux

Windows:

For Windows users, SWI-Prolog is a popular choice due to its extensive features and ease of installation. Follow these steps to install SWI-Prolog on a Windows machine:

1. Visit the SWI-Prolog download page at https://www.swi-prolog.org/Download.html.
2. Under the Windows section, download the appropriate version of the installer, typically the swipl-win64.exe for 64-bit systems.
3. After the download is complete, run the installer by double-clicking the swipl-win64.exe file.
4. Follow the on-screen instructions to complete the installation. The default settings are usually sufficient.
5. Once the installation is complete, you can verify it by opening the command prompt and typing the following command:

```
C:\> swipl
Welcome to SWI-Prolog (threaded, 64 bits, version 8.2.3)
...
?-
```

If you see the SWI-Prolog welcome message, the installation is successful.

macOS:

For macOS users, there are several methods to install SWI-Prolog, with Homebrew being a convenient package manager for this purpose.

1. Open the Terminal application.
2. Install Homebrew if not already installed by running the following command:

```
/bin/bash -c "$(curl -fsSL https://raw.githubusercontent.com/Homebrew/install/
    master/install.sh)"
```

1. Once Homebrew installation is complete, install SWI-Prolog by running:

```
brew install swi-prolog
```

1. After the installation is complete, verify it by typing the following command in the terminal:

```
swipl
```

You should see the SWI-Prolog welcome message, indicating a successful installation.

Linux:

For Linux users, installing SWI-Prolog can vary slightly depending on the distribution. This section covers the installation process for Debian-based distributions, such as Ubuntu, and Red Hat-based distributions, such as Fedora.

Debian/Ubuntu:

1. Open a terminal window.
2. Update the package list by running:

```
sudo apt-get update
```

1. Install SWI-Prolog by running:

```
sudo apt-get install swi-prolog
```

1. After the installation is complete, verify it by typing:

```
swipl
```

The SWI-Prolog welcome message should be displayed, confirming the installation.

Fedora:

1. Open a terminal window.

2. Install SWI-Prolog by running:

```
sudo dnf install swi-prolog
```

1. Verify the installation by typing:

```
swipl
```

The presence of the SWI-Prolog welcome message will confirm a successful installation.

Configuring the Prolog Environment:

Post-installation configuration enhances the usability and efficiency of the Prolog environment.

- Setting Up the Path:
  Ensure that the Prolog executable is in your system's PATH environment variable. This allows you to run Prolog from any terminal or command prompt.

Windows:

1. Open System Properties by right-clicking 'This PC' and selecting 'Properties.'
2. Click 'Advanced system settings' and then 'Environment Variables.'
3. Under 'System variables,' find and select the 'Path' variable, then click 'Edit.'
4. Add the path to the SWI-Prolog bin directory (e.g., C:\Program Files\swipl\bin) and click 'OK.'

- macOS/Linux:

```
echo 'export PATH="/usr/local/bin/swipl:$PATH"' >> ~/.bash_profile
source ~/.bash_profile
```

- Installing an Integrated Development Environment (IDE):
  IDEs streamline development with features like syntax highlighting, debugging, and project management.

SWI-Prolog's Built-in IDE:

SWI-Prolog comes with its built-in graphical interface. You can start it by running:

```
swipl-win
```

- External Editors:
  Alternatively, Atom, Visual Studio Code, and Emacs support Prolog development through plugins and extensions.

Atom:

1. Install the ide-prolog package via the Atom package manager.

Visual Studio Code:

1. Install the vscode-prolog plugin from the Visual Studio Code marketplace.

Emacs:

1. Enable Prolog mode by adding the following lines to your Emacs configuration file:

```
(add-to-list 'load-path "/usr/local/share/emacs/site-lisp")
(require 'prolog)
(setq prolog-system 'swi)
```

Following these steps to install and set up Prolog will prepare your development environment to effectively write and execute Prolog programs.

1.5 Writing Your First Prolog Program

To begin writing a Prolog program, we must first understand its fundamental building blocks: facts, rules, and queries. These components form the basis of any Prolog program and enable us to define relationships and infer new information from known data.

A Prolog program is essentially a database of facts and rules against which queries are executed. Let's explore the process of creating a simple Prolog program:

- Start by declaring some basic facts.
- Define rules that describe relationships between those facts.
- Perform queries on the data to extract meaningful information.

We will illustrate these steps with a classic example relating to family relationships.

Step 1: Declaring Facts

Facts in Prolog are used to assert information about objects or relationships. Each fact is written as a predicate followed by its arguments, enclosed in parentheses and terminated with a period. For instance, let's define some family relationships:

```
parent(tom, bob).
parent(bob, alice).
parent(alice, john).
parent(john, kate).
```

In this example, parent/2 is a predicate representing the parent-child relationship, with the first argument being the parent and the second argument being the child. The term parent/2 denotes that the parent predicate takes two arguments.

Step 2: Defining Rules

Rules are used to describe relationships based on one or more facts. They consist of a head and a body, separated by the :- symbol. The head represents the conclusion that can be drawn if the body is true. For example, we can define a rule to determine if one person is an ancestor of another:

```
ancestor(X, Y) :- parent(X, Y).
ancestor(X, Y) :- parent(X, Z), ancestor(Z, Y).
```

This rule states that:

- X is an ancestor of Y if X is a parent of Y.
- X is an ancestor of Y if X is a parent of Z and Z is an ancestor of Y.

The first line is a base case stating a direct parent-child relationship as an ancestor relationship. The second line is a recursive case ensuring that indirect ancestors are also recognized.

Step 3: Performing Queries

Once we have defined our facts and rules, we can write queries to extract information from our Prolog program. Queries are posed in the same form as facts and rules but do not end with a period. Instead, they end with a question mark and are executed in the Prolog environment.

To check if alice is an ancestor of kate, the query would be:

```
?- ancestor(alice, kate).
```

Upon executing this query, Prolog will return the result based on the defined facts and rules. The output may look like:

```
true.
```

This tells us that alice is indeed an ancestor of kate.

We can also ask Prolog more general queries, such as finding all descendents of a particular ancestor:

```
?- ancestor(bob, X).
```

Prolog will respond with all possible values of X that satisfy the ancestor relationship with bob:

```
X = alice ;
X = john ;
X = kate.
```

Here, the semicolon (;) indicates that there are multiple solutions. The user can press ;, Enter or the appropriate key for their Prolog interpreter to see the next solution.

Practical Example: Defining Sibling Relationships

To further illustrate writing Prolog programs, let's define sibling relationships. Siblings share at least one parent. We can define this with a rule:

```
sibling(X, Y) :- parent(Z, X), parent(Z, Y), X \= Y.
```

In this rule:

- X and Y are siblings if Z is a parent of both X and Y.
- X Y ensures that the two siblings are not the same individual.

To find out if bob and alice are siblings, we perform the query:

```
?- sibling(bob, alice).
```

Given the facts defined earlier, Prolog will respond with:

```
false.
```

This is because there is no common parent between bob and alice defined in the facts. However, if we add another fact:

```
parent(tom, alice).
```

Then, executing the query again will give:

```
true.
```

We can also pose a more generalized query to discover siblings for a given individual:

```
?- sibling(alice, X).
```

The response from Prolog might be:

```
X = bob.
```

This demonstrates the agility of Prolog in handling complex relationships through its logical inferences. Understanding how to declare facts, define rules, and perform queries is foundational to mastering Prolog programming.

1.6 Prolog Development Environments

An efficient and well-structured development environment is crucial for leveraging the full capabilities of Prolog. This section explores various development environments available for Prolog, highlighting their features, advantages, and how to set them up. By understanding these tools, developers can enhance their productivity and facilitate debugging, testing, and deploying Prolog programs.

SWI-Prolog

SWI-Prolog is one of the most widely used Prolog environments. Its rich feature set makes it suitable for both beginners and advanced users. To install SWI-Prolog, navigate to the SWI-Prolog download page and choose the appropriate version for your operating system.

After installation, you can start the SWI-Prolog interpreter by typing swipl in your terminal or command prompt. Once inside the interpreter, you can load Prolog files and run queries directly.

```
?- [my_program].
% my_program compiled 0.00 sec, 0 clauses
true.
```

```
?- my_predicate(X).
```

The output from the above interactive session would be displayed as:

```
X = value ;
false.
```

SWI-Prolog also includes an integrated development environment (IDE) called PceEmacs, offering features like syntax highlighting, code completion, and debugging tools. To open the IDE, run:

```
?- emacs.
```

GNU Prolog

GNU Prolog is another popular choice, known for its efficient compiler and ISO standard compliance. GNU Prolog can be downloaded from the GNU Prolog official page. The installation process depends on the operating system:

For Unix-based systems:

```
$ tar -xvzf gprolog-X.X.X.tar.gz
$ cd gprolog-X.X.X
$ ./configure
$ make
$ sudo make install
```

For Windows, an executable installer is available.

To start the GNU Prolog interpreter, type gprolog in the terminal. The usage is similar to SWI-Prolog:

```
| ?- [my_program].
compiling /path/to/my_program.pl for byte code...
/path/to/my_program.pl compiled, 0 lines read - 1234 bytes written, 9 ms

yes
| ?- my_predicate(X).
```

```
X = value

yes
```

GNU Prolog also supports creating standalone executables from Prolog programs, which can be particularly useful for deploying applications.

SICStus Prolog

SICStus Prolog is a high-performance implementation used extensively in industrial applications. It is a commercial product, and its installation requires a valid license, available from the SICStus Prolog website.

To start SICStus Prolog, run:

```
$ sicstus
```

You can load files and run queries similarly to the other Prolog environments:

```
| ?- [my_program].
% consulting /path/to/my_program.pl
| ?- my_predicate(X).
```

X = value ;
no

SICStus Prolog provides extensive libraries and development tools that support constraint programming, a powerful feature for solving combinatorial problems.

ECLiPSe Prolog

ECLiPSe Prolog focuses on constraint logic programming and offers a robust environment for developing complex applications. ECLiPSe can be downloaded from the ECLiPSe website.

To install ECLiPSe on a Unix-based system:

```
$ tar -xvzf eclipseclp.X.X.X.tar.gz
$ cd eclipseclp_X_X_X
$ ./INSTALL
```

Once installed, run eclipse to start the interpreter:

```
[eclipse]: [my_program].
source_converter.pl compiled traceable 756 bytes in 0.00 seconds

[eclipse]: my_predicate(X).
```

X = value

yes (more solutions?)

ECLiPSe includes a graphical interface, TkECLiPSe, providing a more user-friendly experience. It supports interactive debugging and visualizations of search trees, which can aid in better understanding and optimizing complex constraint logic programs.

Online Development Environments

For users who prefer not to install Prolog on their local machines, several online Prolog development environments are available. Examples include:

- SWISH (SWI-Prolog for SHaring): An online collaborative environment available at SWISH, allowing users to write and share Prolog code in their browsers.

- TDDB: Online platform for running Prolog queries directly, providing a simple interface for learning and experimenting with Prolog.

These platforms offer the convenience of accessing Prolog development tools from any device with an internet connection, making them ideal for educational purposes and lightweight development tasks.

Fine-tuning the development environment to match project requirements and personal preferences can greatly enhance the efficiency and effectiveness of working with Prolog. Selecting the right tools and mastering their features enables developers to focus on solving problems and harnessing the full potential of logic programming.

1.7 Key Concepts: Facts, Rules, and Queries

Prolog programming relies fundamentally on three core constructs: *facts*, *rules*, and *queries*. Understanding these concepts is essential for mastering Prolog and forms the basis for more advanced topics. Each concept plays a significant role in the logical flow and structure of Prolog programs.

Facts represent the simplest form of statements in Prolog. They express basic assertions or truths about the world. Each fact is a predicate that denotes a specific relationship between objects. Facts can be understood as known information that the Prolog database stores. For instance:

```
parent(john, mary).
parent(mary, susan).
```

In this example, parent(john, mary) and parent(mary, susan) are facts indicating that John is a parent of Mary and Mary is a parent of Susan. The predicate parent/2, where /2 indicates arity (number of arguments), describes a parent-child relationship.

Rules provide a way to define relationships between facts through logical inference. A rule in Prolog consists of a head and a body, separated by the symbol :-. The head represents the conclusion, while the body contains a conjunction of goals that need to be satisfied for the rule to hold true. Rules enable the derivation of new knowledge from existing facts. Consider the following example:

```
ancestor(X, Y) :- parent(X, Y).
ancestor(X, Y) :- parent(X, Z), ancestor(Z, Y).
```

Here, the predicate ancestor/2 defines an ancestor relationship. The first rule states that X is an ancestor of Y if X is a parent of Y. The second rule recursively defines an ancestor relationship by stating that X is an ancestor of Y if X is a parent of Z and Z is an ancestor of Y.

Queries allow users to extract information from the Prolog database by posing questions about the facts and rules defined. A query typically seeks to determine if a certain condition holds true based on the existing knowledge. Queries are executed by presenting a goal to the Prolog interpreter, which attempts to satisfy the goal using the available facts and rules. For example:

```
?- parent(john, mary).
```

The query ?- parent(john, mary) asks if John is a parent of Mary. The Prolog interpreter responds with true or false based on the defined facts. Queries can also include variables to request more generalized information:

```
?- parent(X, mary).
```

In this instance, ?- parent(X, mary) asks for all entities X that are parents of Mary. The interpreter returns X = john, providing the matching result.

Prolog's mechanism of *unification* plays a crucial role when processing facts, rules, and queries. Unification is the process of matching terms (constants, variables, and structures) by finding a consistent assignment of variables that makes the terms identical. When evaluating a query, Prolog attempts to unify the query with the relevant facts and rules.

For example, consider the query:

```
?- ancestor(john, susan).
```

Prolog will first attempt to match this query with the head of the ancestor rules. It quickly determines that ancestor(john, susan) :- parent(john, susan) does not hold since parent(john, susan) is not a fact. Next, Prolog attempts the second rule and unifies X with john, Y with susan, leading it to check the subgoal parent(john, Z). This part successfully unifies Z with mary, then continues to verify if ancestor(mary, susan) holds, eventually confirming this by matching it against the parent(mary, susan) fact.

Presenting well-formed queries and writing rules requires a careful understanding of logical relationships and rule recursion to ensure the program executes as intended. Queries drive the execution, as Prolog will dynamically search and infer solutions based on all available information.

Therefore, facts, rules, and queries not only constitute the framework through which Prolog operates, but they also embody the interpretive mechanism of Prolog as a logic programming language, leading logically from established truths to new conclusions and answers.

1.8 Understanding Unification in Prolog

Unification is a fundamental concept in Prolog, enabling the matching of terms, instantiating variables, and thus driving the inference engine. Unification in Prolog tries to make two terms identical by finding a consistent assignment to the variables involved. During this process, Prolog decides if the terms can be made equivalent and, if so, provides the necessary variable bindings.

To comprehend unification thoroughly, it is crucial to first understand the types of terms in Prolog. Terms can be atoms, numbers, variables, or compound terms. Atoms are constants and can be an integer, a floating-point number, or a symbolic identifier. Variables are placeholders for terms and must start with an uppercase letter or an underscore. Compound terms have a functor and a fixed number of arguments (arity), written in the form functor(arg1, arg2, ...,argN).

Consider these basic unification principles:

- An atom unifies with itself.
- A variable unifies with any term.
- Two compound terms unify if they share the same functor and arity, and their corresponding arguments unify.

The unification of two terms follows the elimination of differences between them by applying a series of substitutions until the terms are identical or until no further simplifications are possible.

Let's illustrate unification with a few examples. Suppose we have the query:

```
?- X = 5.
```

Here, the variable X unifies with the number 5, binding X to 5. The output is:

```
X = 5
```

Consider another example:

```
?- father(john, X) = father(john, mary).
```

In this case, Prolog attempts to unify the two terms father(john, X) and father(john, mary). The functor father and the first arguments john are identical, so unification requires the second arguments X and mary to unify. Consequently, X is bound to mary, resulting in:

```
X = mary
```

Now, consider a case where unification fails.

```
?- father(john, X) = father(mary, Y).
```

Here, the functor father is the same, but the first arguments john and mary are different atoms. Prolog concludes that unification is not possible, as these constants do not match.

Unification also works for compound terms with multiple arguments. Examine the query:

```
?- parent(father(john), mother(mary)) = parent(father(F), mother(M)).
```

This term involves several nested compound terms. Prolog performs unification by recursively unifying each component. The functors parent match, and each nested term also matches. As a result, F is unified with john and M with mary, giving:

```
F = john,
M = mary
```

To delve deeper into the implementation, the following pseudocode describes the unification algorithm using the algorithm2e package in LaTeX:

```
Function Unify(Term1, Term2):
    if Term1 and Term2 are identical then
        return True;
    else if Term1 is a variable then
        Bind Term1 to Term2;
        return True;
    else if Term2 is a variable then
        Bind Term2 to Term1;
        return True;
    else if Term1 and Term2 are compound terms with the
     same functor and arity then
        for all corresponding arguments (Arg1, Arg2) do
            if Unify(Arg1, Arg2) is False then
                return False;
        return True;
    else
        return False;
```

This algorithm describes the core steps for unifying two terms, relying on recursive calls to handle compound terms.

Unification in Prolog extends to more nuanced scenarios involving lists and arithmetic expressions. For instance, consider the query involving lists:

```
?- [H|T] = [apples, oranges, bananas].
```

Here, the head H is unified with apples, and the tail T is unified with [oranges, bananas], yielding:

```
H = apples,
T = [oranges, bananas]
```

This demonstrates Prolog's powerful ability to destructure lists, enabling elegant manipulation and matching of list elements within queries and rules.

Understanding unification is pivotal for effective Prolog programming as it underpins the language's pattern matching and logical inference capabilities. As programs grow in complexity, a solid grasp of unification ensures that more sophisticated queries and data structures operate correctly, adhering to Prolog's logical foundations.

1.9 Basics of Pattern Matching

Pattern matching in Prolog is a core component that drives the process of unification and logical inference. Building on the foundational concepts introduced earlier, this section delves deeply into understanding the mechanics and applications of pattern matching within Prolog.

Pattern matching allows Prolog to discern similarities between different data structures, facilitating the unification process fundamental to logic programming. When Prolog attempts to satisfy a query, it checks if the terms can be made identical through pattern matching.

A term in Prolog can be an atom, a number, a variable, or a complex term (composite structure built from functors and smaller terms). Pattern matching occurs during the comparison of these terms. Below, we enumerate the types of terms and the specific rules governing their pattern matching.

- **Atoms and Numbers**: Two atoms or numbers match if and only if they are identical.

```
?- foo = foo.
true.

?- 42 = 42.
true.
```

- **Variables**: A variable matches any term and gets instantiated (bound) to that term if it was previously uninstantiated. If already instantiated, it must match the term to which it is bound.

```
?- X = atom.
X = atom.

?- X = 5, X = 5.
X = 5.

?- X = 5, X = 10.
false.
```

- **Complex Terms**: Recursively match if they share the same functor and arity (number of arguments), and their corresponding arguments match.

```
?- foo(a, b) = foo(a, b).
true.

?- foo(X, b) = foo(a, Y).
X = a,
Y = b.
```

To illustrate pattern matching more comprehensively, consider the following Prolog code snippet:

```
parent_child(parent(tom), child(sam)).
parent_child(parent(bob), child(tina)).

?- parent_child(parent(tom), X).
```

The query ?- parent_child(parent(tom), X). examines the parent_child facts, looking for patterns that match the term parent(tom). The first fact matches, and X is instantiated to child(sam), producing:

```
X = child(sam).
```

Understanding the manner in which Prolog matches patterns is crucial in writing effective programs. Pattern matching in the declarative paradigm harnessed by Prolog ensures that mechanisms tied to data retrieval and logical inference remain both robust and intuitive.

Important considerations during pattern matching are the scope and lifecycle of variables and their bindings:

- **Variable Scope**: A variable in Prolog has local scope within the clause where it is defined. Different variables with the same name in separate clauses or predicates do not interfere with each other.

  ```
  mother(jane, alice).
  father(jane, bob).
  siblings(A, B) :- mother(M, A), mother(M, B),
                    father(F, A), father(F, B), A \neq B.
  ```

  In the example, variables M and F are scoped locally within their respective clauses.

- **Variable Binding Lifecycle**: The lifecycle of a variable's binding exists until the completion of the goal in which it was instantiated or until backtracking occurs. Once backtracking happens, Prolog retracts the most recent instantiation, allowing the variable to be re-bound as needed for further attempts to satisfy the goal.

To better understand backtracking with pattern matching, examine this recursive Prolog definition of the member predicate:

```
member(X, [X|_]).
member(X, [_|T]) :- member(X, T).

?- member(a, [b, a, c]).
```

The query ?- member(a, [b, a, c]). attempts to match a with the head of the list. It fails on the first attempt (head b) causing Prolog to backtrack, then succeeds on the second attempt (head a). The output showcases successful pattern matching after a backtracking step:

```
true.
```

Intrinsic to pattern matching is wildcard usage, represented using the underscore (_) character, denoting an anonymous variable that can match any term but is neither stored nor reused:

```
?- parent_child(parent(_), child(tina)).
```

The query would succeed as it searches for any instance where a parent can be ignored while focusing on child(tina).

Refinement in pattern matching is achievable through constraint introduction and compound conditions ensuring robust and dynamic unifications. Mastery of pattern matching significantly fortifies the proficiency with which Prolog programs address and solve complex logical queries.

1.10 Prolog's Execution Model

Prolog's execution model is rooted in the principles of symbolic logic and resolution. It employs a depth-first search strategy that seeks to resolve goals recursively by matching them against facts and rules defined in the program database. Understanding Prolog's execution model is crucial for debugging, program optimization, and effective problem-solving.

Resolution Strategy and SLD-Resolution (Selective Linear Definite clause resolution)

Prolog utilizes SLD-Resolution, a refinement of the resolution principle which is tuned specifically for definite clauses (clauses with exactly one positive literal). This approach forms the backbone of how Prolog answers queries. The process can be described succinctly through several steps:

- **Goal Selection**: The leftmost goal in the query is selected for resolution.
- **Unification**: Prolog attempts to unify the selected goal with the head of a rule or a fact.
- **Substitution**: If unification succeeds, the goal is replaced by the

body of the rule (applying the necessary substitutions).

- **Backtracking**: If unification fails or subsequent goals cannot be resolved, Prolog backtracks to the previous choice point and attempts the next alternative.

Example Execution

Consider a simple Prolog program consisting of the following facts and rules:

```
parent(tom, bob).
parent(bob, alice).
ancestor(X, Y) :- parent(X, Y).
ancestor(X, Y) :- parent(X, Z), ancestor(Z, Y).
```

To query whether tom is an ancestor of alice, we use the following query:

```
?- ancestor(tom, alice).
```

Prolog's execution for this query involves several steps which we will detail below.

```
1. The goal "ancestor(tom, alice)" is selected.
2. Attempt unification with "ancestor(X, Y) :- parent(X, Y)."
   - Substitution: {X/tom, Y/alice}
   - Check if "parent(tom, alice)" is a fact - fails.
3. Attempt unification with "ancestor(X, Y) :- parent(X, Z), ancestor(Z, Y)."
   - Substitution: {X/tom, Y/alice}
   - Resolve "parent(tom, Z)" to find Z:
     - Z = bob (matches the fact "parent(tom, bob)"), substitution: {Z/bob}
   - Continue with new goal "ancestor(bob, alice)"
4. The goal "ancestor(bob, alice)" is selected.
5. Attempt unification with "ancestor(X, Y) :- parent(X, Y)."
   - Substitution: {X/bob, Y/alice}
   - Check if "parent(bob, alice)" is a fact - succeeds.
6. Since all goals are resolved, the query succeeds with the reported answer: "true".
```

Backtracking Mechanism

Prolog's backtracking mechanism ensures that all potential solutions to a query are explored. If Prolog encounters a failure at any point in its process, it backtracks to the most recent choice point, reattempts alternative clauses or facts, and proceeds forward again. This behavior can be illustrated via modifying the previous example:

```
parent(tom, bob).
parent(bob, alice).
parent(jane, alice).
ancestor(X, Y) :- parent(X, Y).
ancestor(X, Y) :- parent(X, Z), ancestor(Z, Y).
```

Querying for =ancestor(tom, alice)=:

```
?- ancestor(tom, alice).
```

Prolog's backtracking in this case:

```
1. The goal "ancestor(tom, alice)" is selected.
2. Attempt unification with "ancestor(X, Y) :- parent(X, Y)."
   - Substitution: {X/tom, Y/alice}
   - Check if "parent(tom, alice)" is a fact - fails.
3. Attempt unification with "ancestor(X, Y) :- parent(X, Z), ancestor(Z, Y)."
   - Substitution: {X/tom, Y/alice}
   - Resolve "parent(tom, Z)" to find Z:
     - Z = bob (matches the fact "parent(tom, bob)"), substitution: {Z/bob}
   - Continue with new goal "ancestor(bob, alice)"
4. The goal "ancestor(bob, alice)" is selected.
5. Attempt unification with "ancestor(X, Y) :- parent(X, Y)."
   - Substitution: {X/bob, Y/alice}
   - Check if "parent(bob, alice)" is a fact - succeeds.
6. The query initially succeeds with the answer "true".
7. Prolog is ready for backtracking.
8. The goal "ancestor(tom, alice)" is then re-evaluated for any other valid ancestors:
9. Revisits "parent(tom, bob)"; Z is now explored further.
10. Ancestor(jane,alice) confirmed to backtrace all paths.
```

Cut Operator for Controlling Search

Prolog provides the cut operator, denoted by !, to control the backtracking. When Prolog encounters a cut during execution, it discards all choice points generated by the current goal and proceeds without considering alternatives. This operator is particularly useful for optimizing programs and preventing redundant searches.

Example usage of the cut operator:

```
ancestor(X, Y) :- parent(X, Y).
ancestor(X, Y) :- parent(X, Z), !, ancestor(Z, Y).
```

Querying for $ancestor\{tom, alice\}$ again would produce:

```
1. The goal "ancestor(tom, alice)" is selected.
2. Attempt unification with the first clause - fails.
3. Unified with second clause, but involves cut!
4. Once "ancestor(bob, alice)" confirms, any backtrack points are dropped.
5. No alternatives past cut are explored after valid goal resolution.
```

Understanding Prolog's execution model, including SLD-Resolution, backtracking, and the cut operator, equips the programmer to harness the full power of logical programming. This knowledge is essential for developing efficient and effective Prolog programs by ensuring control over the logical flow and search space.

Chapter 2

Basic Concepts of Prolog Programming

This chapter introduces the essential elements of Prolog programming, including atoms, numbers, variables, facts, rules, and queries. It explains variable binding, the scope of variables, and the mechanics of backtracking. The chapter also covers anonymous variables, compound terms, predicate logic, built-in predicates, the cut operator, and how to combine facts, rules, and queries effectively.

2.1 Understanding Atoms, Numbers, and Variables

In Prolog, understanding the fundamental elements such as atoms, numbers, and variables is essential. These elements form the building blocks of Prolog programs and are crucial in defining the facts, rules, and queries that make up a knowledge base. Let's delve deeply into each of these concepts to provide a clear and thorough understanding.

Atoms are the simplest indivisible units in Prolog and represent constants. They can be thought of as symbolic names and are used to denote objects, relations, or functions. Atoms are case-sensitive and can be written in several ways:

- A sequence of lowercase letters, digits, and underscores, starting with a lowercase letter, such as atom_example.
- Enclosed within single quotes if they contain special characters, uppercase letters, or spaces, such as 'Atom Example' or 'Special#Char'.
- Special characters by themselves or in a sequence, such as !, +, :-.

Examples:

```
atom_example.
'anotherAtom'.
'Complex Atom Example'.
!.
+.
:-.
```

Numbers in Prolog represent numeric constants and can be either integers or floating-point numbers. Prolog handles numeric operations and comparisons directly. Numbers are straightforward; they do not have any special syntactic representation beyond the standard forms recognizable from mathematics:

Examples:

```
123.
-456.
0.
7.89.
-3.14.
```

Variables in Prolog hold values and are crucial for pattern matching and unification. A variable name starts with an uppercase letter or an underscore. They can be bound to values (including other variables) during execution, and this binding can change within the scope of a predicate or between predicates due to Prolog's backtracking mechanism. If a variable is not bound to a value, it is considered free.

Examples:

```
X.
Person.
_.
Var_name.
```

Understanding how Prolog handles variable binding and unification is vital. When a variable is unified with a value, it retains that value for the duration of its scope unless backtracking occurs. Backtracking can unbind variables, allowing them to be bound again to different values.

Examples of variable binding:

```
likes(john, apple).
likes(jane, banana).
likes(X, apple). % X will be unified with john
```

In the above example, querying likes(X, apple) will bind X to john. If backtracking occurs, Prolog will attempt to find another value for X that satisfies the predicate.

The scope of a variable is limited to the clause in which it appears. Variables do not retain their bindings across different clauses unless explicitly passed and unified.

These fundamental elements in Prolog offer significant flexibility in how facts, rules, and queries are constructed. Effective usage of atoms, numbers, and variables allows you to create more complex and powerful knowledge bases in Prolog, facilitating sophisticated pattern matching and logical inference.

Here is a simple example integrating atoms, numbers, and variables:

```
% Facts
person(john).
person(jane).
age(john, 30).
age(jane, 25).

% Rule
older(X, Y) :-
    age(X, AgeX),
    age(Y, AgeY),
    AgeX > AgeY.

% Queries
?- person(X).
% Expected Output:
% X = john ;
% X = jane.

?- age(X, 25).
% Expected Output:
% X = jane.

?- older(john, jane).
% Expected Output:
% true.

?- older(jane, john).
% Expected Output:
% false.
```

In this example, john and jane are atoms representing individual persons. The numbers 30 and 25 are associated with these persons representing their ages. The variables X and Y are used to create rules and make queries against these facts.

Thus, understanding how atoms, numbers, and variables function in Prolog equips you with the necessary tools to create and manipulate knowledge bases effectively.

2.2 Defining and Using Facts

Facts represent atomic propositions or assertions about the world in Prolog, establishing basic relationships between objects. In Prolog, facts are the simplest components used to describe the world's state. A fact essentially states that something is true. Facts do not contain variables, only atoms, and numbers.

Syntax of Facts: A Prolog fact typically takes the form of a predicate followed by its arguments, terminated with a period. The general syntax is:

$$\text{predicate(argument1, argument2, ..., argumentN).}$$

Examples of Facts: Consider a simple example that defines family relationships:

```
% Defining parent-child relationships
parent(tom, lily).
parent(mary, lily).
parent(mary, john).

% Defining gender
female(lily).
female(mary).
male(tom).
male(john).
```

In the given example, parent/2 is a predicate with arity 2, indicating it takes two arguments. The arguments tom, mary, lily, and john are atoms representing individuals. Similarly, the predicates female/1 and male/1 indicate the gender of individuals, with arity 1.

Querying Facts: We can extract information from the defined facts using queries. A query in Prolog tests whether certain facts hold in the database. Queries are posed using the '?-' prompt, followed by a predicate and its arguments.

```
% Querying the Prolog database
?- parent(tom, lily).
True.
```

```
?- parent(mary, john).
True.

?- parent(tom, john).
False.
```

In the example, querying parent(tom, lily) returns True because it directly matches the fact stated in the database. Conversely, querying parent(tom, john) returns False because no such fact exists in the database.

Facts with Numbers: Facts can also involve numerical arguments. Consider an example involving the ages of individuals:

```
% Defining ages
age(tom, 40).
age(mary, 38).
age(lily, 10).
age(john, 15).
```

Here, the age/2 predicate denotes the ages of individuals, with the second argument being a number.

Combining Facts: Facts can be combined to form more complex relationships. For instance, we can define if an individual is a mother, father, or sibling based on existing facts:

```
% Defining complex relationships
mother(X, Y) :-
    parent(X, Y),
    female(X).

father(X, Y) :-
    parent(X, Y),
    male(X).

sibling(X, Y) :-
    parent(Z, X),
    parent(Z, Y),
    X \= Y.
```

Here, rules such as mother/2 and father/2 extend the definition of parent/2 by adding conditions about gender. The sibling/2 predicate establishes if two individuals share the same parent but are not the same individual.

Negation of Facts: In Prolog, negation can be used to query the absence of a fact. This uses the built-in predicate \+/1 which denotes negation as failure. For instance:

```
% Querying negated facts
?- \+ parent(tom, john).
True.
```

The query $\backslash+$ parent(tom, john) checks if tom is not a parent of john, returning True because no such parent-child relationship is defined in the database.

Developing a clear understanding of the structure, querying, and combination of facts is pivotal for constructing more advanced Prolog programs. Concepts such as rules and queries build upon these foundational elements to define complex logic and inference mechanisms within the Prolog system. Understanding the intricate mechanics of defining and utilizing facts provides a robust basis for mastering Prolog's logical reasoning capabilities.

2.3 Defining and Using Rules

A rule in Prolog serves as a formal statement that relates a conclusion to a set of conditions. Rules are fundamental to Prolog's declarative nature, facilitating logical inference based on given facts and relationships. Rules are constructed using a head and a body, connected by the ':-' operator, which is read as "if".

The syntax of a rule is:

```
head :- body.
```

Here, the head is a single goal, and the body is a conjunction of one or more goals. The rule states that the head is true if the body is true.

Consider the example of defining the rule is_parent:

```
parent(X, Y) :- father(X, Y).
parent(X, Y) :- mother(X, Y).
```

In this example, two rules are defined for the parent/2 predicate. The first rule states that X is a parent of Y if X is the father of Y. The second rule asserts that X is a parent of Y if X is the mother of Y.

Rules enable abstraction and reduce redundancy by capturing recurring logical patterns. In larger programs, this abstraction facilitates maintenance and readability.

Unification in Rules A critical mechanism behind Prolog rules is unification. Unification attempts to make different terms identical by finding a suitable substitution for the variables. This feature is crucial when matching the head of a rule with a query. Consider the rule:

```
ancestor(X, Y) :- parent(X, Y).
```

```
ancestor(X, Y) :- parent(X, Z), ancestor(Z, Y).
```

This example introduces recursive rules for the ancestor/2 predicate. The first rule states that X is an ancestor of Y if X is a direct parent of Y. The second rule states that X is an ancestor of Y if X is a parent of some Z, and Z is an ancestor of Y. This recursive definition enables the inference of ancestral relationships across multiple generations.

Ordering and Execution of Rules Prolog's execution model follows a top-down approach where it attempts to satisfy goals by trying rules in the order they are defined until a match is found. Consider:

```
sibling(X, Y) :- parent(Z, X), parent(Z, Y), X \= Y.
elder_sibling(X, Y) :- sibling(X, Y), age(X, AgeX), age(Y, AgeY), AgeX > AgeY.
```

The sibling/2 rule states that X and Y are siblings if they share a common parent Z and are not the same individual (X Y). The elder_sibling/2 rule builds upon this definition by adding conditions that X and Y are siblings and that X is older than Y.

Combining Facts and Rules Effective Prolog programs interleave facts and rules to model complex relationships. Consider the family tree modeling:

```
% Facts
father(john, mary).
mother(susan, mary).
father(john, mark).
mother(susan, mark).

% Rules
parent(X, Y) :- father(X, Y).
parent(X, Y) :- mother(X, Y).
sibling(X, Y) :- parent(Z, X), parent(Z, Y), X \= Y.
```

Given these facts and rules, a query:

```
?- sibling(mary, mark).
```

Prolog evaluates the sibling(mary, mark) query by first matching it with the sibling/2 rule. It verifies that mary and mark share common parents john and susan, confirming them as siblings.

Cut Operator in Rules The cut operator (!) is used within rules to control backtracking, providing a way to optimize program behavior by pruning unnecessary computations. For instance:

```
max(X, Y, X) :- X >= Y, !.
max(_, Y, Y).
```

In this example, the max/3 predicate determines the maximum of two numbers. If X is greater than or equal to Y, the first rule succeeds and the cut operator prevents further backtracking, ensuring the next rule won't be attempted.

Prolog rules empower the modeling of intricate logical relationships and support advanced inference capabilities, critical for solving complex problems efficiently.

2.4 Formulating Queries to Extract Information

In Prolog, queries are the primary means for retrieving information from a knowledge base composed of facts and rules. A query, also referred to as a goal, asks the Prolog system whether certain facts hold true or whether certain predicates can be satisfied based on the given rules and facts.

A basic query in Prolog takes the form of a goal, which Prolog attempts to satisfy by searching through its set of known facts and rules. When Prolog finds a match, it confirms the query by returning true; otherwise, it returns false.

To illustrate the formulation of queries, consider the following simple database:

```
% Facts
parent(john, mary).
parent(jane, mary).
parent(mary, lisa).
parent(mary, tom).

% Rules
ancestor(X, Y) :-
    parent(X, Y).
ancestor(X, Y) :-
    parent(X, Z),
    ancestor(Z, Y).
```

In this example, the database contains four facts indicating parent-child relationships and a rule defining the ancestor predicate. The rule for ancestor states that an ancestor is either a direct parent or a parent of an ancestor.

To extract information using queries, we proceed by formulating goals that Prolog can attempt to satisfy. Here are some examples of queries based on our database:

1. **Simple Query for Facts:**

```
?- parent(john, mary).
```

Prolog will search for a fact that matches parent(john, mary). Since such a fact exists in the database, Prolog returns:

```
true.
```

2. **Query for Rules:**

```
?- ancestor(john, lisa).
```

Prolog utilizes the defined rules to verify this query. It finds that John is a parent of Mary, who is in turn a parent of Lisa. Therefore, Prolog returns:

```
true.
```

3. **Query with Variables:**

```
?- parent(mary, X).
```

Here, X is a variable, and the query asks Prolog to find all values of X that satisfy parent(mary, X). Prolog finds two matching facts and returns:

```
X = lisa ;
X = tom.
```

If the user requests more solutions by typing a semicolon (;) after each result, Prolog continues searching until all possible values have been exhausted.

4. **Complex Queries Using Multiple Variables:**

```
?- ancestor(X, lisa).
```

This query asks Prolog to determine all possible values of X such that X is an ancestor of Lisa. Based on the rules, Prolog finds:

```
X = mary ;
X = john ;
X = jane.
```

Prolog uses backtracking to explore different paths and relationships defined in the rules and facts.

5. **Conjunctions in Queries:**

```
?- parent(john, Y), parent(Y, lisa).
```

In this query, we use a conjunction (the comma operator) to specify that both goals must be true. Prolog first finds that Y can be mary from the first goal, and then it verifies if parent(mary, lisa) holds. Since both conditions are satisfied, Prolog returns:

Y = mary.

6. **Disjunctions in Queries:**

```
?- parent(jane, X); parent(john, X).
```

Here, the disjunction (the semicolon operator) specifies that at least one of the goals must be true. Prolog searches for any X such that either Jane or John is a parent of X. This results in:

X = mary.Prolog returns all solutions satisfying either part of the disjunction.

Formulating queries to extract information involves understanding the structure and relationships within the knowledge base and leveraging Prolog's goal resolution and backtracking mechanisms to retrieve the desired data. Users can combine facts, rules, and complex query constructs to answer intricate questions and derive new insights from the knowledge base.

2.5 Variable Binding and Scope

In Prolog, variable binding and scope are fundamental concepts that significantly influence how the language operates and how queries are resolved. A clear understanding of these concepts is crucial for effective Prolog programming.

Variables in Prolog begin with an uppercase letter or an underscore. When a variable is first introduced in a query or a rule, it is unbound, meaning it does not have a specific value at that point. Once a variable is assigned a value, it becomes bound. This binding remains throughout the current scope until the query or rule evaluation concludes or backtracking occurs. A standard example can illustrate basic variable binding and scope:

```
% Define a simple fact
parent(john, mary).

% Query involving variable binding
?- parent(X, mary).
```

In this example, X is introduced as an unbound variable in the query. When Prolog evaluates the query, it binds X to john, as parent(john, mary) is a known fact.

X = john.

Once the variable is bound, it cannot be rebound within the same scope. If we extend the query or introduce additional conditions, the current binding of the variable will influence the behavior of the query:

```
% Define additional facts
parent(john, mary).
parent(john, sam).
parent(alice, mary).

% Complex query
?- parent(X, mary), parent(X, sam).
```

Prolog will attempt to find a consistent binding for X that satisfies both conditions. In this case, X cannot be both john (parent of mary and sam) and alice (parent of mary), leading to:

```
false.
```

false indicates that no consistent binding satisfies both parts of the query simultaneously.

The scope of a variable in Prolog is determined by the rule or query in which it is introduced. Each variable can have a scope limited to a single clause or can span multiple clauses in a predicate definition. When a variable appears in multiple rules, each occurrence is treated independently unless the rules are part of the same compound term.

Consider the following example to demonstrate variable scopes:

```
% Compound Prolog rules
ancestor(X, Y) :- parent(X, Y).
ancestor(X, Y) :- parent(X, Z), ancestor(Z, Y).

% Queries on these rules
?- ancestor(john, mary).
?- ancestor(alice, mary).
```

Examining the first rule, ancestor(X,Y) :- parent(X,Y), the scope of X and Y is limited to this rule. Similarly, in the second rule, ancestor(X, Y) :- parent(X, Z), ancestor(Z, Y), the variables X, Y, and Z are scoped to the rule. However, when evaluating the rules, Prolog tries to find bindings such that each individual query clause is resolved consistently within the rule's scope.

```
% For the query ancestor(john, mary):
true.

% For the query ancestor(alice, mary):
false.
```

In cases involving multiple rules or clauses, Prolog must backtrack to find all possible solutions. Backtracking involves undoing variable bindings and retrying with different values until no further possibilities remain or a solution is found. This automatic backtracking mechanism distinguishes Prolog from many other programming languages:

```
% Additional complex query
?- parent(john, X), parent(X, Y).
```

Prolog first binds X to mary (since parent(john, mary) is true), then tries to find Y such that parent(mary, Y) is true. If it fails, it backtracks and considers X bound to sam, finding Y accordingly.

```
X = mary, Y = ...
X = sam, Y = ...
```

It is important to mention that the use of underscores allows defining anonymous variables, which are placeholders for values we care to bind. They are useful when the specific value is not relevant:

```
% Example using anonymous variables
?- parent(john, _).
```

This query simply checks if john is a parent to anyone, without necessitating the binding of a specific child.

When variables are used within recursive predicates, careful consideration of scope and binding is required to avoid logical errors and ensure correct solutions. Prolog performs variable binding through unification, attempting to make terms identical by finding a consistent set of bindings for variables.

Understanding how variable binding and scope interact and influence Prolog computations is essential for proficient programming and debugging. It ensures precise control over logical constructs and correct formulation of queries, leading to desired outcomes.

2.6 Understanding Backtracking

Backtracking is a fundamental concept in Prolog programming, allowing the language to explore multiple possibilities in problem-solving and logic inference. Backtracking permits Prolog to systematically search through different paths and possibilities when trying to satisfy a goal or query. This systematic search is at the core of Prolog's ability to find solutions to complex problems.

When Prolog attempts to solve a goal, it searches through the database of facts and rules to find a matching clause. If a solution is not found immediately, Prolog will backtrack or return to the most recent decision point to try a different path. This process continues until all possibilities are exhausted or a solution is found.

Consider the following Prolog code example, which contains facts and rules about familial relationships:

```
parent(john, mary).
parent(john, alice).
parent(peter, john).
parent(peter, kate).

sibling(X, Y) :-
    parent(Z, X),
    parent(Z, Y),
    X \= Y.
```

In this example, the parent/2 predicate defines the parent-child relationships. The sibling/2 predicate determines whether two individuals share at least one parent but are not the same person.

To query for siblings of john, the following query can be made:

```
?- sibling(john, Sibling).
```

Prolog's execution proceeds as follows:

- The sibling/2 predicate invokes parent/2 to find a common parent for john and another potential sibling.
- The first parent/2 fact is parent(john, mary), with john as the parent. Since john is not equal to john, this path is discarded.
- The second parent/2 fact is parent(john, alice). Here, john is the parent, but mary and alice are different individuals.
- This branch is explored further, but no valid sibling is found for john.
- Prolog backtracks and searches for other possible instances where the parent/2 clause could hold and finds another fact, parent(peter, john).
- The sibling/2 predicate tries to satisfy parent(peter, john) and subsequent clauses to identify 'Sibling'.

Prolog's systematic search and backtracking mechanism ensures that each path is explored fully before moving on to another potential solution path. This can be visualized by a search tree.

Consider a case where Prolog's backtracking is illustrated by solving the following query:

```
?- sibling(john, Sibling).
```

Possible execution trace and results demonstrated by the verbatim environment:

```
| ?- sibling(john, Sibling).
|   callee: sibling(john, _2056)
|       call: parent(_2129, john) ?
|           exit: parent(peter, john) ?
|               call: parent(peter, Sibling) ?
|                   exit: parent(peter, john)
|                       fail: X = john
|                   redo: parent(peter, Sibling) ?
|                       exit: parent(peter, kate)
Sibling = kate
```

In this example, Prolog tries to satisfy the sibling/2 predicate by instantiating Sibling with john, and then backtracks to other possible Sibling values until it finds kate, who satisfies the sibling/2 predicate.

This is a simplified illustration; Prolog's backtracking can handle vastly more complex situations due to its depth-first search approach and rule-driven logic. Understanding the nuances of backtracking enables the programmer to structure Prolog code effectively, anticipating how the backtracking mechanism will navigate through the logical constructs provided.

In practical terms, backtracking can also be controlled using the cut operator ('¡) to limit search space and prevent Prolog from exploring unnecessary alternatives, thus optimizing the search process.

Efficient use of backtracking and understanding its implications are pivotal to mastering Prolog programming. By strategically utilizing and controlling backtracking, complex logical relationships can be articulated and solutions derived effectively.

2.7 Using Anonymous Variables

In Prolog programming, an anonymous variable is represented by the underscore symbol _. Anonymous variables serve as placeholders where the specific value is not important, or when the value is not used. They are particularly useful in queries, facts, and rules, especially when pattern matching is required without retaining the associated value.

Anonymous variables are unique in that each occurrence of _ is treated as a different variable. Contrast this with named variables in Prolog, where the same name refers to the same variable instance throughout the scope of the clause.

Consider the following example where an anonymous variable is used in a fact:

```
likes(john, pizza).
likes(mary, sushi).
```

If we are interested in finding who likes sushi, we can form a query as follows:

```
?- likes(Who, sushi).
```

This query binds Who to mary. However, if we want to check the presence of someone liking sushi without caring about who it is, we can use an anonymous variable:

```
?- likes(_, sushi).
```

The query's result will indicate true if there is at least one fact where someone likes sushi, without providing who that someone is.

In rule definitions, anonymous variables are also useful when certain parts of the rule may involve values that do not require explicit handling. Examining a rule definition helps illustrate this further:

```
eats(human, Food) :- likes(_, Food), available(Food).
```

In the above rule, the variable _ is used to signify that likes predicate's first argument is irrelevant to the condition we are defining. The rule states that a human eats a certain food if that food is liked by someone (who is unspecified) and the food is available.

Additionally, anonymous variables are crucial when defining facts that inherently contain irrelevant or unused values. For example, if we wish to indicate that a certain event happens regardless of a specific parameter, we can use _:

```
occursAt(Event, Location) :- eventOccurrence(Event, Location, _).
```

Here, the rule determines if an event occurs at a location without considering the third argument of the eventOccurrence predicate.

Anonymous variables help in simplifying predicates by ignoring unnecessary details while focusing on the relevant logic. Consider a scenario where we need to find students enrolled in any course but are not interested in the course name. If we have:

```
enrolled(john, calculus).
enrolled(mary, physics).
```

A query to find any students enrolled in some course, without caring about the specific course, would be:

```
?- enrolled(Student, _).
```

This query binds Student to each value found in the facts, showcasing that John and Mary are enrolled in some course.

It is important to remember that each occurrence of _ is treated as a new and distinct variable. This means that in a query like:

```
?- enrolled(_, _).
```

The system checks if there is any enrolled fact with two unspecified values, effectively ignoring both arguments and merely verifying predicate existence.

Moreover, incorrect usage of anonymous variables could lead to unintended logical gaps. For instance:

```
happy(Person) :- likes(Person, Food), nutritious(Food, _), not(allergic(Person, _)).
```

Here, it indicates that a person is happy if they like any food, it is nutritious irrespective of what makes it so, and the person is not allergic to something. The use of _ within not(allergic(Person, _)) should be reviewed carefully to ensure that the logic aligns with the expectation that the person is not allergic to any entity in the system.

Using anonymous variables judiciously helps keep the Prolog programs succinct and efficient, allowing programmers to abstract away unnecessary details and focus on the core logic and relationships within the data.

2.8 Working with Compound Terms

Compound terms in Prolog are fundamental constructs that consist of a functor and a fixed number of arguments. A compound term's structure allows it to represent more complex data and relationships than simple atoms or numbers. The general form of a compound term is:

```
functor(argument1, argument2, ..., argumentN)
```

The functor is an atom that provides the name of the compound term, while the arguments enclosed in parentheses are terms themselves, which can be atoms, numbers, variables, or other compound terms.

Example of Compound Terms

Consider the following examples to illustrate compound terms:

```
person(john, doe, 30).
date(2023, october, 15).
address(street('Main St', 123), city('New York'), zipcode(10001)).
```

Here, person/3, date/3, and address/3 are compound terms. The notation /N expresses that the functor has N arguments.

Unification with Compound Terms

Unification is a key mechanism in Prolog, fundamental to matching goals with facts or rules. When dealing with compound terms, unification requires both the functor and corresponding arguments to match.

```
?- person(john, doe, Age) = person(john, doe, 30).
```

```
Age = 30
true.
```

In this example, the variable Age is unified with the value 30, demonstrating successful unification.

Decomposing Compound Terms

Prolog provides methods to decompose or destructure compound terms into their constituent parts, enabling more detailed inquiry or manipulation.

One commonly used approach to decomposing compound terms is with the built-in predicate =../2, often referred to as the "univ" operator. This predicate can convert between a compound term and a list representation where the first element is the functor and the remainder are the arguments.

```
?- date(2023, october, 15) =.. L.
```

```
L = [date, 2023, october, 15].
true.
```

Conversely, we can construct a compound term from a list using the =../2 operator:

```
?- Term =.. [functor, arg1, arg2].
```

```
Term = functor(arg1, arg2).
true.
```

Nested Compound Terms

Compound terms can be nested, allowing even richer and more complex data representations. Consider an address with structured components:

```
address(street('Main St', 123), city('New York'), zipcode(10001)).
```

To query nested components, Prolog allows pattern matching directly within the goal:

```
?- address(street(Name, Number), City, Zip) = address(street('Main St', 123), city('
    New York'), zipcode(10001)).
```

```
Name = 'Main St',
Number = 123,
City = city('New York'),
Zip = zipcode(10001).
true.
```

This query extracts the individual components of the nested structure using pattern matching.

Creating and Using Complex Data Structures

Prolog's ability to handle compound terms makes it suitable for creating and manipulating complex data structures like trees or graphs. Consider the following binary tree representation:

```
tree(value, left_subtree, right_subtree).
```

An example binary tree:

```
tree(10, tree(5, nil, nil), tree(15, nil, nil)).
```

Using pattern matching to discriminate tree structures:

```
?- tree(Value, Left, Right) = tree(10, tree(5, nil, nil), tree(15, nil, nil)).
```

```
Value = 10,
Left = tree(5, nil, nil),
Right = tree(15, nil, nil).
true.
```

This query successfully decomposes the tree into its root value and subtrees.

Defining and Manipulating Lists with Compound Terms

Lists in Prolog are a special form of compound terms using the dot/2 (./2) functor and the empty list constant []. A list such as [1, 2, 3] is internally represented as:

```
.(1, .(2, .(3, []))).
```

List structures can thus be handled using compound term techniques:

```
?- [Head|Tail] = [1, 2, 3].
```

```
Head = 1,
Tail = [2, 3].
true.
```

This simple decomposition yields the head and tail of the list.

By comprehensively understanding and utilizing compound terms, Prolog programmers can create and manipulate more elaborate and meaningful representations of data.

2.9 Exploring Predicate Logic

Predicate logic is a fundamental aspect of Prolog programming, enabling the expression of complex relationships and rules. It incorporates not only propositional logic but also quantifiers and predicates, which significantly enhance its expressive power. Predicates represent relations between objects and can take arguments, which are terms that the predicate relates.

In Prolog, a predicate is primarily defined by its name and arity (the number of arguments it takes). Predicates are used to assert facts, define rules, and formulate queries. Consider the predicate parent/2, which could be used to denote the relationship between a parent and their child. Here, the number 2 denotes that the predicate parent takes two arguments.

```
parent(john, mary).
parent(mary, susan).
parent(susan, alice).
```

The above facts define a simple family tree. The predicate parent/2 relates two individuals, the first being the parent of the second.

To formulate more complex relationships, Prolog allows the combination of multiple predicates into rules. For example, to define the ancestor/2 predicate, which denotes that one person is an ancestor of another, we can use the following rule:

```
ancestor(X, Y) :- parent(X, Y).
```

```
ancestor(X, Y) :- parent(X, Z), ancestor(Z, Y).
```

This rule states that X is an ancestor of Y if X is a parent of Y. Additionally, X is an ancestor of Y if X is a parent of Z, and Z is an ancestor of Y.

To query this knowledge base and find all ancestors of alice, we can use:

```
?- ancestor(X, alice).
```

This query returns:

```
X = susan ;
X = mary ;
X = john.
```

Predicate logic in Prolog becomes more potent with the use of logical connectives and quantifiers. Logical connectives such as conjunction (','), and disjunction (';') allow the combination of multiple conditions within rules.

For example, to define a sibling/2 predicate:

```
sibling(X, Y) :- parent(P, X), parent(P, Y), X \= Y.
```

This rule states that X is a sibling of Y if they share at least one parent P, and X is not equal to Y.

Quantifiers are used implicitly in Prolog, typically through the use of variables. For instance, the rule:

```
uncle(X, Y) :- parent(Z, Y), sibling(X, Z).
```

This indicates that X is an uncle of Y if Z is a parent of Y, and X is a sibling of Z. The variables X, Y, and Z implicitly cover all possible individuals in the knowledge base.

The expressive power of predicate logic in Prolog is further demonstrated by the ability to define rules involving inequality and arithmetic operations. For instance, to define a rule to check if two numbers are in ascending order:

```
ascending(X, Y) :- X =< Y.
```

The predicate $=</2 is a built-in predicate that succeeds if the first argument is less than or equal to the second.

Logical representation of more complex relationships might involve nested structures and compound terms. For example, to represent a complex term defining a date:

```
date(Day, Month, Year).
```

A specific date can be represented as a fact:

```
date(25, dec, 2021).
```

This predicate can be part of more comprehensive rules involving dates. For example, to define a predicate that expresses a relationship between two dates:

```
earlier(date(D1, M1, Y1), date(D2, M2, Y2)) :-
    Y1 < Y2 ;
    (Y1 =:= Y2, M1 < M2) ;
    (Y1 =:= Y2, M1 =:= M2, D1 < D2).
```

This rule uses conjunction and disjunction to cover various scenarios where one date is considered earlier than the other.

Prolog leverages predicate logic to perform not only simple data retrieval but also to solve complex problems involving relationships and constraints. Understanding these principles is pivotal for mastering Prolog programming and effectively leveraging its capabilities in knowledge representation and problem-solving.

2.10 Prolog's Built-in Predicates

Prolog offers a variety of built-in predicates that facilitate fundamental programming tasks without requiring developers to define these predicates explicitly. Understanding and effectively utilizing these built-in predicates is crucial for efficient Prolog programming. This section explores several key built-in predicates including those for list manipulation, arithmetic, input/output operations, and control structures.

The member/2 predicate checks if an element is a member of a list. It succeeds if the element is in the list and fails otherwise. The syntax is as follows:

```
member(Element, List).
```

For example:

```
?- member(a, [a, b, c]).
```

```
true.
```

The append/3 predicate concatenates two lists, producing a third list. It can be used for both appending and splitting lists. The syntax is:

```
append(List1, List2, Result).
```

An example usage is:

```
?- append([a, b], [c, d], Result).
```

Result = [a, b, c, d].

Arithmetic operations in Prolog are performed using the is/2 predicate, which assigns the value of an arithmetic expression to a variable. The syntax is:

```
Variable is Expression.
```

Consider this example:

```
?- X is 3 + 4.
```

X = 7.

Comparison predicates such as $=:=/2$, $=\backslash=/2$, $</2$, $>/2$, $=</2$, and $>=/2$ evaluate arithmetic expressions and compare their values. Their usage is straightforward. For instance:

```
?- 4 =:= 2 + 2.
```

true.

For handling input and output, Prolog provides numerous predicates like write/1, read/1, nl/0, and format/2. The write/1 predicate outputs its argument to the standard output:

```
write(Term).
```

Example usage:

```
?- write('Hello, world!').
```

Hello, world!
true.

The read/1 predicate reads a Prolog term from the current input stream:

```
read(Term).
```

Using read/1:

```
?- read(X).
```

|: hello.
X = hello.

nl/0 outputs a newline. Its usage is:

```
?- nl.
```

true.

The format/2 predicate is used for formatted text output. It is similar to printf in other languages:

```
format(Format, Arguments).
```

An example:

```
?- format('The value of X is ~d and Y is ~d.\n', [10, 20]).
```

The value of X is 10 and Y is 20.
true.

Control predicates such as !, fail/0, and true/0 are crucial for managing the flow of Prolog programs. The ! (cut) operator commits to the choices made so far and prunes alternatives. The syntax for fail/0 and true/0 are:

```
fail.
```

```
true.
```

A sample use case:

```
?- (write('Hello'), !, write('World')) ; write('Fail').
```

HelloWorld
true.

The fail/0 predicate always fails, causing backtracking. Its use is demonstrated here:

```
?- (write('Hello'), fail ; write('World')).
```

HelloWorld
true.

Lastly, true/0 is a predicate that always succeeds, often used for syntactic purposes:

```
?- (true, write('Success')).
```

Success
true.

Efficiently utilizing these built-in predicates allows for concise, readable, and effective Prolog programs.

2.11 Failures and Cut Operator

Prolog's approach to problem-solving involves systematic exploration of potential solutions through a process called backtracking. While the backtracking mechanism is powerful, controlling the flow of execution is crucial in practical applications. The cut operator, denoted as !, serves as a pivotal tool in controlling backtracking and managing the logical flow of Prolog programs. This section delves into the nature of failures in Prolog and explores the functioning and application of the cut operator.

Failures occur when a query cannot be satisfied under the given rules and facts. When Prolog encounters a failure, it backtracks to the most recent choice point and attempts an alternative path. The systematic exploration continues until all possible solutions are examined or a solution is found. Consider the following example, which illustrates the failure and backtracking process:

```
parent(john, mary).
parent(john, tom).
parent(mary, susan).

ancestor(X, Y) :- parent(X, Y).
ancestor(X, Y) :- parent(X, Z), ancestor(Z, Y).
```

Query: ancestor(john, Y).

```
Y = mary ;
Y = tom ;
Y = susan ;
false.
```

Here, the ancestor/2 predicate initiates with the base case. If parent(X, Y) matches the query, Prolog succeeds immediately. If a match is not found, it moves to the recursive case, seeking an intermediate ancestor.

However, consider scenarios requiring precise control over backtracking. Suppose we need to enforce that once Prolog finds a solution, it should not backtrack to find alternative solutions:

```
male(john).
male(tom).
female(mary).
female(susan).
```

```
is_male(X) :- male(X), !.
is_male(X) :- \+female(X).
```

Query: is_male(john).

```
true.
```

Query: is_male(mary).

```
false.
```

Here, the cut operator `!` is used in the is_male/1 predicate, preventing further exploration once a male is found. Adding `!` ensures Prolog does not consider the subsequent rule if the first condition succeeds, thus optimizing performance and ensuring logical integrity.

To fully understand the implications of the cut operator, let's examine an illustrative example representing a more sophisticated scenario:

```
grade(mary, 90).
grade(tom, 85).
grade(susan, 92).

scholarship(X) :- grade(X, G), G > 85, !, write('Scholarship granted to: '), write(X), nl.
scholarship(X) :- write('No scholarship for: '), write(X), nl.
```

Query: scholarship(mary).

```
Scholarship granted to: mary
true.
```

Query: scholarship(tom).

```
No scholarship for: tom
true.
```

In this example, the cut operator ensures that once Prolog grants a scholarship (with a grade greater than 85), it does not attempt the second rule, which could negate the decision. The presence of `!` thus serves as a commitment point.

Awareness of cut usage avoids unintended consequences like "cut-fail" combinations, often causing undesirable termination of logical paths. Consider the following cautionary example:

```
test(X) :- A = 1, !, (B = 1 ; B = 2).
test(X) :- A = 2.
```

Query: test(1).

```
true.
```

Query: test(2).

```
false.
```

In this case, the cut operator within test/1 restricts Prolog from considering the second alternative rule, demonstrating the need for strategic placement and thorough understanding.

Mastering the cut operator empowers Prolog programmers to fine-tune logical flow, enhancing both efficiency and clarity in program execution. Proper utilization demands awareness of potential pitfalls and the logic's structural integrity.

2.12 Combining Facts, Rules, and Queries

To leverage Prolog's full potential, we must understand how to combine facts, rules, and queries effectively. In this section, we will explore how these elements interact to create a powerful querying system that can answer complex questions based on the provided logical premises.

Facts form the fundamental units of information in Prolog. Each fact is typically a predicate that expresses a relationship or a state of affairs. For example:

```
parent(john, mary).
parent(mary, susan).
```

In the above listing, parent(john, mary) indicates that John is the parent of Mary, and similarly, parent(mary, susan) indicates that Mary is the parent of Susan.

Rules, on the other hand, define logical implications that extend the facts. A rule is generally composed of a head and a body, connected by the implication operator :-. The head is true if the body of the rule is true. For example:

```
grandparent(X, Y) :- parent(X, Z), parent(Z, Y).
```

This rule states that X is a grandparent of Y if X is a parent of Z and Z is a parent of Y. Thus, rules enable Prolog to infer new relationships from existing facts.

A query is a request for information based on the facts and rules in the Prolog database. When Prolog executes a query, it tries to find instances that satisfy the conditions specified. For instance, the query:

```
?- grandparent(john, Y).
```

will prompt Prolog to determine who, if anyone, is the grandchild of John. Given the facts and rules provided earlier, Prolog would deliver the response:

```
Y = susan.
```

Let us delve deeper into a more complex example to fully appreciate how facts, rules, and queries come together.

```
% Facts
male(john).
male(bob).
female(mary).
female(susan).
parent(john, mary).
parent(mary, susan).
parent(bob, susan).

% Rules
father(X, Y) :- parent(X, Y), male(X).
mother(X, Y) :- parent(X, Y), female(X).
sibling(X, Y) :- parent(Z, X), parent(Z, Y), X \= Y.
```

With these definitions, several types of queries can be formulated and resolved by Prolog:

1. **Identifying parents**: The query ?- parent(john, Y). returns all children of John. 2. **Determining specific relationships**: The query ?- father(john, Y). identifies the children for whom John is the father. 3. **Finding siblings**: The query ?- sibling(mary, Y). figures out if Mary has any siblings in the database. 4. **Checking parenthood**: The query ?- parent(X, susan). reveals Susan's parents.

Consider the execution of the sibling rule. The query ?- sibling(mary, Y). will prompt Prolog to determine if Mary has any siblings by checking if there is another person Y who shares the same parent as Mary but is not Mary herself. Prolog would follow this logic:

```
Y = susan ; % considering both parents
no.
```

In this scenario, the answer indicates that Susan and John could potentially have common parents given specific facts.

Handling more complex rules, the power of backtracking becomes evident. Suppose we introduce another set of rules intended for more hierarchical family relations:

```
ancestor(X, Y) :- parent(X, Y).
ancestor(X, Y) :- parent(X, Z), ancestor(Z, Y).
```

Here, ancestor/2 is defined recursively to denote that X is an ancestor of Y if X is a parent of Y, or X is a parent of Z and Z is an ancestor of Y. Testing this with a query:

```
?- ancestor(john, Y).
```

Prolog processes through facts and rules, concluding all descendants of John:

```
Y = mary ;
Y = susan ;
no.
```

Illustrating recursive relationships highlights Prolog's efficiency in handling nested and interconnected data structures.

Combining facts, rules, and queries effectively roots in the understanding of how Prolog unifies data, follows logical implications, and employs backtracking. This proficiency allows us to construct databases that can articulate complex systems and solve intricate problems logically.

Chapter 3

Working with Lists and Recursion

This chapter delves into lists and recursion in Prolog, covering list creation, manipulation, and fundamental operations such as accessing the head and tail. It explores recursive definitions, base cases, and list processing techniques, including appending, reversing, searching, and sorting lists. The chapter also addresses the use of accumulators for efficiency, handling nested lists, advanced list patterns, and practical examples of recursive algorithms, as well as debugging recursive list programs.

3.1 Introduction to Lists in Prolog

Prolog, being a logic programming language, excels at handling symbolic data and structures. Lists are one of the fundamental data structures in Prolog, providing a versatile way to manage collections of elements. A solid understanding of lists and their manipulation is crucial because they play a pivotal role in various logical operations and algorithms.

A list in Prolog is an ordered sequence of elements, which can comprise integers, atoms, variables, compound terms, or even other lists. Lists are enclosed in square brackets, with elements separated by commas. For instance, the list containing the atoms apple, banana, and cherry is written as:

```
[apple, banana, cherry]
```

An essential characteristic of Prolog lists is their recursive definition. Conceptually, a list is either empty or consists of a head and a tail, where the head is the first element, and the tail is a list of the remaining elements. This recursive nature simplifies many operations on lists.

To declare an empty list in Prolog, we use:

```
[]
```

A list with a single element, say the atom apple, is:

```
[apple]
```

A longer list, such as one containing three elements, can be represented as:

```
[apple, banana, cherry]
```

Within the context of head and tail, the above list can be decomposed recursively. For the list [apple, banana, cherry], the head is apple, and the tail is [banana, cherry].

Prolog provides robust pattern matching capabilities, allowing us to describe and manipulate list structures succinctly. For example, we can define a predicate to check if a list has a specific form using pattern matching:

```
is_three_elements([_, _, _]).
```

Here the predicate is_three_elements/1 succeeds if its argument is a list with exactly three elements, regardless of their actual values.

We frequently decompose lists into their head and tail to perform recursive operations. The head/tail notation [H|T] captures this pattern, where H is the first element, and T is the remaining list. For instance, consider the following simple predicate that checks if the list starts with a particular element:

```
starts_with(Element, [Element|_]).
```

The variable Element is matched against the head of the list, while the tail is ignored using the anonymous variable _. This form of pattern matching is central to recursive list processing.

Complex lists and nested lists are also supported in Prolog. For example, a list containing other lists can be represented as:

```
[[1, 2], [3, 4], [5, 6]]
```

Operations on nested lists require depth-aware processing, often using recursive predicates that traverse the structure.

While manipulating lists, one often encounters the need for list concatenation. This operation combines two lists into one. It can be achieved with the built-in predicate append/3. For instance:

```
append([1, 2], [3, 4], Result).
```

After execution, Result will unify with [1, 2, 3, 4]. The append/3 predicate leverages recursion:

```
append([], L, L).
append([H|T], L, [H|R]) :-
    append(T, L, R).
```

The base case unifies an empty list with the second list, and the recursive case builds the result list by prepending the head of the first list to the result of the recursive call.

Prolog's strengths in symbolic processing make it exceptionally powerful for handling lists. We can leverage the inherent recursive structure of lists to define and analyze list-processing algorithms concisely. Understanding these core concepts lays the foundation for more advanced list operations and recursive algorithms.

3.2 Creating and Manipulating Lists

In Prolog, lists are fundamental structures used to represent and process collections of elements. Understanding how to create and manipulate lists is crucial for efficient programming in Prolog.

Creating Lists: Lists in Prolog are defined using square brackets, [].

- An empty list is denoted by [].
- A list with elements can be written as [E1, E2, ..., En], where E1, E2, ..., En are the elements.

For example, the list containing integers 1, 2, and 3 is written as:

```
[1, 2, 3]
```

Constructing Lists: Lists can also be constructed using the [Head|Tail] notation, where Head represents the first element and Tail is a list of the remaining elements.

```
[1|[2, 3]] -> [1, 2, 3]
```

Manipulating Lists: There are several built-in predicates for performing common list manipulations:

member/2: Checks if an element is a member of a list.

```
member(X, [1, 2, 3]).
```

This will be true if X matches any of the elements in the list.

append/3: Concatenates two lists.

```
append([1, 2], [3, 4], L).
```

This results in L = [1, 2, 3, 4].

length/2: Computes the length of a list.

```
length([1, 2, 3], Len).
```

This results in Len = 3.

reverse/2: Reverses the order of elements in a list.

```
reverse([1, 2, 3], L).
```

This results in L = [3, 2, 1].

Example of List Manipulation: Consider a case where we are required to insert an element into a specific position within a list.

We define the predicate insert_at/4.

```
insert_at(X, 1, L, [X|L]).
insert_at(X, N, [H|T], [H|R]) :-
    N > 1,
    N1 is N - 1,
    insert_at(X, N1, T, R).
```

This predicate operates as follows:

- insert_at(X, 1, L, [X|L]) inserts X at the head (first position).
- insert_at(X, N, [H|T], [H|R]) handles the recursive case.

- The recursive case ensures that the element is inserted at the correct position by decrementing the position counter N until it reaches 1.

Example Usage:

```
insert_at(a, 2, [b, c, d], L).
```

Results in:

```
L = [b, a, c, d].
```

Another Example: Removing an Element from a List:

We define the predicate remove/3.

```
remove(_, [], []).
remove(X, [X|T], L) :-
    remove(X, T, L).
remove(X, [H|T], [H|R]) :-
    X \= H,
    remove(X, T, R).
```

This predicate works as follows:

- remove(_, [], []) defines the base case for an empty list.
- remove(X, [X|T], L) removes the head if it matches X.
- remove(X, [H|T], [H|R]) maintains the head if it does not match X and continues recursively.

Example Usage:

```
remove(c, [a, b, c, d], L).
```

Results in:

```
L = [a, b, d].
```

Understanding how to create and manipulate lists in Prolog unlocks powerful and efficient programming techniques, particularly when combined with recursion and logical reasoning inherent in the language. Lists, along with their associated operations, form the backbone of many Prolog programs, providing a versatile means of data representation.

3.3 List Operations: Head and Tail

Understanding the concept of head and tail is fundamental when working with lists in Prolog. This notion allows us to decompose lists, which in turn facilitates recursive processing and various list manipulations.

In Prolog, lists are constructed using the dot operator (.), which separates the head from the tail of the list. The head is the first element, and the tail is the remainder of the list. For example, in the list $[H|T]$, H represents the head, while T signifies the tail.

To illustrate, consider the following examples:

```
% Example 1: Head and tail extraction
?- [H|T] = [apple, banana, cherry].
H = apple,
T = [banana, cherry].

% Example 2: Nested lists
?- [H|T] = [[1,2], [3,4], [5,6]].
H = [1,2],
T = [[3,4], [5,6]].
```

It is critical to understand that the tail itself is always a list, which may be empty. This property enables the recursive traversal and manipulation of lists.

Common list operations often rely on this pattern for definition. Let us delve into several fundamental operations, demonstrating how the notions of head and tail are applied.

```
% Finding the head of a list
head([H|_], H).

% Finding the tail of a list
tail([_|T], T).
```

These predicates can be used as follows:

```
?- head([apple, banana, cherry], H).
H = apple.

?- tail([apple, banana, cherry], T).
T = [banana, cherry].
```

Accessing Specific Elements

Having understood how to access the head and tail, we can define predicates to access specific elements within a list. For instance, accessing the second element would involve retrieving the head of the tail:

```
second_element([_|T], Second) :-
```

```
    head(T, Second).
```

Applying this to a query:

```
?- second_element([apple, banana, cherry], E).
E = banana.
```

Recursively Defining List Operations

By employing recursive definitions, we can create more complex list operations. For instance, summing the elements of a list of numbers involves processing the head and recursively summing the tail:

```
% Base case: an empty list sums to zero
sum_list([], 0).

% Recursive case: head added to the sum of the tail
sum_list([H|T], Sum) :-
    sum_list(T, SumTail),
    Sum is H + SumTail.
```

This predicate usage is:

```
?- sum_list([1, 2, 3, 4], Sum).
Sum = 10.
```

Constructing and Deconstructing Lists

Constructing and deconstructing lists are frequent operations that use head and tail. For constructing, we can define a predicate that prepends an element to a list:

```
prepend(X, List, [X|List]).
```

This allows:

```
?- prepend(apple, [banana, cherry], NewList).
NewList = [apple, banana, cherry].
```

Practical Applications

A practical application of manipulating head and tail is the creation of predicates for common tasks such as finding the maximum element in a list. This operation can employ the head and tail:

```
% Base case: the maximum of a single-element list is the element itself
max_list([X], X).

% Recursive case: compare head with the maximum of the tail
max_list([H|T], Max) :-
    max_list(T, MaxTail),
    Max is max(H, MaxTail).
```

Executing this predicate:

```
?- max_list([1, 5, 3, 8, 2], Max).
Max = 8.
```

Through these examples, the concept of head and tail becomes a powerful tool for list manipulation in Prolog, enabling recursive definitions and efficient processing.

3.4 Recursive Definitions and Base Case

To effectively utilize recursion in Prolog, it is imperative to grasp the underlying principles of recursive definitions and base cases. A recursive definition specifies how a problem can be broken down into simpler, smaller instances of the same problem. In Prolog, recursion is both a powerful and natural paradigm for defining operations on lists and other recursive data structures.

A typical recursive definition in Prolog comprises two main components: the base case and the recursive case. The base case provides the termination criterion for the recursion, ensuring that it does not proceed indefinitely. The recursive case, on the other hand, specifies how the problem can be reduced to smaller instances that converge toward the base case.

Consider the following example, which computes the length of a list:

```
% Base case: The length of an empty list is 0.
list_length([], 0).

% Recursive case: The length of a non-empty list is 1 + the length of the tail.
list_length([_|Tail], Length) :-
    list_length(Tail, TailLength),
    Length is TailLength + 1.
```

In the given definition, list_length/2 is defined as a predicate with two arguments. The first argument is the list whose length is to be measured, and the second argument is the resulting length. The base case list_length([], 0) states that the length of an empty list is zero. The recursive case list_length([|_]|Tail], Length) decomposes the list into its head and tail, recursively computing the length of the tail and then adding one to account for the head.

The execution of the recursive case proceeds as follows:

- Deconstruct the list into its head and tail.

- Recursively call list_length/2 with the tail.
- On returning from the recursive call, add one to the length of the tail to obtain the total length.

Let us analyze an example query:

```
?- list_length([a, b, c], Length).
```

The execution process is as follows:

```
list_length([a, b, c], Length)
 --> list_length([b, c], TailLength), Length is TailLength + 1
   --> list_length([c], TailLength), Length is TailLength + 1
     --> list_length([], TailLength), Length is TailLength + 1
       --> TailLength = 0
     <-- TailLength is 0 + 1 = 1
   <-- TailLength is 1 + 1 = 2
 <-- TailLength is 2 + 1 = 3
```

The base case ensures termination when the list is empty, while the recursive case breaks down the problem into manageable subproblems, each getting closer to the base case.

A more complex example involving lists is the computation of the sum of all elements in a list:

```
% Base case: The sum of an empty list is 0.
list_sum([], 0).

% Recursive case: The sum of a non-empty list is the head plus the sum of the tail.
list_sum([Head|Tail], Sum) :-
    list_sum(Tail, TailSum),
    Sum is Head + TailSum.
```

In this example, the base case list_sum([], 0) specifies that the sum of an empty list is zero. The recursive case list_sum([Head|Tail], Sum) breaks the list into its head and tail, recursively computes the sum of the tail, and then adds the head element to the sum of the tail.

Evaluating this with a specific query:

```
?- list_sum([1, 2, 3, 4], Sum).
```

The execution proceeds:

```
list_sum([1, 2, 3, 4], Sum)
 --> list_sum([2, 3, 4], TailSum), Sum is 1 + TailSum
   --> list_sum([3, 4], TailSum), Sum is 2 + TailSum
     --> list_sum([4], TailSum), Sum is 3 + TailSum
       --> list_sum([], TailSum), Sum is 4 + TailSum
         --> TailSum = 0
       <-- Sum is 4 + 0 = 4
     <-- Sum is 3 + 4 = 7
   <-- Sum is 2 + 7 = 9
 <-- Sum is 1 + 9 = 10
```

Another pertinent example is the concatenation of two lists:

```
% Base case: Concatenating an empty list with List2 yields List2.
list_concat([], List2, List2).

% Recursive case: Concatenate List1's head with the concatenation of
% its tail and List2.
list_concat([Head|Tail1], List2, [Head|Tail3]) :-
    list_concat(Tail1, List2, Tail3).
```

In the above example, list_concat/3 concatenates two lists. The base case list_concat([], List2, List2) states that concatenating an empty list with another list results in the latter. The recursive case list_concat([Head|Tail1], List2, [Head|Tail3]) deconstructs the first list into its head and tail, concatenates the tail with the second list, and then constructs the resultant list by prepending the head.

3.5 List Processing Techniques

In Prolog, mastering list processing techniques is fundamental to efficient programming. This section focuses on core techniques for manipulating lists, including concatenation, length determination, checking membership, concatenating a list, selecting elements, and partitioning a list. These operations are pivotal in various recursive algorithms and play a significant role in problem-solving within Prolog.

Concatenation of Lists:

To concatenate two lists, Prolog provides standard predicate append/3. The predicate append/3 takes three arguments: the first two are the lists to be concatenated, and the third is the resultant list.

```
append([], L, L).
append([H|T1], L2, [H|T3]) :- append(T1, L2, T3).
```

The base case specifies that appending an empty list to any list L simply results in L. The recursive case states that to append [H|T1] to L2, we append T1 to L2 first and then prepend H to the result.

Determining the Length of a List:

To compute the length of a list, the predicate length/2 is commonly utilized. This predicate succeeds if the second argument unifies with the number of elements in the first argument, which is a list.

```
length([], 0).
length([_|T], N) :- length(T, N1), N is N1 + 1.
```

In the base case, the length of an empty list is 0. The recursive case decrements the list, calling length/2 on the tail T, and increments the count by 1.

Checking Membership in a List:

The predicate member/2 checks if an element is present in the list. It is defined as follows:

```
member(X, [X|_]).
member(X, [_|T]) :- member(X, T).
```

The base case checks if the head of the list is the element X we are looking for. The recursive case checks the tail of the list if X is not the head.

Selecting and Removing Elements from a List:

Selection and removal of elements are managed with the predicate select/3. This predicate succeeds if the third argument is the list obtained by removing the first occurrence of the item specified in the first argument from the list in the second argument.

```
select(X, [X|T], T).
select(X, [H|T], [H|R]) :- select(X, T, R).
```

In the base case, if the head of the list is X, then the resultant list is the tail of the list. In the recursive case, select/3 searches through the tail of the list, reconstructing the list as it proceeds.

Partitioning a List:

Partitioning a list breaks it into two parts based on a pivot element. The predicate partition/4 can be defined to achieve this:

```
partition(_, [], [], []).
partition(Pivot, [H|T], [H|L], G) :- H =< Pivot, partition(Pivot, T, L, G).
partition(Pivot, [H|T], L, [H|G]) :- H > Pivot, partition(Pivot, T, L, G).
```

In this predicate, the base case maintains that an empty list produces two empty partitions. If the head of the list is less than or equal to the pivot, it is added to the first partition (list L). Otherwise, it is added to the second partition (list G).

Filtering Elements from a List:

Filtering elements based on a condition is implemented with predicates such as include/3 and exclude/3. The include/3 predicate includes elements that satisfy a given condition:

```
include(_, [], []).
```

```
include(Pred, [H|T], [H|R]) :-
    call(Pred, H),
    include(Pred, T, R).
include(Pred, [_|T], R) :-
    include(Pred, T, R).
```

Here, the base case defines that filtering an empty list results in an empty list. The first recursive clause checks if the element satisfies the predicate, retaining the element in the resultant list. The second clause excludes elements that don't satisfy the predicate.

Understanding these fundamental list processing techniques is vital for developing proficiency in Prolog. These capabilities provide the underpinnings for more complex algorithms and applications, facilitating efficient data manipulation within the language's logical programming paradigm.

3.6 Appending and Reversing Lists

In Prolog, appending and reversing lists are fundamental operations that can be elegantly handled using recursive predicates. Understanding these operations deepens the comprehension of list manipulation and recursion principles. This section will cover the implementation of these functionalities and provide insight into their recursive nature.

Appending two lists involves creating a new list that contains elements from both input lists in sequence. The general approach to appending lists utilizes pattern matching and recursion. Let's define the predicate $\mathrm{append}/3$, where $\mathrm{append}(\mathrm{List1}, \mathrm{List2}, \mathrm{Result})$ signifies that Result is the concatenation of $\mathrm{List1}$ and $\mathrm{List2}$.

The base case for an empty $\mathrm{List1}$ is straightforward:

```
append([], List2, List2).
```

For the recursive case, we decompose $\mathrm{List1}$ into its head H and tail T, and prepend H to the recursive result of appending T and $\mathrm{List2}$:

```
append([H|T], List2, [H|Result]) :-
    append(T, List2, Result).
```

Full definition of $\mathrm{append}/3$ in Prolog:

```
append([], List2, List2).
append([H|T], List2, [H|Result]) :-
    append(T, List2, Result).
```

To illustrate this with an example, consider appending [1, 2] and [3, 4]. The predicate call append([1, 2], [3, 4], Result) should yield Result = [1, 2, 3, 4].

```
?- append([1, 2], [3, 4], Result).
Result = [1, 2, 3, 4].
```

Reversing a list is another common operation that involves creating a new list wherein the elements are in the reverse order of the original list. The predicate reverse/2, where reverse(List, ReversedList), serves this purpose.

The base case for reversing an empty list is:

```
reverse([], []).
```

For the recursive case, we can use an auxiliary predicate and an accumulator to efficiently manage the intermediate results. Let's define an auxiliary predicate reverse_acc/3 such that reverse_acc(List, Acc, ReversedList) reverses List into ReversedList using Acc as an accumulator.

Starting with an accumulator initially set to an empty list:

```
reverse(List, ReversedList) :-
    reverse_acc(List, [], ReversedList).
```

Within reverse_acc/3, the base case occurs when the input List is empty:

```
reverse_acc([], Acc, Acc).
```

For the recursive case, we decompose the list into head H and tail T, and recursively reverse T while accumulating H at the front of Acc:

```
reverse_acc([H|T], Acc, ReversedList) :-
    reverse_acc(T, [H|Acc], ReversedList).
```

Combining these definitions provides the complete implementation of list reversal:

```
reverse([], []).
reverse(List, ReversedList) :-
    reverse_acc(List, [], ReversedList).

reverse_acc([], Acc, Acc).
reverse_acc([H|T], Acc, ReversedList) :-
    reverse_acc(T, [H|Acc], ReversedList).
```

Using an accumulator optimizes the reversal process as it avoids repeated concatenation operations seen in less efficient implementations.

For instance, reversing the list [1, 2, 3] should provide ReversedList = [3, 2, 1].

```
?- reverse([1, 2, 3], ReversedList).
ReversedList = [3, 2, 1].
```

These methods exemplify the power of recursion and pattern matching in Prolog. Understanding and implementing these list operations fosters a deeper grasp of list processing techniques and the efficiency considerations inherent in recursive programming.

3.7 Searching and Sorting Lists

Searching and sorting are critical operations in list processing. Effective use of these operations can significantly enhance the functionality of a Prolog program. This section explores several search and sorting algorithms implemented recursively in Prolog, such as linear search and binary search, and elaborate on sorting techniques like bubble sort, insertion sort, and quicksort.

Searching Lists:

Searching for an element in a list involves checking if an element exists and retrieving its position. Prolog's unification feature makes this process straightforward using recursive definitions. Below is an implementation of a linear search that checks whether an element exists in a list.

```
% Linear search to determine if Element exists in List
element_exists(Element, [Element|_]). % Element is the head of the list
element_exists(Element, [_|Tail]) :-
    element_exists(Element, Tail). % Recursive call with the tail of the list
```

To search for the position of an element in a list, one can augment the linear search algorithm slightly by keeping track of the current index.

```
% Search for the position of Element in List, returns 1-based Index
element_position(Element, List, Index) :-
    element_position_helper(Element, List, 1, Index).

element_position_helper(Element, [Element|_], Index, Index).
element_position_helper(Element, [_|Tail], CurrentIndex, Index) :-
    NextIndex is CurrentIndex + 1,
    element_position_helper(Element, Tail, NextIndex, Index).
```

Sorting Lists:

Sorting algorithms arrange the elements in lists in a particular order. Here, we examine several sorting algorithms from basic to more advanced methods, each defined recursively.

Bubble Sort:

Bubble sort repeatedly steps through the list, compares adjacent elements, and swaps them if they are in the wrong order. This process continues until the list is sorted.

```
% Bubble sort implementation
bubble_sort(List, SortedList) :-
    bubble_sort_pass(List, PartialSortedList, Flag),
    (Flag = true -> bubble_sort(PartialSortedList, SortedList) ; SortedList = List).

bubble_sort_pass([A, B | T], [B | NT], Flag) :-
    A > B, !,
    bubble_sort_pass([A | T], NT, _),
    Flag = true.
bubble_sort_pass([A | T], [A | NT], Flag) :-
    bubble_sort_pass(T, NT, Flag).
bubble_sort_pass([], [], false).
```

While easy to implement, bubble sort is inefficient for large lists due to its $O(n^2)$ time complexity.

Insertion Sort:

Insertion sort works by maintaining a sorted sublist and iteratively inserting elements from the unsorted sublist into the correct position within the sorted sublist.

```
% Insertion sort implementation
insertion_sort([], []).
insertion_sort([H|T], SortedList) :-
    insertion_sort(T, SortedTail),
    insert_sorted(H, SortedTail, SortedList).

insert_sorted(Element, [H|T], [H|NT]) :-
    Element > H, !,
    insert_sorted(Element, T, NT).
insert_sorted(Element, List, [Element|List]).
```

Insertion sort is more efficient on small lists or nearly sorted lists but still holds a time complexity of $O(n^2)$ in the worst case.

Quicksort:

Quicksort is a more sophisticated and efficient sorting algorithm, utilizing a divide-and-conquer strategy. It selects a pivot element and partitions the list into sublists with elements less than and greater than the pivot, recursively sorting each sublist.

```
% Quicksort implementation
quicksort([], []).
quicksort([Pivot|Rest], SortedList) :-
    partition(Pivot, Rest, Less, Greater),
    quicksort(Less, SortedLess),
```

```
    quicksort(Greater, SortedGreater),
    append(SortedLess, [Pivot|SortedGreater], SortedList).

partition(_, [], [], []).
partition(Pivot, [H|T], [H|Less], Greater) :-
    H =< Pivot, !,
    partition(Pivot, T, Less, Greater).
partition(Pivot, [H|T], Less, [H|Greater]) :-
    partition(Pivot, T, Less, Greater).
```

By efficiently dividing the list, quicksort achieves a better average-case performance with a time complexity of $O(n \log n)$.

Practical Considerations:

Understanding the performance and characteristics of these algorithms allows selecting the most appropriate one for a given problem. Efficiency in Prolog can often be enhanced using accumulators or tail-recursion optimization, especially for large lists. Further exploration of these optimization techniques is provided in subsequent sections. Debugging strategies for recursive logic is essential to ensure correctness and performance, which is addressed in the concluding chapters of our text.

These basic search and sorting mechanisms form foundational tools in Prolog, crucial for developing more complex algorithms and data processing tasks. Efficiently manipulating lists is a stepping stone towards achieving expert proficiency in Prolog programming.

3.8 Using Accumulators for Efficiency

Understanding how accumulators enhance efficiency in Prolog programs is crucial for optimizing recursive algorithms, especially when dealing with lists. Accumulators serve as additional arguments in recursive predicates, maintaining partial results as the recursion progresses. This technique significantly reduces the overhead associated with standard recursive processes by converting recursive operations into tail-recursive ones, thus enabling optimizations by Prolog's internal mechanisms.

Consider a classic problem—computing the sum of all elements in a list. The naive recursive approach might look as follows:

```
sum_list([], 0).
sum_list([Head|Tail], Sum) :-
    sum_list(Tail, SumTail),
    Sum is Head + SumTail.
```

This method is intuitive but not tail-recursive. Each recursive call must wait for the result of sum_list(Tail, SumTail) before proceeding, leading to increased memory usage and potential stack overflow for large lists.

Transforming this example to use an accumulator involves defining a helper predicate that carries the running total through each recursive call:

```
sum_list(List, Sum) :-
    sum_list_acc(List, 0, Sum).

sum_list_acc([], Acc, Acc).
sum_list_acc([Head|Tail], Acc, Sum) :-
    NewAcc is Acc + Head,
    sum_list_acc(Tail, NewAcc, Sum).
```

Here, sum_list/2 acts as a wrapper to initialize the accumulation process. The sum_list_acc/3 predicate is tail-recursive—passing the accumulating sum Acc to each subsequent call. This structure allows Prolog to optimize memory usage effectively.

Similarly, reversing a list can benefit from accumulators. The naive approach is:

```
reverse_list([], []).
reverse_list([Head|Tail], Rev) :-
    reverse_list(Tail, RevTail),
    append(RevTail, [Head], Rev).
```

This method is highly inefficient due to the repeated append/3 operation, each of which has a linear complexity. Introducing an accumulator provides a tail-recursive solution:

```
reverse_list(List, Rev) :-
    reverse_list_acc(List, [], Rev).

reverse_list_acc([], Acc, Acc).
reverse_list_acc([Head|Tail], Acc, Rev) :-
    reverse_list_acc(Tail, [Head|Acc], Rev).
```

In this formulation, the accumulator Acc collects elements, constructing the reversed list progressively. The recursion terminates when the input list is exhausted, with the accumulator holding the reversed result.

Accumulators are equally valuable in list concatenation algorithms. Consider concatenating multiple lists into a single list:

```
concat_lists([], []).
concat_lists([List|Lists], Res) :-
    concat_lists(Lists, ResTail),
    append(List, ResTail, Res).
```

Each append/3 operation within this natural recursive solution incurs substantial overhead. Leveraging accumulators, we propose:

```
concat_lists(Lists, Res) :-
    concat_lists_acc(Lists, [], Res).

concat_lists_acc([], Acc, Acc).
concat_lists_acc([List|Lists], Acc, Res) :-
    append(Acc, List, NewAcc),
    concat_lists_acc(Lists, NewAcc, Res).
```

To further optimize, consider directly incorporating elements from each sublist:

```
concat_lists_lin(Lists, Res) :-
    concat_lists_lin_acc(Lists, [], Res).

concat_lists_lin_acc([], Acc, Acc).
concat_lists_lin_acc([List|Lists], Acc, Res) :-
    append_lists_direct(List, Acc, NewAcc),
    concat_lists_lin_acc(Lists, NewAcc, Res).

append_lists_direct([], Acc, Acc).
append_lists_direct([H|T], Acc, Res) :-
    append_lists_direct(T, [H|Acc], Res).
```

In this optimized approach, append_lists_direct/3 accumulates list elements without invoking append/3, directly enhancing performance.

Accumulators can even assist in computation-heavy operations like finding the maximum value in a list:

```
max_list([H|T], Max) :-
    max_list_acc(T, H, Max).

max_list_acc([], Acc, Acc).
max_list_acc([H|T], Acc, Max) :-
    NewAcc is max(H, Acc),
    max_list_acc(T, NewAcc, Max).
```

By maintaining Acc as the maximum encountered thus far, max_list_acc/3 efficiently narrows down the largest value through tail-recursive calls.

Accumulators are essential in recursively solving problems more efficiently, transforming algorithms into tail-recursive alternatives where the time complexity remains linear and space complexity is minimized. Prolog's internal optimizations leverage these patterns to handle extensive data structures effectively.

3.9 Nested Lists and Converting Structures

In Prolog, lists can contain other lists as elements, allowing for the creation of hierarchical or nested list structures. This capability is essential for representing more complex data and performing advanced manipulations. Understanding nested lists is crucial for proficiently handling various problems requiring hierarchical data representations.

A nested list in Prolog is a list in which one or more elements are themselves lists. For instance, the list [1, [2, 3], 4] contains another list [2, 3] as its second element. Nested lists are represented using the same syntactic rules as regular lists, with elements separated by commas and enclosed in square brackets.

Consider the following Prolog example demonstrating a nested list:

```
nested_list([a, [b, c], [d, [e, f]], g]).
```

In this example, the list [a, [b, c], [d, [e, f]], g] comprises several nested structures. The first element is a, followed by the list [b, c], then another nested list [d, [e, f]], and finally the element g.

To work effectively with nested lists, various operations, such as flattening and accessing nested elements, become necessary. We shall explore key techniques for manipulating nested lists and converting structures, aiding in the efficient handling of complex list configurations.

Flattening a Nested List

Flattening a nested list involves transforming it into a single-level list by recursively extracting elements from nested sublists. The flattening operation is particularly useful for simplifying the processing of hierarchical data. A typical approach to flattening a nested list uses recursion and pattern matching.

Below is a Prolog predicate flatten/2 that achieves this:

```
flatten([], []).
flatten([Head|Tail], FlatList) :-
    flatten(Head, FlatHead),
    flatten(Tail, FlatTail),
    append(FlatHead, FlatTail, FlatList).
flatten(NonList, [NonList]).
```

Explanation of flatten/2:

- The first clause handles the base case where an empty list [] is flattened to an empty list [].

- The second clause addresses the case where the head of the list is itself a list. It recursively flattens both the head and the tail, then concatenates the flattened head and tail to produce the final flattened list.
- The third clause manages the case where the element is a non-list (i.e., an atomic element), placing it as a single-element list.

For example, flattening $[1, [2, [3], 4], 5]$ yields:

```
?- flatten([1, [2, [3], 4], 5], Result).
Result = [1, 2, 3, 4, 5].
```

Accessing Nested Elements

Accessing elements within nested lists requires traversing the list structure until the desired element is found. This necessitates recursive access functions that can navigate through multiple list levels.

Consider the following predicate to retrieve an element at a specific position within a nested list:

```
nth_nested(1, [Head|_], Head).
nth_nested(N, [_|Tail], Elem) :-
    N > 1,
    N1 is N - 1,
    nth_nested(N1, Tail, Elem).
```

This predicate nth_nested/3 provides access to the N-th element of a (potentially nested) list:

- The first clause returns the head of the list if the position is 1.
- The second clause recursively decrements the position and processes the tail of the list until the desired position is reached.

However, for deeply nested structures, more sophisticated approaches are required to handle various levels of depth correctly.

Converting Other Structures to Nested Lists

Other Prolog structures, such as trees, can be converted to nested lists for simplified manipulation. For example, a binary tree is a common data structure that can be represented as a nested list where each node is a list containing its value and its subtrees.

Below is an example of converting a binary tree into a nested list:

```
tree_to_list(nil, []).
tree_to_list(t(Value, Left, Right), [Value|NestedList]) :-
    tree_to_list(Left, LeftList),
    tree_to_list(Right, RightList),
    append(LeftList, RightList, NestedList).
```

Explanation of tree_to_list/2:

- The first clause handles the base case where an empty tree (denoted by nil) converts to an empty list [].
- The second clause processes a tree node by recursively converting its left and right subtrees to lists, then concatenating these lists with the node value.

For example, given a tree represented by t(1, t(2, nil, nil), t(3, nil, nil)), the conversion yields:

```
?- tree_to_list(t(1, t(2, nil, nil), t(3, nil, nil)), List).
List = [1, 2, 3].
```

This approach ensures a consistent and manageable representation of complex hierarchical data structures within the Prolog environment.

By mastering nested lists and the conversion techniques presented, one gains the ability to robustly handle, manipulate, and transform complex hierarchical data structures using Prolog's recursive power.

3.10 Advanced List Patterns

In complex Prolog programs, advanced list patterns emerge as essential tools for managing intricate data manipulations. Building on fundamental list operations and recursive techniques, these patterns demonstrate Prolog's versatility in handling diverse and nested list structures. Here, detailed examples will be examined to illustrate these advanced concepts effectively.

Pattern Matching with Lists of Lists

One common scenario necessitates working with lists of lists. Consider a list where each element is itself a list. In such cases, pattern matching requires careful attention to each nested level. For instance, matching the head of a list of lists can be done as follows:

```
% Defining a predicate to match the head of a list of lists
head_of_list_of_lists([[HeadList|_]|_], HeadList).
```

In this example, [[HeadList|_]|_] is the argument pattern, where HeadList captures the head of the first inner list. Given the query:

```
?- head_of_list_of_lists([[1,2,3],[4,5,6],[7,8,9]], Head).
```

the output is:

```
Head = 1.
```

List Flattening

Flattening a list is another advanced pattern, particularly useful when converting nested lists into a single list by removing all internal list structures. This process can be implemented recursively:

```
% Predicate to flatten a list
flatten([], []).
flatten([Head|Tail], FlatList) :-
    flatten(Head, FlatHead),
    flatten(Tail, FlatTail),
    append(FlatHead, FlatTail, FlatList).

% Base case for non-list elements
flatten(Element, [Element]) :-
    \+ is_list(Element).
```

Here, flatten/2 checks if the Head is a list. If so, it recursively flattens Head and Tail, and then appends the results. The base case handles non-list elements directly.

Zip and Unzip Operations

Zip and unzip operations combine and split lists element-wise, respectively, which are particularly handy for manipulating data structured in pairs. To implement zipping:

```
% Zips two lists into a list of pairs
zip([], [], []).
zip([H1|T1], [H2|T2], [(H1,H2)|T]) :-
    zip(T1, T2, T).
```

Given:

```
?- zip([1,2,3], [a,b,c], Zipped).
```

the result is:

```
Zipped = [(1,a), (2,b), (3,c)].
```

Conversely, unzipping can be achieved by separating pairs back into two lists:

```
% Unzips a list of pairs into two separate lists
unzip([], [], []).
unzip([(H1,H2)|T], [H1|T1], [H2|T2]) :-
    unzip(T, T1, T2).
```

Difference Lists

Difference lists optimize certain list operations by using a pair of lists representing the difference between them. These can simplify list concatenation. A difference list D for appending lists can be defined as:

```
% Difference list representation for append
append_dl(A-B, B-C, A-C).
```

To use this, consider:

```
?- append_dl([1,2|R1]-R1, [3,4|R2]-R2, Result-R2).
```

producing:

```
Result = [1,2,3,4|R2].
```

This pattern significantly enhances efficiency by avoiding repeated appending operations.

Accumulator Patterns

Accumulators are an advanced recursive technique for efficient list processing, especially for tasks like reversing a list. Unlike naive recursion that rebuilds lists at each step, accumulators carry intermediate results:

```
% Reverse a list using an accumulator
reverse(List, Reversed) :-
    reverse_acc(List, [], Reversed).

reverse_acc([], Acc, Acc).
reverse_acc([Head|Tail], Acc, Reversed) :-
    reverse_acc(Tail, [Head|Acc], Reversed).
```

Using:

```
?- reverse([1,2,3], R).
```

yields:

```
R = [3,2,1].
```

This efficiency stems from building the final result in the Acc parameter without reconstructing intermediary lists.

Sets and Bagof/3

Finally, managing sets involves unique patterns. The bagof/3 predicate can collect all solutions of a goal in a list, respecting variable bindings:

```
% Example usage of bagof/3
bagof(X, member(X, [1,2,2,3]), Bag).
```

results in:

```
Bag = [1, 2, 2, 3].
```

For sets (unique elements), setof/3 ensures the list contains no duplicates and is ordered:

```
% Example usage of setof/3
setof(X, member(X, [3,2,2,1]), Set).
```

produces:

```
Set = [1, 2, 3].
```

The comprehensive understanding of these advanced list patterns equips the reader with essential tools for efficient and robust Prolog programming, allowing complex data manipulations and optimizations to be performed seamlessly.

3.11 Examples of Recursive Algorithms on Lists

Examining recursive algorithms on lists allows us to understand the fundamental mechanisms that drive many Prolog operations. Recursive list processing is a cornerstone of functional logic programming, enabling us to perform complex transformations and queries succinctly and efficiently.

Example 1: Calculating the Sum of Elements

To begin, consider a simple recursive algorithm that calculates the sum of elements in a list. The process involves two primary operations: a base case that handles an empty list and a recursive step that processes the non-empty list.

```
% sum_list(List, Sum) - sums up the elements of List producing Sum.
sum_list([], 0).
```

```
sum_list([Head|Tail], Sum) :-
    sum_list(Tail, SumTail),
    Sum is Head + SumTail.
```

The predicate sum_list/2 operates by recursively summing the tail of the list and accumulating the sum in the variable Sum. When the list is empty, the sum is initialized to 0.

Example 2: Finding the Length of a List

Another common recursive operation is determining the length of a list. This can be accomplished using a similar approach: processing each element recursively and incrementing a count.

```
% length_list(List, Length) - computes the length of List.
length_list([], 0).
length_list([_|Tail], Length) :-
    length_list(Tail, LengthTail),
    Length is LengthTail + 1.
```

Here, the predicate length_list/2 counts elements by recursively processing the tail and incrementing the length for each head of the list.

Example 3: Reversing a List

Reversing a list involves appending the head of the list to the result of reversing the tail. This is efficiently achieved via recursion.

```
% reverse_list(List, Reversed) - produces the reversed version of List.
reverse_list(List, Reversed) :-
    reverse_list(List, [], Reversed).

% reverse_list(List, Acc, Reversed) - uses an accumulator to store the result.
reverse_list([], Acc, Acc).
reverse_list([Head|Tail], Acc, Reversed) :-
    reverse_list(Tail, [Head|Acc], Reversed).
```

The predicate reverse_list/2 calls a helper predicate reverse_list/3 with an accumulator that collects the reversed list.

Example 4: Checking for Membership

Determining if an element belongs to a list can be achieved through recursion by checking each head against the desired element.

```
% member(Element, List) - checks if Element is in List.
member(Element, [Element|_]).
member(Element, [_|Tail]) :-
    member(Element, Tail).
```

The predicate member/2 succeeds if the element matches the head of the list, or if it can be located in the tail through recursive descent.

Example 5: Duplicating Elements

To duplicate each element in the list, we employ a recursive approach that creates a new list with each element appearing twice.

```
% duplicate_list(List, Duplicated) - duplicates each element of List.
duplicate_list([], []).
duplicate_list([Head|Tail], [Head, Head|DuplicatedTail]) :-
    duplicate_list(Tail, DuplicatedTail).
```

In the predicate duplicate_list/2, each head is placed twice in the resulting list, followed by recursive duplication of the tail.

Example 6: Filtering Elements

Filtering elements based on a condition involves recursively processing each element and including it in the result if it satisfies the condition.

```
% filter_list(List, Condition, Filtered) - filters elements that satisfy Condition.
filter_list([], _, []).
filter_list([Head|Tail], Condition, [Head|FilteredTail]) :-
    call(Condition, Head),
    filter_list(Tail, Condition, FilteredTail).
filter_list([_|Tail], Condition, FilteredTail) :-
    filter_list(Tail, Condition, FilteredTail).
```

The predicate filter_list/3 uses the built-in call/2 predicate to evaluate the condition and construct the filtered list.

Example 7: Mapping a Function over a List

Applying a function to each element in a list is a fundamental operation that can be elegantly implemented using recursion.

```
% map_list(List, Function, Mapped) - applies Function to each element yielding
      Mapped.
map_list([], _, []).
map_list([Head|Tail], Function, [MappedHead|MappedTail]) :-
    call(Function, Head, MappedHead),
    map_list(Tail, Function, MappedTail).
```

The predicate map_list/3 utilizes call/2 to apply the function, generating a list wherein each element is the result of the function application.

Example 8: Flattening a Nested List

Flattening a nested list involves recursively traversing each sublist and concatenating the elements into a single list.

```
% flatten_list(NestedList, FlatList) - flattens a nested list structure.
flatten_list([], []).
flatten_list([Head|Tail], FlatList) :-
    flatten_list(Head, FlatHead),
    flatten_list(Tail, FlatTail),
    append(FlatHead, FlatTail, FlatList).
```

```
flatten_list(Element, [Element]) :-
    \+ is_list(Element).
```

The predicate flatten_list/2 processes both atomic elements and lists, producing a flattened list representation.

These examples collectively demonstrate the versatility and power of recursive algorithms in list processing within Prolog, providing foundational techniques essential for advanced programming tasks.

3.12 Debugging Recursive List Programs

Debugging recursive list programs in Prolog involves a systematic approach to identifying and fixing errors that can arise from the nature of recursion and list processing. This section will explore techniques and best practices for debugging recursive Prolog code, with a specific focus on list operations. We will discuss common issues such as infinite loops, stack overflows, and incorrect outputs, and provide methods to track and resolve these issues effectively.

Trace Facility:

The primary tool for debugging in Prolog is the trace facility, which allows you to follow the execution of your program step by step. You can invoke the trace facility by using the trace/0 predicate. This tool is especially useful for understanding the flow of recursive calls and pinpointing where the logic might be failing.

```
% Example: Tracing a simple recursive definition

trace.
member(X, [X|_]).
member(X, [_|T]) :- member(X, T).

% Query
?- member(3, [1, 2, 3, 4]).
```

```
Call: (10) member(3, [1, 2, 3, 4])
Call: (11) member(3, [2, 3, 4])
Call: (12) member(3, [3, 4])
Exit: (12) member(3, [3, 4])
Exit: (11) member(3, [2, 3, 4])
Exit: (10) member(3, [1, 2, 3, 4])
```

Analyzing the trace output helps understand how Prolog processes each recursive call. This visibility into the call stack can help identify deviations from the expected behavior.

Common Issues and Solutions:

Several common issues can arise when working with recursive list programs. Here we discuss them alongside strategies for debugging and resolving these issues.

1. Infinite Loops:

Infinite loops occur when the base case of a recursive predicate is never reached. This typically results from missing or incorrect termination conditions.

```
% Faulty Example: Infinite loop due to missing base case

print_list([H|T]) :-
    write(H), nl,
    print_list(T).

% Correct Example: Proper base case included

print_list([]).
print_list([H|T]) :-
    write(H), nl,
    print_list(T).
```

Using the trace facility, we can see that without the base case, the recursion would never terminate:

```
Call: (10) print_list([a, b, c])
Call: (11) print_list([b, c])
Call: (12) print_list([c])
Call: (13) print_list([])
Exit: (13) print_list([])
```

2. Incorrect Outputs:

Wrong outputs often stem from logic errors in recursive rules. Ensuring that recursive rules and base cases are correctly defined and that they collectively cover all possible input cases is crucial.

```
% Example: Wrongly implemented list reversal

reverse_list([H|T], Rev) :-
    reverse_list(T, RevT),
    append(RevT, [H], Rev).

reverse_list([], []).

% Query
?- reverse_list([1, 2, 3], Rev).
```

```
Call: (10) reverse_list([1, 2, 3], _G123)
Call: (11) reverse_list([2, 3], _G123)
Call: (12) reverse_list([3], _G124)
Call: (13) reverse_list([], _G125)
Exit: (13) reverse_list([], [])
Exit: (12) reverse_list([3], [3])
Exit: (11) reverse_list([2, 3], [3, 2])
Exit: (10) reverse_list([1, 2, 3], [3, 2, 1])
```

This is correct. However, adjusting the rule without the base case first can provide insight into why it's necessary.

Annotated outputs and unit tests can be used to verify the correctness of each component before integrating them into larger recursive procedures.

3. Stack Overflows:

Stack overflow errors occur when recursion depth exceeds the system's stack limits. This often results from unnecessarily deep recursion due to inefficient recursive logic.

Consider the example of calculating the Fibonacci sequence recursively, which can lead to significant redundancy and inefficiency:

```
% Inefficient Example: Fibonacci sequence calculation

fib(0, 0).
fib(1, 1).
fib(N, F) :-
    N > 1,
    N1 is N - 1,
    N2 is N - 2,
    fib(N1, F1),
    fib(N2, F2),
    F is F1 + F2.

% Query
?- fib(30, F).
```

While the implementation above correctly calculates Fibonacci numbers, it recomputes the values multiple times, leading to an exponential time complexity. This inefficiency can be mitigated by using memoization or iterative approaches.

```
% Efficient Example: Fibonacci with memoization

:- dynamic fib_mem/2.

fib_mem(0, 0).
fib_mem(1, 1).
fib_mem(N, F) :-
    N > 1,
    ( fib_mem(N, F)
    -> true
    ; N1 is N - 1,
        N2 is N - 2,
```

```
        fib_mem(N1, F1),
        fib_mem(N2, F2),
        F is F1 + F2,
        assertz(fib_mem(N, F))).

% Query
?- fib_mem(30, F).
```

Using the assertz/1 predicate saves previously computed results, avoiding redundant calculations and significantly improving performance.

Annotated Tracing:

Annotating recursive processes helps track variable states and flow of logic more explicitly. Adding print statements within recursion provides insight into intermediate variables and recursion depth.

```
% Adding print statements for debugging

reverse_list([H|T], Rev) :-
    reverse_list(T, RevT),
    write('Reversing: '), write(T), nl,
    append(RevT, [H], Rev).

reverse_list([], []) :-
    write('Base case reached'), nl.
```

This approach clarifies whether the recursion is processing the list correctly and whether the expected base case logic is activated.

Through these systematic techniques, debugging recursive programs in Prolog, especially those involving lists, becomes a controlled and resolvable task. Monitoring the execution with trace, ensuring proper base cases, correcting logic errors, avoiding excessive recursion depth, and using annotations are essential methods to refine and verify recursive predicates.

Chapter 4

Prolog Arithmetic and Operations

This chapter covers arithmetic in Prolog, including basic operations and the use of arithmetic operators. It explains the evaluation of expressions using is/2, comparison operators, and the implementation of arithmetic functions. Topics also include handling integer and float types, generating random numbers, dealing with arithmetic errors, and practical problem-solving examples using Prolog arithmetic.

4.1 Introduction to Arithmetic in Prolog

Arithmetic in Prolog allows the evaluation and manipulation of numerical expressions using standard arithmetic operators. Unlike traditional procedural languages, Prolog approaches arithmetic through a declarative paradigm, providing unique methods for performing and evaluating mathematical computations.

Arithmetic expressions in Prolog are evaluated using a predefined set of arithmetic operators and predicates. It's crucial to understand that arithmetic operations in Prolog are not inherently performed during the unification process. Instead, arithmetic expressions must be explicitly evaluated using specific predicates.

Prolog supports typical arithmetic operations such as addition, subtraction, multiplication, division, and exponentiation. These operations can be performed on integers and floating-point numbers. An arithmetic expression in Prolog might look similar to expressions found in other programming languages, but the way they are evaluated differs significantly.

```
% Example arithmetic operations in Prolog
A = 5 + 3, % This will store the term '5 + 3' in A, not evaluate it
B is 5 + 3, % This will evaluate '5 + 3' and store the result (8) in B
C is 7 * 2.5, % This will evaluate '7 * 2.5' and store the result (17.5) in C
```

In the example above, $A = 5 + 3$ simply assigns the unevaluated expression $5 + 3$ to the variable A. To actually perform the arithmetic operation and store the result, the $is/2$ predicate is used, as demonstrated with variables B and C.

The $is/2$ predicate is fundamental to arithmetic in Prolog since it directs the interpreter to evaluate the arithmetic expression on the right-hand side and unify the result with the variable on the left-hand side. Failure to use $is/2$ where necessary can lead to type errors or unexpected behavior, as Prolog treats unevaluated arithmetic terms as data structures rather than numerical values.

```
% Erroneous usage example
D = 5 + 3 * 2 / 1 - 4, % This stores the whole expression in D
```

Arithmetic expressions in Prolog can also leverage parentheses for controlling precedence, similar to other languages. The typical arithmetic operator precedence rules apply, with parentheses allowing explicit grouping of subexpressions to override default precedence.

```
% Using parentheses to control precedence
E is (5 + 3) * 2, % This evaluates '(5 + 3) * 2' and stores 16 in E
F is 5 + (3 * 2), % This evaluates '5 + (3 * 2)' and stores 11 in F
```

Prolog supports both integer and floating-point arithmetic. Conversion between these types occurs automatically as needed, allowing mixed-type arithmetic operations. Nevertheless, care must be taken to avoid unintentional type-related issues, particularly when precision is a consideration.

```
% Mixed-type arithmetic
G is 7 / 2, % This evaluates '7 / 2' as 3.5 and stores it in G
H is 7 // 2, % This performs integer division, storing the result 3 in H
I is 7 mod 4. % This calculates the remainder of '7 / 4', storing 3 in I
```

The $//$ operator is used specifically for integer division, discarding any fractional component, while the mod operator computes the remainder from integer division.

A key consideration in Prolog arithmetic is the handling of variables and ensuring they are instantiated appropriately before arithmetic evaluation. Attempting to evaluate an arithmetic expression with uninstantiated variables will result in errors.

```
% Error example due to uninstantiated variables
J is X + 3. % This will produce an error if X is not previously instantiated
```

Arithmetic predicate behavior varies slightly among Prolog implementations, but the foundational concepts remain consistent. Programmers must familiarize themselves with the specific arithmetic operations detailed in their Prolog system's documentation to ensure compatibility and correct usage.

Prolog's declarative nature requires a different mindset from imperative languages when performing arithmetic operations. By mastering the use of arithmetic predicates, operators, and their appropriate contexts, one can effectively leverage Prolog's arithmetic capabilities for problem-solving and computation.

4.2 Basic Arithmetic Operations

In Prolog, basic arithmetic operations follow specific syntax conventions and utilize operators such as addition, subtraction, multiplication, and division. Understanding these operations is fundamental for performing calculations and forming the foundation for more complex arithmetic expressions.

Prolog supports four primary arithmetic operations:

- **Addition** (+)
- **Subtraction** (-)
- **Multiplication** (*)
- **Division** (/)

When performing these operations, Prolog adheres to standard operator precedence and associativity rules. Let us delve into each operation with practical examples.

Addition: The + operator is used to add two numbers. For instance, to add 5 and 3, one would write:

```
?- X is 5 + 3.
```

The output will be:

X = 8In this example, the is/2 predicate is used to evaluate the arithmetic expression on the right-hand side of is and assign the result to the variable X.

Subtraction: The - operator subtracts one number from another. To subtract 3 from 7, the expression is:

```
?- Y is 7 - 3.
```

The output will be:

Y = 4This indicates that the value of Y is 4 after the subtraction operation.

Multiplication: The * operator multiplies two numbers together. For example, multiplying 4 by 5 is achieved by:

```
?- Z is 4 * 5.
```

The output is:

Z = 20Here, Z holds the product of the two numbers.

Division: The / operator divides one number by another. Dividing 10 by 2 can be written as:

```
?- A is 10 / 2.
```

The output is:

A = 5.0Prolog returns a floating-point number as the result of division, hence the output is 5.0.

Prolog also supports integer division using the // operator and the modulus operation using the mod operator. These operations provide results pertinent to integer arithmetic.

Integer Division: The // operator divides one integer by another and returns the integer quotient:

```
?- B is 10 // 3.
```

The result is:

B = 3Here, the division discards the remainder and only returns the integer part.

Modulus Operation: The mod operator returns the remainder of an integer division:

```
?- C is 10 mod 3.
```

The result is:

C = 1In this case, C is 1 because the remainder when 10 is divided by 3 is 1.

To handle these operations effectively, it is important to understand how Prolog evaluates expressions. The following code snippet demonstrates combining various arithmetic operators:

```
?- Result is (5 + 2) * (8 - 3) / 5.
```

The output will be:

Result = 7.0In the above example, Prolog evaluates the expression inside the parentheses first, following the precedence rules: addition and subtraction before multiplication and division.

Proper use of parentheses can override default precedence, ensuring expressions are evaluated in the intended order. This is crucial in complex calculations to avoid unexpected results.

Understanding basic arithmetic operations in Prolog is essential for further delving into the intricacies of arithmetic expressions and comparisons. The ability to perform and combine these operations is the foundation upon which more advanced arithmetic functionalities are built. Proper comprehension of these operations will facilitate the effective use of Prolog for solving computational problems.

4.3 Using Arithmetic Operators

In Prolog, arithmetic operators enable the manipulation and evaluation of numerical expressions. Prolog supports a variety of arithmetic operators that can be employed to perform fundamental calculations. These operators include addition (+), subtraction (-), multiplication (*), division (/), integer division (//), modulus (mod), and exponentiation (**). Understanding their usage is essential for solving arithmetic problems effectively.

Addition (+):

The addition operator, denoted by +, adds two numbers.

```
?- Result is 5 + 3.
Result = 8.
```

Subtraction (-):

The subtraction operator, represented by -, subtracts the second number from the first number.

```
?- Result is 5 - 3.
Result = 2.
```

Multiplication (*):

Multiplication is performed using the asterisk symbol (*), multiplying two numbers.

```
?- Result is 5 * 3.
Result = 15.
```

Division (/):

The division operator, indicated by the forward-slash (/), divides the first number by the second number. Note that it returns a floating-point result.

```
?- Result is 5 / 2.
Result = 2.5.
```

Integer Division (//):

Integer division is represented by a double forward-slash (//). It performs division but discards the remainder, returning an integer result.

```
?- Result is 5 // 2.
Result = 2.
```

Modulus (mod):

The modulus operator, denoted as mod, calculates the remainder of the division of the first number by the second number.

```
?- Result is 5 mod 2.
Result = 1.
```

Exponentiation (**):

Exponentiation, or raising a number to a power, is performed using the double asterisk (**).

```
?- Result is 5 ** 3.
Result = 125.0.
```

Prolog also provides other arithmetic operators and functions, such as absolute value, trigonometric functions, and logarithms. For example, the absolute value operator is abs/1, and it returns the non-negative value of its argument:

```
?- A = -5, B is abs(A).
A = -5,
B = 5.
```

To ensure arithmetic expressions are correctly evaluated, they must be used within the context of the is/2 predicate or another suitable arithmetic predicate. The is/2 predicate assigns the evaluated result of an expression on its right side to a variable on its left side. Without is/2, Prolog treats the arithmetic expression as a symbolic term rather than evaluating it.

For instance, the following query does not produce the desired arithmetic result:

```
?- Result = 5 + 3.
Result = 5 + 3.
```

In this case, Result is simply bound to the term 5 + 3. By using is/2, the expression is evaluated:

```
?- Result is 5 + 3.
Result = 8.
```

Logical operators, such as =:= for equality and =\= for inequality, also play a critical role in arithmetic comparisons. The operator =:= is used to compare two expressions for equality:

```
?- 5 + 3 =:= 8.
true.
```

Similarly, =\= checks for inequality between two expressions:

```
?- 5 + 3 =\= 8.
false.
```

Combining arithmetic operations with logical comparisons facilitates the construction of more intricate conditions and rules within a Prolog program:

```
larger(X, Y, Z) :-
    Z is max(X, Y).
```

```
?- larger(10, 20, Result).
Result = 20.
```

Understanding and applying these arithmetic operators correctly allows the creation of complex mathematical and logical constructs, enhancing the ability to solve diverse problems within the Prolog environment.

4.4 Understanding Arithmetic Expressions

Prolog provides robust support for operations involving arithmetic expressions. An arithmetic expression in Prolog can include numbers, variables, arithmetic operators, and function calls that result in numerical values. Understanding how to construct and evaluate these expressions is crucial for performing mathematical computations in Prolog.

An arithmetic expression can be as simple as a single number or as complex as a series of operations involving multiple variables and functions. The primary arithmetic operators available in Prolog are as follows:

- Addition: $+$
- Subtraction: -
- Multiplication: $*$
- Division: $/$

Additionally, Prolog supports integer division using the div operator and modulo operations with the mod operator. To illustrate, consider the following arithmetic expression:

$$3 + 5 * 2 - 8/4$$

Prolog follows conventional operator precedence rules when evaluating such expressions. Multiplication and division are performed before addition and subtraction. Parentheses can be used to alter the default precedence, as shown in the following examples:

```
Result1 is 3 + (5 * 2) - (8 / 4).
Result2 is (3 + 5) * 2 - 8 / 4.
```

In the above expressions, $\mathrm{Result1}$ will yield 10, while $\mathrm{Result2}$ will yield 14.

Variables in arithmetic expressions can hold numerical values, allowing for dynamic calculations based on variable assignments. The example below demonstrates this:

```
A = 4,
B = 7,
Result is A + B * 2.
```

Here, the variable Result will resolve to 18, since B * 2 evaluates to 14 and adding A results in 18.

Functions within arithmetic expressions can further extend their utility. Prolog provides a variety of built-in functions for mathematical computations including sqrt/1, abs/1, sin/1, cos/1, and log/1. Consider the following examples:

```
X = 16,
Y = sqrt(X).
```

In this case, Y will be assigned the value 4.0, as it is the square root of 16.

Expressions can also be nested, combining variables, numbers, and functions:

```
A = 4,
B = 16,
Result is A + sqrt(B).
```

Here, Result will resolve to 8.0, as the square root of 16 is 4.0 and adding A gives 8.0.

When working with arithmetic expressions in Prolog, the is/2 operator is commonly used to force the evaluation of the right-hand side and assign the resulting value to the left-hand side variable. Importantly, the right-hand side expression must be fully evaluable at the time of execution. Consider the following examples illustrating correct and incorrect usage:

Correct usage:

```
X = 10,
Y = 2,
Result is X + Y * 3.
```

Incorrect usage:

```
Result is X + Y * 3.
X = 10,
Y = 2.
```

In the incorrect example, X and Y are unbound when Result is evaluated, leading to an error. All variables on the right-hand side of an is/2 operation must be bound to numerical values before the expression is evaluated.

Prolog also supports the evaluation of comparisons within arithmetic expressions using comparison operators. Although detailed exploration of comparison operators is provided in the subsequent section, a fundamental understanding is essential for comprehending arithmetic expressions:

- Equality: =:=
- Inequality: =\=
- Less than: <
- Greater than: >
- Less than or equal to: =<
- Greater than or equal to: >=

The equality operator =:= is used to compare the values of two expressions. For instance,

```
X = 5,
Y = 3 + 2,
X =:= Y.
```

This evaluation will succeed since both X and Y resolve to 5.

Mastering the construction and evaluation of arithmetic expressions in Prolog is foundational for leveraging its full computational capabilities. Understanding the principles of operator precedence, the role of the is/2 operator, the use of variables and functions within expressions, and the appropriate application of comparison operators are key components of this understanding.

4.5 Evaluating Expressions with is/2

Evaluating expressions in Prolog requires a thorough understanding of the is/2 operator. The is/2 operator is a built-in predicate used to evaluate arithmetic expressions and assign the resulting value to a variable.

Proper usage of is/2 involves two key points: the left-hand side should be an unbound or partially bound variable, and the right-hand side must be an arithmetic expression.

Syntax:

```
Variable is ArithmeticExpression
```

The ArithmeticExpression can include numerical values, variables, or more complex expressions constructed using arithmetic operators and functions. The evaluation process adheres to the precedence and associativity rules defined in Prolog.

Example 1: Basic Usage

Consider a simple example where an arithmetic expression is evaluated and assigned to a variable.

```
?- X is 2 + 3 * 4.
```

Upon execution, the arithmetic expression 2 + 3 * 4 is evaluated, yielding a result of 14 due to the precedence of multiplication over addition.

```
X = 14.
```

Example 2: Using Variables in Expressions

Variables can be included in expressions. Before evaluation, ensure that the variables already have assigned numeric values.

```
?- A = 5, B = 10, X is A + B / 2.
```

In this case, variables A and B are instantiated with values 5 and 10, respectively. The expression A + B / 2 evaluates to 10, where the division operation is performed prior to addition.

```
A = 5,
B = 10,
X = 10.
```

Example 3: Complex Expressions

More complex arithmetic expressions involving multiple operators or nested sub-expressions can also be evaluated using is/2.

```
?- X is (4 + 2) * (10 / 5) - 3^2.
```

Here, the expression (4 + 2) * (10 / 5) - 3^2 is evaluated within the parentheses with correct precedence, resulting in (6 * 2) - 9, ultimately yielding 3.

```
X = 3.
```

Important Considerations

Several important aspects must be considered while using is/2:

- **Groundedness**: The variable on the left-hand side of is/2 should be unbound or partially bound. If it is already bound to a numeric value, Prolog attempts to reassign the value without causing inconsistency.
- **Arithmetic Types**: Prolog distinguishes between integers and floating-point numbers. The arithmetic expression must respect these types; however, mixed-type operations are automatically handled.

Type Conversion

Prolog transparently handles type conversion between integers and floats during arithmetic evaluations. For instance:

```
?- X is 5 + 2.0.
```

The integer 5 and the floating-point 2.0 are converted and the result will be a float.

```
X = 7.0.
```

Another scenario involves reactions to arithmetic errors or invalid operations. Understanding these potential outcomes enhances the robustness of Prolog programs.

Handling Arithmetic Errors

When evaluating expressions, Prolog performs checks to prevent common errors such as division by zero, non-numeric operands, or invalid expressions. For example:

```
?- X is 10 / 0.
```

Executing the above query will result in a runtime error due to the division by zero condition.

```
ERROR: 10 / 0: evaluation error: zero_divisor
```

Usage in Conditional Statements

The is/2 operator can also be utilized within conditional statements to perform arithmetic evaluations conditionally.

```
max(A, B, Max) :-
    ( A > B -> Max is A
```

```
    ; Max is B
    ).
```

In the example above, the predicate $\max/3$ calculates the maximum of two numbers by evaluating the expression using $is/2$ conditionally based on the comparison of A and B.

Best Practices

When using $is/2$:

- Always ensure that the right-hand side is a valid arithmetic expression.
- Utilize parentheses to explicitly define precedence and improve readability.
- Be cautious with operations that might lead to runtime errors, such as division by zero.
- Consider edge cases and invalid inputs to enhance robustness.

Logical correctness and clarity of the arithmetic expressions evaluated using $is/2$ contribute to the accuracy and reliability of Prolog programs. Careful adherence to the discussed principles and examples ensures effective utilization of arithmetic operations in Prolog.

4.6 Comparison Operators in Prolog

Comparison operators in Prolog are integral to evaluating predicates and making logical decisions based on numerical values. They enable Prolog programs to compare numbers and determine relationships such as equality, inequality, less than, greater than, and more complex relations between numerical expressions. The core comparison operators in Prolog include $=:=$, $=\backslash=$, $<$, $>$, $=\backslash=$, and $>=$. Each of these operators serves a specific purpose and is used with the $is/2$ predicate or within conditional statements. It is important to understand the syntax and semantics of these operators to effectively utilize them in Prolog programming.

The operator $=:=$ checks for numerical equality of two arithmetic expressions. It succeeds if the evaluated expressions to its left and right are numerically equal.

```
?- X is 10, Y is 5 + 5, X =:= Y.
X = 10,
Y = 10.
```

In this example, the Prolog query succeeds because both X and Y evaluate to 10, making the expression $X =:= Y$ true.

The operator $=\backslash=$ is used to determine numerical inequality. It succeeds if the evaluated expressions to its left and right are not numerically equal.

```
?- X is 10, Y is 5 + 3, X =\textbackslash= Y.
X = 10,
Y = 8.
```

Here, the query succeeds since X evaluates to 10 and Y evaluates to 8, making the expression $X =\backslash= Y$ true.

The less than operator $<$ is used to test if the expression on the left evaluates to a value less than the one on the right.

```
?- X is 10, Y is 20, X < Y.
X = 10,
Y = 20.
```

In this query, X is 10 and Y is 20. The condition $X < Y$ holds true, resulting in a successful query.

Conversely, the greater than operator $>$ checks if the value on the left side is greater than the value on the right.

```
?- A is 20, B is 10, A > B.
A = 20,
B = 10.
```

Here, the query returns true as A evaluates to 20, and B evaluates to 10, and 20 is indeed greater than 10.

The operator $=\backslash=$ tests for less than or equal to conditions. It succeeds if the expression on the left evaluates to a value that is less than or equal to the value on the right.

```
?- C is 15, D is 15, C =\textbackslash= D.
C = 15,
D = 15.
```

This query succeeds because C is equal to D, satisfying the $=\backslash=$ condition.

Lastly, the $>=$ operator is used to verify if the expression on the left is greater than or equal to the expression on the right.

```
?- E is 25, F is 20, E >= F.
E = 25,
F = 20.
```

In this scenario, the query succeeds as E (25) is greater than F (20).

It is crucial to note that all these operators necessitate the expressions on both sides to be fully evaluable to numerical values for the comparison to make sense. Therefore, variables involved in the comparisons should be instantiated or directly capable of being evaluated through expressions with $is/2$ or similar arithmetic contexts.

When utilizing these comparison operators within Prolog rules and predicates, one can build more complex logic by combining multiple conditions with logical operators. This capability enables constructing intricate decision-making processes.

```
greater_than_and_odd(X, Y) :-
    X > Y,
    X mod 2 =:= 1.
```

The above predicate $greater\_than\_and\_odd/2$ will succeed if X is greater than Y and X is an odd number. This demonstrates how comparison operators can be embedded in user-defined predicates for more advanced control structures.

Effective use of comparison operators can significantly enhance the decision-making and control flow of Prolog programs, allowing for efficient and correct evaluation of arithmetic conditions and ensuring logical consistency within the computational logic.

4.7 Implementing Arithmetic Functions

In this section, we delve into the implementation of arithmetic functions in Prolog. Arithmetic functions in Prolog allow us to perform various calculations and complex operations within our programs. These functions are defined using predicates and can include built-in arithmetic operators and user-defined calculations. Proper implementation of these functions is crucial for solving problems that involve numerical computations.

Arithmetic functions often involve the use of recursive definitions, accumulation patterns, and direct calculations. We will explore several examples to illustrate these concepts effectively.

Factorial Function: The factorial of a number is a classic example of a recursive arithmetic function. In Prolog, the factorial function can be implemented using a recursive predicate to handle the multiplication of the sequence.

```
factorial(0, 1). % Base case: factorial of 0 is 1.

factorial(N, F) :-
    N > 0, % Ensure N is positive.
    N1 is N - 1, % Decrement N.
    factorial(N1, F1), % Recursive call.
    F is N * F1. % Calculate factorial.
```

When we query factorial/2, Prolog evaluates the expression recursively until it reaches the base case. The final result is computed as the product of the series of decrements.

Power Function: Another common arithmetic function is exponentiation, where a base number is raised to a power. This can be implemented in Prolog using a similar recursive approach.

```
power(_, 0, 1). % Base case: any number to the power of 0 is 1.

power(Base, Exponent, Result) :-
    Exponent > 0, % Ensure Exponent is positive.
    E1 is Exponent - 1, % Decrement Exponent.
    power(Base, E1, R1), % Recursive call.
    Result is Base * R1. % Calculate power.
```

Querying power/3 with specific Base and Exponent values triggers recursive evaluation until the exponent reaches zero.

Summation Function: To further illustrate arithmetic functions, consider a summation function that calculates the sum of all integers from 1 to N. This can be efficiently implemented using recursion with an accumulator pattern.

```
sum_to_n(N, Sum) :- sum_to_n(N, 0, Sum).

sum_to_n(0, Acc, Acc). % Base case: accumulator contains the sum.

sum_to_n(N, Acc, Sum) :-
    N > 0,
    Acc1 is Acc + N, % Update accumulator.
    N1 is N - 1, % Decrement N.
    sum_to_n(N1, Acc1, Sum). % Recursive call.
```

Here, sum_to_n/3 ensures the accumulation process and terminates when N reaches zero.

Greatest Common Divisor (GCD): The GCD of two integers can be calculated using the Euclidean algorithm, a well-known efficient recursive method.

```
gcd(A, 0, A). % Base case: GCD of A and 0 is A.

gcd(A, B, G) :-
    B > 0,
    Rem is A mod B, % Compute remainder.
    gcd(B, Rem, G). % Recursive call.
```

Querying gcd/3 recursively applies modulo operations until the remainder is zero, returning the last non-zero divisor.

Fibonacci Sequence: Calculating Fibonacci numbers can also be defined recursively. However, naive recursion leads to exponential time complexity. Below is a basic implementation followed by an optimized version using memoization.

```
% Naive recursive approach.
fibonacci(0, 0).
fibonacci(1, 1).

fibonacci(N, F) :-
    N > 1,
    N1 is N - 1,
    N2 is N - 2,
    fibonacci(N1, F1),
    fibonacci(N2, F2),
    F is F1 + F2.
```

The optimized version uses an auxiliary predicate to store intermediate computations.

```
% Optimized approach with memoization.
:- dynamic fib/2.

fibonacci_optimized(0, 0).
fibonacci_optimized(1, 1).

fibonacci_optimized(N, F) :-
    N > 1,
    ( fib(N, F) -> true % Check memoized result.
    ; N1 is N - 1,
        N2 is N - 2,
        fibonacci_optimized(N1, F1),
        fibonacci_optimized(N2, F2),
        F is F1 + F2,
        assertz(fib(N, F)) % Store result.
    ).
```

With these implementations, Prolog can handle a variety of arithmetic computations efficiently. Understanding and utilizing these patterns greatly enhance our problem-solving capabilities in Prolog.

4.8 Working with Integer and Float Types

Prolog supports two primary numeric types: integers and floats. Understanding the properties and operations applicable to these types is crucial for writing effective and accurate arithmetic expressions in Prolog.

Integers are whole numbers, and their representation in Prolog is straightforward. They can be positive, negative, or zero. For example, 42, -5, and 0 are all valid integer literals. Floats, on the other hand, represent real numbers and include a fractional component. They are typically written using a decimal point, such as 3.14, -0.001, or 2.0.

In Prolog, the type of a numeric value influences how expressions are evaluated and how results are interpreted. It is essential to be aware of the differences in behavior between integers and floats to avoid unexpected results in arithmetic computations.

Type Identification

Prolog provides built-in predicates to check the type of a number. The primary predicates for this purpose are $\mathrm{integer}/1$ and $\mathrm{float}/1$. These predicates succeed if the argument is of the respective type and fail otherwise.

```
% checks if a number is an integer
?- integer(42).
true.

% checks if a number is a float
?- float(3.14).
true.

% fails because the number is an integer
?- float(5).
false.
```

Implicit Type Conversion

Prolog performs type conversion implicitly in certain arithmetic operations. When an integer and a float are involved in an expression, the integer is converted to a float, and the result is computed as a float. This automatic conversion ensures that operations yield consistent results by maintaining a single type within the expression.

Consider the following example:

```
% the integer 2 is implicitly converted to a float
% the result of the division is a float
?- X is 2 / 2.0.
X = 1.0.
```

Arithmetic Operations

Arithmetic operations can involve both integers and floats. The precision and type of the result depend on the operands. Prolog supports common arithmetic operations, such as addition (+), subtraction (-), multiplication (*), and division (/).

```
% addition of an integer and a float
?- X is 5 + 2.5.
X = 7.5.

% multiplication of an integer and a float
?- Y is 4 * 0.5.
Y = 2.0.
```

It is important to note that the division operator (/) always produces a float result, even if both operands are integers. For integer division, Prolog provides the div/2 operator, which yields the quotient of the division.

```
% float division
?- Z is 5 / 2.
Z = 2.5.

% integer division
?- W is 5 div 2.
W = 2.
```

Modulo Operation

For integer computations, Prolog offers the mod/2 operator to obtain the remainder of an integer division. This is useful in scenarios where cyclic behaviors or interval-based calculations are required.

```
% modulo operation
?- Remainder is 17 mod 5.
Remainder = 2.
```

Type-Specific Functions

Prolog includes functions specifically designed for integer and float types. For instance, the floor/1 and ceiling/1 functions convert floats to the nearest lower or higher integer, respectively. The round/1 function rounds a float to the nearest integer, and the truncate/1 function removes the fractional part of a float, effectively converting it to an integer.

```
% floor function example
?- X is floor(3.9).
X = 3.
```

```
% ceiling function example
?- Y is ceiling(3.1).
Y = 4.

% round function example
?- Z is round(3.5).
Z = 4.

% truncate function example
?- W is truncate(3.9).
W = 3.
```

Handling Precision

Care must be taken when working with floats due to their inherent inaccuracy resulting from the finite precision of floating-point representation. Small errors can accumulate in computations, leading to significant inaccuracies. It is advisable to use appropriate rounding functions or precision handling techniques, especially in applications requiring high numerical accuracy.

Floats in Prolog follow the IEEE 754 standard for binary floating-point arithmetic, which includes specific behavior for operations like overflow, underflow, and rounding. Understanding these behaviors helps mitigate precision-related issues in arithmetic computations.

Working with integers and floats in Prolog requires an understanding of type-specific behaviors and operations. Using appropriate predicates and handling implicit type conversions ensures correct and efficient arithmetic processing. Taking care of the precision in floating-point operations is crucial for accurate results, especially in complex numerical computations.

4.9 Random Number Generation

Random number generation is a crucial feature for various computational tasks, such as simulations, randomized algorithms, and games. Prolog provides built-in predicates to facilitate random number generation, allowing for the creation of integers and floating-point numbers within specified ranges.

To generate a random integer within a given range, use the random/3 predicate. The syntax for this predicate is:

```
random(Low, High, Result)
```

where Low is the inclusive lower bound, High is the exclusive upper bound, and Result is the variable that will be unified with the randomly generated integer. The random/3 predicate ensures that Low and High are integers, and that Result will be an integer such that Low =< Result < High.

For example, to generate a random integer between 1 and 10:

```
?- random(1, 11, X).
```

The output may look like this:

X = 7.Each invocation of random/3 will yield a different result within the specified range.

For generating random floating-point numbers within the range [0.0, 1.0), use the random/1 predicate. The syntax is:

```
random(Result)
```

where Result will be unified with a random floating-point number in the specified range. This can be useful for applications requiring higher precision or for generating fractions.

An example of generating a random floating-point number:

```
?- random(X).
```

The output will resemble:

X = 0.453321.

When it is necessary to generate random floating-point numbers within a specific range [Low, High), a common practice is to use arithmetic operations in conjunction with random/1:

```
generate_random_float(Low, High, Result) :-
    random(R),
    Result is Low + (High - Low) * R.
```

Calling generate_random_float/3 with appropriate bounds will yield a floating-point number within the desired range:

```
?- generate_random_float(5.0, 10.0, X).
```

The output could be:

X = 7.145897.

In certain scenarios, applications may require a random selection from a list of elements. The random_member/2 predicate serves this purpose efficiently. The syntax is:

```
random_member(Element, List)
```

where Element will be unified with a randomly chosen element from List.

Consider selecting a random element from a predefined list:

```
?- random_member(X, [a, b, c, d, e]).
```

The output can be:

X = c.Ensuring different outcomes within repeated trials.

For reproducibility and testing purposes, random seed control is essential. Use the set_random/1 predicate to set the seed value:

```
set_random(seed(Seed))
```

where Seed is an integer. This practice guarantees that sequences of random numbers will be consistent across different runs with the same seed.

For example:

```
?- set_random(seed(42)).
```

Subsequent calls to random/3 or random/1 will produce the same sequence of numbers given the seed 42. Verifying the functionality:

```
?- random(1, 100, X).
```

The generated number:

X = 53.

Understanding and utilizing these predicates and techniques enables precise and efficient random number generation in Prolog.

4.10 Handling Arithmetic Errors

Handling errors is a crucial part of any programming language, and Prolog is no exception. Arithmetic errors can arise from various situations, such as division by zero, overflow, underflow, or attempting to evaluate non-numeric expressions. Knowing how to detect and manage these errors effectively ensures that your Prolog programs are robust and reliable.

Prolog's error handling mechanism involves both system-specific error messages and the ability to defend against possible arithmetic pitfalls through careful programming practices.

Division by Zero: One of the most common arithmetic errors in any programming language is division by zero. When Prolog encounters this error, it typically raises an exception and terminates the goal where the error occurred.

For example:

```
?- X is 5 / 0.
```

The Prolog interpreter will emit an error message similar to the following:

```
ERROR: /: arithmetic expression '5/0' is undefined
```

To handle such errors gracefully, you can use a conditional check before performing the division.

```
safe_division(Numerator, Denominator, Result) :-
    (Denominator \= 0 -> Result is Numerator / Denominator; Result = 'undefined').
```

This safe_division/3 predicate ensures that the division only occurs if the Denominator is not zero. Otherwise, it assigns the atom 'undefined' to Result.

Overflow and Underflow: Given that Prolog typically uses underlying libraries written in C or other low-level languages, it inherits similar constraints for number representations. Overflow errors occur when an arithmetic operation produces a number larger than the maximum representable value, while underflow occurs for numbers smaller than the minimum representable value.

Consider an example of handling these scenarios:

```
check_overflow(Expression, Result) :-
    catch(Result is Expression, error(evaluation_error(float_overflow), _), Result = '
        overflow'),
    catch(Result is Expression, error(evaluation_error(float_underflow), _), Result = '
        underflow').
```

In this example, the use of catch/3 allows for trapping overflow and underflow errors, providing an alternative result when these errors occur.

Invalid Arithmetic Expressions: Prolog will also raise an error if an arithmetic operation is attempted on non-numeric expressions. Consider the following erroneous query:

```
?- X is 5 + foo.
```

This results in an error message similar to:

```
ERROR: is/2: Arithmetic: 'foo/0' is not a function
```

To avoid such errors, ensure that variables involved in arithmetic expressions are properly validated.

```
valid_number(X) :- number(X).

safe_addition(A, B, Result) :-
    valid_number(A), valid_number(B),
    Result is A + B.
```

Here, valid_number/1 serves as a guard to check if both A and B are numbers before performing the addition.

Use of catch/3 **and** throw/1: Both catch/3 and throw/1 are integral for exception handling in Prolog. The catch/3 predicate allows capturing exceptions, while throw/1 can be used to raise exceptions.

Example of catch/3:

```
safe_arithmetic(Operation, Default, Result) :-
    catch(Operation, error(E, _), (write(E), nl, Result = Default)).
```

You can call this predicate with specific arithmetic operations encapsulated in goals:

```
?- safe_arithmetic((X is 5 / 0), 'error', Result).
```

This would capture the division by zero error, print the error message, and assign 'error' to Result.

Undefined Evaluations: Handling other forms of undefined evaluations, like square roots of negative numbers, can be done similarly:

```
safe_sqrt(Number, Result) :-
    (Number >= 0 -> Result is sqrt(Number); Result = 'undefined').
```

This ensures that the square root operation is only performed on non-negative numbers.

Robust error handling in Prolog arithmetic ensures programs can manage erroneous conditions gracefully, without termination or unhandled exceptions disrupting normal execution. Applying these principles enhances code stability, especially in complex problem-solving scenarios.

4.11 Example Problems with Prolog Arithmetic

To solidify our understanding of arithmetic in Prolog, we will examine several example problems, addressing a variety of scenarios where arithmetic operations play a crucial role. Each example showcases the use of arithmetic operators, evaluation of expressions, and application of arithmetic functions in Prolog.

Example 1: Calculating the Sum of a List of Numbers

This problem involves calculating the sum of a list of numbers. We will define a predicate sum_list/2 that takes a list and a variable to store the sum.

```
sum_list([], Sum) :-
    Sum is 0.

sum_list([Head|Tail], Sum) :-
    sum_list(Tail, SumTail),
    Sum is Head + SumTail.
```

The base case specifies that the sum of an empty list is 0. The recursive clause breaks down the problem, adding the head of the list to the sum of the remaining elements. Here is an example interaction:

```
?- sum_list([1, 2, 3, 4], Sum).
Sum = 10.
```

Example 2: Finding the Maximum in a List

We aim to identify the maximum element in a list. We define the predicate max_list/2 to perform this task.

```
max_list([X], X).

max_list([Head|Tail], Max) :-
    max_list(Tail, MaxTail),
    Max is max(Head, MaxTail).
```

The base case considers a list with a single element as the maximum. The recursive clause compares the head with the maximum of the tail, using the max/2 function. Example interaction:

```
?- max_list([10, 2, 33, 4], Max).
Max = 33.
```

Example 3: Computing the Factorial of a Number

The factorial of a number n (denoted as $n!$) is the product of all positive integers up to n. We define factorial/2 to calculate this.

```
factorial(0, 1).

factorial(N, F) :-
    N > 0,
    N1 is N - 1,
    factorial(N1, F1),
    F is N * F1.
```

The base case specifies that the factorial of 0 is 1. The recursive clause computes the factorial for N by multiplying N with the factorial of $N-1$. Example interaction:

```
?- factorial(5, F).
F = 120.
```

Example 4: Generating Fibonacci Numbers

The Fibonacci sequence is defined as $F(0) = 0$, $F(1) = 1$, and $F(n) = F(n-1) + F(n-2)$ for $n > 1$. We define fibonacci/2 to compute it.

```
fibonacci(0, 0).

fibonacci(1, 1).

fibonacci(N, F) :-
    N > 1,
    N1 is N - 1,
    N2 is N - 2,
    fibonacci(N1, F1),
    fibonacci(N2, F2),
    F is F1 + F2.
```

The base cases handle $F(0)$ and $F(1)$. The recursive clause sums the two preceding Fibonacci numbers to compute $F(N)$. Example interaction:

```
?- fibonacci(7, F).
F = 13.
```

Example 5: Summing Elements in a Matrix

To sum all elements in a matrix (represented as a list of lists), we define sum_matrix/2 utilizing sum_list/2 from our first example.

```
sum_matrix([], 0).

sum_matrix([Row|Rows], Sum) :-
    sum_list(Row, RowSum),
    sum_matrix(Rows, SumRest),
    Sum is RowSum + SumRest.
```

The base case handles an empty matrix (sum is 0). The recursive clause sums the elements of the current row and the sum of the remaining rows. Example interaction:

```
?- sum_matrix([[1, 2], [3, 4], [5, 6]], Sum).
Sum = 21.
```

Example 6: Solving the Quadratic Equation

The quadratic equation $ax^2 + bx + c = 0$ is solved by the formula $x = \frac{-b \pm \sqrt{b^2 - 4ac}}{2a}$. We create $\text{quadratic\_roots}/4$ to find the roots.

```
quadratic_roots(A, B, C, Roots) :-
    Discriminant is B * B - 4 * A * C,
    ( Discriminant > 0
    -> Root1 is (-B + sqrt(Discriminant)) / (2 * A),
       Root2 is (-B - sqrt(Discriminant)) / (2 * A),
       Roots = [Root1, Root2]
    ; Discriminant =:= 0
    -> Root is -B / (2 * A),
       Roots = [Root]
    ; Roots = []
    ).
```

This predicate calculates the discriminant, then determines roots based on its value: two roots if positive, one root if zero, and no real roots if negative. Example interaction:

```
?- quadratic_roots(1, -3, 2, Roots).
Roots = [2.0, 1.0].

?- quadratic_roots(1, 2, 1, Roots).
Roots = [-1.0].

?- quadratic_roots(1, 0, 1, Roots).
Roots = [].
```

Each example consolidates the understanding of arithmetic operations and functions within Prolog, providing practical applications and reinforcing the syntax and logic required to implement solutions.

Chapter 5

Managing Data Structures in Prolog

This chapter explores data structures in Prolog, focusing on tuples, compound data structures, and dictionaries. It examines tree structures, including binary trees, and graph representations. The chapter discusses set manipulation, nested data structures, persistence, and pattern matching with complex data. Practical examples illustrate these concepts and their applications in Prolog.

5.1 Introduction to Data Structures in Prolog

Prolog, as a logic programming language, employs various robust data structures to effectively manage and manipulate data. Understanding these data structures is foundational for constructing efficient Prolog programs. This section introduces the essential data structures used in Prolog, including atoms, lists, and terms, to set the groundwork for the more complex data structures discussed in subsequent sections.

An atom in Prolog is a general-purpose, named constant. Atoms can be any string of characters enclosed in single quotes, e.g., $\mathrm{'tom'}$, or a sequence of alphanumeric characters starting with a lowercase letter, e.g., tom. Atoms are the simplest form of data and are often used to represent individual objects or identifiers.

Prolog lists are a fundamental and flexible data structure, akin to arrays in other programming languages. A list in Prolog is an ordered collection of elements, written as a sequence of terms separated by commas and enclosed in square brackets, e.g., [a, b, c]. Lists can be nested, allowing for lists of lists, and can contain any Prolog data type.

```
% Example of a Prolog list
my_list([apple, banana, cherry]).
nested_list([[1,2], [3,4], [5,6]]).
```

Terms, or compound terms, are the building blocks for more complex data structures in Prolog. A compound term consists of a functor and a sequence of arguments, which can themselves be atoms, numbers, variables, or other terms. The arity of a term is the number of arguments it contains.

```
% Example of a compound term
family(person(tom, male, 30), person(anna, female, 29), [child(julie, female, 5)]).
```

Variables in Prolog are placeholders for terms and are represented by strings of characters starting with an uppercase letter or an underscore. Variables are dynamically bound to values during the execution of queries.

```
% Example using variables
likes(Who, pizza).
```

Queries and predicates play a significant role in manipulating these data structures. A query is a request to determine if a certain condition is true based on the defined predicates and facts. A predicate is a relation among terms, and it operates on these terms to yield true or false.

```
% Example of a fact and a query
fruit(apple).
fruit(banana).

% Query to check for fruit
?- fruit(apple).
```

The outputs of the above code would be:

```
true.
```

Lists can be dissected using the | operator, termed the head and tail notation, where the head is the first element and the tail is the remainder of the list. For instance, [H|T] = [1,2,3] would bind H to 1 and T to [2,3].

```
% Example of head and tail notation
decompose_list([H|T]) :-
```

```
    write('Head: '), write(H), nl,
    write('Tail: '), write(T), nl.
```

Calling the above predicate with decompose_list([1, 2, 3]) results in the output:

```
Head: 1
Tail: [2,3]
```

Combining lists and compound terms, more complex structures such as trees and graphs can be represented. Trees are often expressed using nested terms, while graphs may be represented using lists of edges or adjacency lists. An understanding of these basic forms lays the groundwork for more advanced data manipulation techniques to be explored.

```
% Representation of a binary tree
binary_tree(node(left(leaf, 2, leaf)), 1, node(right(leaf, 3, leaf))).
```

binary_tree/1 demonstrates a binary tree where each node is either a leaf or a node with left and right branches. These branches can recursively contain more nodes or leaves.

```
% Example of a graph represented as a list of edges
graph([edge(a, b), edge(a, c), edge(b, d), edge(c, d)]).
```

Understanding these basic concepts and structures is essential for mastering more advanced topics in Prolog. These structures provide a firm foundation for creating efficient and complex data manipulations, enhancing the capabilities of Prolog programs significantly.

5.2 Defining and Using Tuples

Tuples in Prolog are utilized to group a fixed number of items together. They are a form of compound data structure that is fundamental in representing complex data. In Prolog, tuples can be defined using the functor and arguments notation. This resembles the typical combination of elements in other programming languages but with syntactical differences.

In Prolog, a tuple is essentially an n-ary term where the functor represents the name of the tuple, and the arguments are the elements within the tuple. Consider the following example defining a tuple to represent a point in a 2-dimensional space:

```
point(X, Y).
```

Here, point/2 is a tuple with the functor point and two arguments, X and Y, representing coordinates in a 2-dimensional space. The notation point/2 indicates a functor named point with arity 2.

To instantiate this tuple, we create specific tuples by providing actual values:

```
P1 = point(3, 4),
P2 = point(-1, 5).
```

In these examples, P1 and P2 are instances of tuples where P1 represents the point with coordinates $(3, 4)$ and P2 represents the point with coordinates $(-1, 5)$.

To retrieve and manipulate the elements within a tuple, unification is employed. Consider the following example where we extract the coordinates of a point:

```
point(X, Y) = point(3, 4).
```

After unification, X will be bound to 3 and Y will be bound to 4. This demonstrates the straightforward nature of accessing tuple elements using Prolog's built-in pattern matching capabilities.

Tuples can also be nested within other tuples to form more complex structures. For instance, a 3-dimensional point can be represented by nesting a 2-dimensional point within another tuple:

```
point3D(X, Y, Z) = point3D(point(3, 4), 5).
```

In this tuple, point3D has a nested point for the first two dimensions, and a third element representing the Z-coordinate. To access these nested elements, the unification process can be applied recursively:

```
point3D(point(X, Y), Z) = point3D(point(3, 4), 5).
```

Here, X will be bound to 3, Y to 4, and Z to 5, effectively unwrapping the nested structure.

Prolog's support for tuples extends to operational contexts where functions or predicates return tuples. A predicate may not only take tuples as arguments but also produce tuples as output. This enables the encapsulation of multiple values in a single return structure, facilitating complex data manipulations. Consider the following predicate that creates a 2-dimensional point from given coordinates:

```
create_point(X, Y, point(X, Y)).
```

This predicate, create_point/3, takes X and Y as inputs and encapsulates them into a tuple point(X, Y).

To extend this concept further, we can define predicate operations that handle tuples for calculations. For example, calculating the distance between two 2-dimensional points:

```
distance(point(X1, Y1), point(X2, Y2), Distance) :-
    DiffX is X2 - X1,
    DiffY is Y2 - Y1,
    Distance is sqrt(DiffX * DiffX + DiffY * DiffY).
```

In this distance calculation predicate, distance/3, we take two points as tuples and compute the Euclidean distance between them. The tuple elements are accessed directly within the predicate, demonstrating practical tuple usage in functional operations.

```
?- distance(point(3, 4), point(-1, 5), Distance).
Distance = 4.123105625617661
```

This example query calculates the distance between the points $(3, 4)$ and $(-1, 5)$, returning approximately 4.123105625617661.

Understanding and utilizing tuples in Prolog enriches the ability to handle complex data structures efficiently. By leveraging the inherent unification mechanism, tuple manipulation becomes an intuitive and powerful tool in Prolog programming.

5.3 Working with Compound Data Structures

Compound data structures in Prolog, often referred to as terms, play a critical role in representing and manipulating related pieces of information collectively. Unlike simple data structures, compound data structures are nested data representations that can recursively include other terms, allowing for the creation of complex models suited for various applications.

functor/3 and arg/3 are central predicates used to work with compound terms.

Forming Compound Data Structures

Compound data structures are commonly constructed using functors. A functor is akin to a function name, and the arguments are the components combined by the functor. A typical functor in Prolog takes the form FunctorName(Arg1, Arg2, ..., ArgN). For instance:

```
person(john, doe, 30).
date(2023, october, 10).
```

In the above constructs, person/3 and date/3 are compound terms where person and date are functors, and the following arguments are encapsulated within these structures.

Extracting Components from Compound Terms

To decompose or inspect the elements of a compound term, Prolog provides the functor/3 and arg/3 predicates.

functor/3 unifies the functor name and arity of a term:

```
?- functor(person(john, doe, 30), Functor, Arity).
Functor = person,
Arity = 3.
```

This returns the functor person and the number of arguments, 3.

arg/3 retrieves the value of a specific argument:

```
?- arg(2, person(john, doe, 30), LastName).
LastName = doe.
```

This demonstrates how to access the second element within the person/3 compound term.

Using Compound Data Structures Effectively

By leveraging compound data structures, it is possible to implement a variety of complex models with nested terms. Here is an illustrative example of a hierarchical data structure for representing a company organizational chart:

```
employee(ceo,
  person(john, doe, 50), [
    employee(manager,
      person(jane, smith, 40), [
        employee(developer, person(tom, brown, 30), [])
      ]),
    employee(manager,
      person(susan, taylor, 38), [
        employee(developer, person(emily, white, 28), [])
      ])
  ]).
```

The above structure demonstrates nested functors to represent an employee hierarchy. The employee/3 compound term includes the position, personal details, and a list of subordinates.

Pattern Matching with Compound Terms

Compound data structures facilitate dynamic pattern matching, an essential feature in logic programming. Prolog's unification mechanism automatically matches patterns between terms, providing a foundation for recursive and declarative programming. Consider the following pattern-matching rule to identify a manager in an employee hierarchy:

```
is_manager(employee(manager, _, _)).
```

Here, the predicate is_manager/1 checks if an employee is a manager.

Handling Lists Within Compound Structures

Compound terms and lists can coexist seamlessly. It is common to mix these structures for representing more elaborate models. Consider a data structure modeling a book catalog:

```
book_catalog([
  book('Prolog Programming for Beginners',
       author('John', 'Smith'),
       date(2022, april, 10)),
  book('Advanced Prolog Concepts',
       author('Alice', 'Johnson'),
       date(2021, july, 25))
]).
```

Accessing elements from such mixed structures uses the same principles of pattern matching and recursion. For instance, to retrieve all book titles:

```
retrieve_titles([]) :- !.
retrieve_titles([book(Title, _, _)|Rest]) :-
  writeln(Title),
  retrieve_titles(Rest).
?- book_catalog(Catalog), Catalog = [Books], retrieve_titles(Books).
```

This employs a recursive approach to iterate through the list of books within the book_catalog/1 structure.

Compound data structures, therefore, empower the representation and manipulation of complex and nested data efficiently, forming the foundation for sophisticated Prolog programming.

5.4 Creating and Using Dictionaries

Dictionaries in Prolog offer a versatile way to manage key-value pairs, akin to associative arrays or hash maps in other programming languages. They are particularly useful for tasks that require efficient lookups, insertions, and updates. Prolog dictionaries can be implemented using various techniques such as lists, trees, or built-in dictionary predicates, depending on the Prolog dialect.

To illustrate the fundamental use of dictionaries in Prolog, we will use the SWI-Prolog implementation, which provides robust support for dictionary operations through its built-in ‘dict‘ module. We will delve into dictionary creation, key-value pair manipulation, and query operations.

Dictionary Creation

In SWI-Prolog, a dictionary can be created using the {...} syntax. The keys and values are specified within the braces, separated by commas. Here is an example of creating a simple dictionary:

```
Dict = _{name: "John", age: 30, occupation: "Engineer"}.
```

Accessing Values

Accessing values in a dictionary can be done using the dot notation or the get/3 predicate. The dot notation is straightforward:

```
Name = Dict.name,
Age = Dict.age.
```

Alternatively, the get/3 predicate can be used:

```
get(Dict, name, Name),
get(Dict, age, Age).
```

Adding and Updating Key-Value Pairs

To add or update key-value pairs in a dictionary, the put/4 predicate is used. This predicate creates a new dictionary with the specified key updated to the given value:

```
put(Dict, city, "New York", NewDict).
```

This results in NewDict containing all original key-value pairs plus the new key-value pair city: "New York". If the key city already exists in Dict, its value will be updated.

Removing Key-Value Pairs

To remove a key-value pair from a dictionary, you can use the del/3 predicate. This predicate produces a new dictionary without the specified key:

```
del(Dict, age, UpdatedDict).
```

After executing the above, UpdatedDict will be a dictionary without the key age.

Checking for Keys and Values

It is often necessary to check whether a key exists in a dictionary or to retrieve all keys and values. The get/3 predicate can determine the existence of a key:

```
( get(Dict, name, Name)
-> writeln(Name)
; writeln('Key not found')
).
```

To retrieve all keys or values, the 'keys/2' and 'vals/2' predicates can be used:

```
keys(Dict, Keys), % Retrieves all keys
vals(Dict, Values). % Retrieves all values
```

These predicates are especially useful when you need to iterate over all elements of a dictionary.

Example: Managing a Contact List

Consider a scenario where we need to manage a contact list, where each contact is a dictionary. We will perform operations like adding a new contact, updating an existing contact's information, removing a contact, and querying for specific details.

```
% Initialize a contact list
Contact1 = _{name: "Alice", phone: "1234", email: "alice@example.com"},
Contact2 = _{name: "Bob", phone: "5678", email: "bob@example.com"}.

% Add contacts to a list
ContactList = [Contact1, Contact2].

% Add a new contact
Contact3 = _{name: "Charlie", phone: "9101", email: "charlie@example.com"},
NewContactList = [Contact3 | ContactList].

% Update Bob's phone number
select(Contact2, ContactList, UpdatedList),
put(Contact2, phone, "8765", UpdatedContact2),
UpdatedContactList = [UpdatedContact2 | UpdatedList].

% Remove Alice from the contact list
delete(ContactList, Contact1, FinalContactList).
```

This example illustrates the fundamental operations on dictionaries within a list context, showcasing insertion, update, and deletion.

Efficient Data Retrieval

When dealing with larger datasets, the efficiency of data retrieval operations becomes paramount. Using dictionaries ensures that lookups and updates are performed in constant time, O(1), due to their underlying implementation, which typically leverages hash tables.

Dictionaries in Prolog provide a powerful mechanism for managing dynamic associations between keys and values. Their efficient operations and ease of use make them an indispensable tool for various applications, ranging from simple data storage to complex pattern matching and beyond.

5.5 Understanding Trees in Prolog

In Prolog, trees are a crucial data structure used to represent hierarchical relationships. A tree is composed of nodes connected by edges, with one node designated as the root. Each node contains a value and potentially one or more child nodes. Trees can implement various algorithms efficiently due to their hierarchical nature.

In Prolog, trees are typically represented using compound terms. A node can be expressed as a term with the node's value and a list representing the child nodes. For example, a binary tree can be represented with a nested structure such as:

```
tree(Value, LeftSubtree, RightSubtree).
```

A simpler general tree may be represented as:

```
node(Value, Children).
```

where Value represents the data contained in the node, and $\mathrm{Children}$ is a list of subtrees.

Consider the following example of a binary tree representation:

```
tree(1,
    tree(2,
        tree(4, nil, nil),
        tree(5, nil, nil)),
    tree(3,
        tree(6, nil, nil),
        tree(7, nil, nil))).
```

This structure can be illustrated as follows:

```
    1
   / \
  2   3
 /|   |\
4 5   6 7
```

Tree Traversals in Prolog

Traversal refers to the process of visiting all the nodes in a tree in a specific order. Common tree traversal methods include preorder, inorder, and postorder traversals.

Preorder Traversal:

Visit the root node first, then recursively traverse the left and right subtrees.

Result: Preorder traversal of a tree

```
Function preorder(tree(Value, Left, Right)):
    Visit(Value);
    preorder(Left);
    preorder(Right);
Function preorder(nil):
    return;
```

Inorder Traversal:

Recursively traverse the left subtree, visit the root node, and then recursively traverse the right subtree.

Result: Inorder traversal of a tree

```
Function inorder(tree(Value, Left, Right)):
    inorder(Left);
    Visit(Value);
    inorder(Right);
Function inorder(nil):
    return;
```

Postorder Traversal:

Recursively traverse the left and right subtrees, then visit the root node.

Result: Postorder traversal of a tree

```
Function postorder(tree(Value, Left, Right)):
    postorder(Left);
    postorder(Right);
    Visit(Value);
Function postorder(nil):
    return;
```

To implement these traversals in Prolog, we define predicates for each traversal method.

```
% Preorder traversal
preorder(nil, []).
preorder(tree(Value, Left, Right), [Value|Nodes]) :-
    preorder(Left, LeftNodes),
    preorder(Right, RightNodes),
    append(LeftNodes, RightNodes, Nodes).

% Inorder traversal
inorder(nil, []).
inorder(tree(Value, Left, Right), Nodes) :-
    inorder(Left, LeftNodes),
    inorder(Right, RightNodes),
    append(LeftNodes, [Value|RightNodes], Nodes).

% Postorder traversal
postorder(nil, []).
postorder(tree(Value, Left, Right), Nodes) :-
    postorder(Left, LeftNodes),
    postorder(Right, RightNodes),
    append(LeftNodes, RightNodes, SubtreeNodes),
    append(SubtreeNodes, [Value], Nodes).
```

Executing the above predicates on the binary tree example will yield the following results:

```
?- preorder(tree(1,
            tree(2,
                tree(4, nil, nil),
                tree(5, nil, nil)),
            tree(3,
                tree(6, nil, nil),
                tree(7, nil, nil))), Result).
Result = [1, 2, 4, 5, 3, 6, 7].

?- inorder(tree(1,
           tree(2,
               tree(4, nil, nil),
               tree(5, nil, nil)),
           tree(3,
               tree(6, nil, nil),
               tree(7, nil, nil))), Result).
Result = [4, 2, 5, 1, 6, 3, 7].

?- postorder(tree(1,
             tree(2,
                 tree(4, nil, nil),
                 tree(5, nil, nil)),
             tree(3,
                 tree(6, nil, nil),
                 tree(7, nil, nil))), Result).
Result = [4, 5, 2, 6, 7, 3, 1].
```

Understanding tree structures and traversal methods in Prolog is instrumental for developing programs that manage hierarchical data efficiently. Traversal algorithms facilitate processing nodes in specific orders, enabling operations such as search, sort, and more. Practicing with various tree structures deepens comprehension of their applications and manipulation in Prolog.

5.6 Constructing and Traversing Binary Trees

Binary trees are a fundamental data structure in computer science, widely used for various tasks such as searching, sorting, and representing hierarchical data. In Prolog, binary trees can be elegantly defined and manipulated using the language's inherent strengths in pattern matching and recursion.

A binary tree in Prolog is typically represented using a compound term. A common representation might be tree(Left, Value, Right), where Left and Right are the left and right subtrees, respectively, and Value is the value stored at the node.

```
% A binary tree with a single node containing the value 10,
% and two empty subtrees.
tree(nil, 10, nil).
```

```
% A binary tree with root value 5, left subtree containing a single node 3,
% and right subtree containing a single node 7.
tree(tree(nil, 3, nil), 5, tree(nil, 7, nil)).
```

The above examples illustrate the structure of binary trees in Prolog. The atom nil is used to represent an empty subtree. Compound terms like tree(tree(nil, 3, nil), 5, tree(nil, 7, nil)) can represent more complex trees.

To construct a binary tree dynamically, one can write Prolog predicates that insert elements into the tree. The following example demonstrates inserting a value into a binary search tree.

```
% insert(+Tree, +Value, -NewTree)
% Inserts Value into Tree, producing NewTree.
insert(nil, Value, tree(nil, Value, nil)).
insert(tree(Left, Root, Right), Value, tree(NewLeft, Root, Right)) :-
    Value < Root, !, insert(Left, Value, NewLeft).
insert(tree(Left, Root, Right), Value, tree(Left, Root, NewRight)) :-
    insert(Right, Value, NewRight).
```

This predicate, insert/3, allows for the insertion of a value into a binary search tree. Pattern matching checks various conditions: if the tree is empty (nil), a new tree node is created. If the value to be inserted is less than the current node's value, the predicate inserts it into the left subtree. Otherwise, it goes into the right subtree.

Traversing a binary tree is another fundamental operation. Traversals can be categorized mainly into preorder, inorder, and postorder. Each traversal has different applications and explores the tree in a unique pattern.

In inorder traversal, the tree is traversed in the following sequence: left subtree, root, right subtree. The following predicate performs an inorder traversal of a binary tree.

```
% inorder(+Tree, -List)
% Traverses Tree inorder, producing List of values.
inorder(nil, []).
inorder(tree(Left, Value, Right), List) :-
    inorder(Left, LList),
    inorder(Right, RList),
    append(LList, [Value|RList], List).
```

In the inorder/2 predicate, inorder(nil, []) handles the base case where the tree is empty, returning an empty list. The recursive case splits the tree into its left and right subtrees, traverses each recursively, and then concatenates the results, placing the root value between the lists of values from the left and right subtrees.

Preorder traversal visits the root first, followed by the left subtree and then the right subtree.

```
% preorder(+Tree, -List)
% Traverses Tree in preorder, producing List of values.
preorder(nil, []).
preorder(tree(Left, Value, Right), [Value|List]) :-
    preorder(Left, LList),
    preorder(Right, RList),
    append(LList, RList, List).
```

In the preorder/2 predicate, the root value is placed at the head of the resulting list, followed by the concatenation of the preorder traversals of the left and right subtrees.

Postorder traversal, in contrast, processes the left subtree first, then the right subtree, and finally the root node.

```
% postorder(+Tree, -List)
% Traverses Tree in postorder, producing List of values.
postorder(nil, []).
postorder(tree(Left, Value, Right), List) :-
    postorder(Left, LList),
    postorder(Right, RList),
    append(LList, RList, TempList),
    append(TempList, [Value], List).
```

In the postorder/2 predicate, the lists produced by the postorder traversals of the left and right subtrees are concatenated first, and the root value is appended at the end of the resulting list.

It's crucial to note that the append/3 predicate is used to concatenate lists in these traversal predicates. This built-in Prolog predicate has the form append(List1, List2, Result), where Result is the concatenation of List1 and List2.

Binary tree traversal predicates illustrate Prolog's strengths in recursion and pattern matching, offering a powerful and expressive way to manipulate such data structures. By carefully combining these techniques, Prolog can efficiently handle various binary tree operations, providing a foundation for more advanced algorithms and data manipulations. Here is the corrected LaTeX text for the section:

"'latex

5.7 Using Graph Structures

Graphs are pivotal structures in computer science, utilized for representing a myriad of relationships and connections between objects. In Prolog, graphs can be represented and manipulated with great flexibility, allowing for efficient problem-solving in domains such as network analysis, pathfinding, and social network modeling.

A graph is defined by a set of vertices (nodes) and edges (connections between nodes). Formally, a graph G is denoted as $G = (V, E)$, where V is the set of vertices and E is the set of edges. Depending on the application, graphs may be directed (where edges have a direction) or undirected (where edges do not have a direction).

Representation of Graphs in Prolog

In Prolog, graphs can be represented using various methods. One common approach is to represent graphs using adjacency lists, where each vertex is associated with a list of vertices to which it is directly connected. Another approach is to use edge lists, where each edge is explicitly listed as a predicate.

Adjacency List Representation

Here, each vertex is represented as a fact with a list of adjacent vertices. Consider the following simple undirected graph:

```
% Graph representation using adjacency lists
% Format: vertex(Vertex, [List of Adjacent Vertices]).

vertex(a, [b, c]).
vertex(b, [a, d, e]).
vertex(c, [a, f]).
vertex(d, [b]).
vertex(e, [b, f]).
vertex(f, [c, e]).
```

In this representation, each vertex is defined using the vertex/2 predicate, which associates the vertex with its list of adjacent vertices.

Edge List Representation

Here, each edge is represented as a fact, specifying the pair of connected vertices. The same graph can be represented as follows:

```
% Graph representation using edge lists
% Format: edge(Vertex1, Vertex2).

edge(a, b).
edge(a, c).
edge(b, d).
```

```
edge(b, e).
edge(c, f).
edge(e, f).
```

This representation uses the edge/2 predicate to specify the connections between vertices. Note the absence of duplicate edges for undirected graphs, assuming the edges are bidirectional.

Graph Traversal

Traversal algorithms are fundamental operations on graphs, enabling searches through the nodes to locate specific vertices or paths. Two common traversal strategies are Depth-First Search (DFS) and Breadth-First Search (BFS).

Depth-First Search (DFS)

DFS explores as far as possible along each branch before backtracking. Below is a Prolog implementation for graph traversal using DFS:

Algorithm 1: Depth-First Search in Prolog

Data: Graph represented as adjacency lists
Result: Traversal path from Start to Goal

```
Function dfs(Start, Goal, Path):
    dfs (Start, Goal, [Start], Path)
Function dfs(Goal, Goal, PathAcc, Path):
    reverse(PathAcc, Path)
Function dfs(Current, Goal, PathAcc, Path):
    vertex(Current, AdjList);
    member(Next, AdjList);
    not(member(Next, PathAcc));
    dfs (Next, Goal, [Next|PathAcc], Path)
```

The dfs function initiates the traversal, maintaining a list of visited nodes to avoid cycles. The search continues recursively until the goal is found.

Breadth-First Search (BFS)

BFS explores all vertices at the present depth level before moving on to vertices at the next depth level. The following Prolog implementation demonstrates BFS:

Algorithm 2: Breadth-First Search in Prolog

Data: Graph represented as adjacency lists
Result: Traversal path from Start to Goal

Function bfs(*Start, Goal, Path*):
    bfs ([(Start, [Start])], Goal, Path)

Function bfs(*[(Goal, PathAcc)|_]), Goal, Path*:
    reverse(PathAcc, Path)

Function bfs(*[(Current, PathAcc)|Rest]), Goal, Path*:
    findall(Next, (vertex(Current, AdjList), member(Next, AdjList), not(member(Next, PathAcc))), NextNodes);
    append(Rest, NextNodes, NewQueue);
    bfs (NewQueue, Goal, Path)

The bfs function maintains a queue of paths to explore, expanding the breadth level-wise until the goal is reached.

Graph Search Example

Consider querying the path from vertex a to vertex f in the previously defined graph:

```
?- dfs(a, f, Path).
Path = [a, c, f].

?- bfs(a, f, Path).
Path = [a, c, f].
```

Both DFS and BFS successfully find the path. The choice of algorithm depends on the specific problem requirements, such as finding the shortest path or deeply nested structures.

Representation and traversal are foundational to leveraging graph structures in Prolog. Mastery of these concepts equips one with powerful tools to tackle complex relational problems effectively.

5.8 Representing and Manipulating Sets

In Prolog, sets are typically represented as unordered collections of unique elements. This section delves into the various methods to represent and manipulate sets in Prolog, including operations such as set construction, membership testing, union, intersection, and difference.

To represent a set, a common approach is to use a list that contains the set elements without duplication. For instance, the set $\{1, 2, 3\}$ can be represented as the list $[1, 2, 3]$.

To illustrate basic set operations, we will define auxiliary predicates for membership testing, set construction, and set manipulation.

```
% Predicate to test if an element is in a set (list)
member_set(Element, [Element|_]).
member_set(Element, [_|Tail]) :-
    member_set(Element, Tail).
```

The member_set/2 predicate verifies if Element is contained in the list [Element|_] or recursively checks the tail of the list.

Let's define a predicate add_element/3 that adds an element to a set (list) if it is not already present:

```
% Predicate to add an element to a set
add_element(Element, Set, Set) :-
    member_set(Element, Set), !.
add_element(Element, Set, [Element|Set]).
```

The add_element/3 predicate ensures that Element is not duplicated in Set. If Element is already in the set, the set remains unchanged; otherwise, Element is added to the front.

For constructing a set from a list of elements, we use a predicate list_-to_set/2:

```
% Predicate to construct a set from a list
list_to_set([], []).
list_to_set([Head|Tail], Set) :-
    list_to_set(Tail, TailSet),
    add_element(Head, TailSet, Set).
```

With list_to_set/2, even if the input list contains duplicate elements, the resulting set will not have any duplicates.

To concatenate two sets, a union_set/3 predicate can be defined:

```
% Predicate to find the union of two sets
union_set([], Set, Set).
union_set([Head|Tail], Set, Union) :-
    union_set(Tail, Set, PartialUnion),
    add_element(Head, PartialUnion, Union).
```

The union_set/3 predicate recursively adds each element of the first set to the second set, ensuring no duplicates in the resulting union.

For intersection, we define intersection_set/3 to compute the elements common to both sets:

```
% Predicate to find the intersection of two sets
```

```
intersection_set([], _, []).
intersection_set([Head|Tail], Set, [Head|Intersection]) :-
    member_set(Head, Set),
    intersection_set(Tail, Set, Intersection).
intersection_set([_|Tail], Set, Intersection) :-
    intersection_set(Tail, Set, Intersection).
```

The intersection_set/3 predicate checks if each element of the first set is a member of the second set. If so, it is included in the intersection.

Similarly, the difference_set/3 predicate computes the set difference:

```
% Predicate to find the difference of two sets
difference_set([], _, []).
difference_set([Head|Tail], Set, Difference) :-
    member_set(Head, Set),
    difference_set(Tail, Set, Difference).
difference_set([Head|Tail], Set, [Head|Difference]) :-
    difference_set(Tail, Set, Difference).
```

The difference_set/3 predicate includes elements from the first set that are not found in the second set in the resulting difference.

Enumerating all subsets of a set can be achieved with the following subsets/2 predicate:

```
% Predicate to find all subsets of a set
subsets([], [[]]).
subsets([Head|Tail], Subsets) :-
    subsets(Tail, TailSubsets),
    add_to_all(Head, TailSubsets, AdditionalSubsets),
    append(TailSubsets, AdditionalSubsets, Subsets).

% Helper predicate to add an element to all subsets
add_to_all(_, [], []).
add_to_all(Element, [Subset|Rest], [[Element|Subset]|More]) :-
    add_to_all(Element, Rest, More).
```

The subsets/2 predicate finds all subsets of a given set by recursively constructing subsets that include or exclude each element. The helper predicate add_to_all/3 assists this operation by adding an element to each subset.

These foundational operations cover essential manipulations for set representation in Prolog. Practitioners can extend these building blocks to develop more complex algorithms and operations tailored to specific applications.

5.9 Handling Nested Data Structures

Nested data structures are hierarchical constructs where elements can themselves be data structures. Prolog's flexibility with terms allows it to elegantly represent and manipulate nested data structures, which are crucial for various complex applications.

Consider processing a nested list of numbers. Nested lists can have varying depths, making handling more complex than flat lists. Prolog provides a concise syntax for nested lists and powerful recursion to process them.

A nested list can be defined as follows:

```
nested_list([1, [2, 3], [4, [5, 6], 7], 8]).
```

To flatten a nested list into a single-level list, a recursive approach can be employed.

```
Data: Nested List
Result: Flattened List
Function flatten(Nested, Flattened):
    if Nested is empty then
        Flattened := []
    else
        Head := first element of Nested;
        Tail := rest of Nested;
        if Head is a list then
            FlattenedHead := Flat_list(Head);
            FlattenedTail := Flat_list(Tail);
            Flattened := FlattenedHead concatenated with
              FlattenedTail;
        else
            FlattenedTail := Flat_list(Tail);
            Flattened := [Head] concatenated with FlattenedTail;
```

Implementing this in Prolog:

```
% Flatten a nested list
flat_list([], []).
flat_list([Head|Tail], Flat) :-
    flat_list(Head, FlatHead),
    flat_list(Tail, FlatTail),
    append(FlatHead, FlatTail, Flat).
flat_list(Head, [Head]).
```

Executing the flatten function on nested_list([1, [2, 3], [4, [5, 6], 7], 8]) yields:

```
?- flat_list([1, [2, 3], [4, [5, 6], 7], 8], Flat).
Flat = [1, 2, 3, 4, 5, 6, 7, 8].
```

For another complex scenario, consider nested dictionaries where each key maps to a value that can be another dictionary.

An example nested dictionary:

```
nested_dict(
    {person, {name, 'John'},
             {address, {city, 'New York', zip, '10001'}},
             {age, 30}}
).
```

Querying nested structures involves pattern matching and recursion. The following example demonstrates retrieving nested values:

```
% Get a value from a dictionary
get_value(Key, {Key, Value}, Value).
get_value(Key, {K, V|Dict}, Value) :-
    ( is_dict(V) -> get_value(Key, V, Value) ) ;
    get_value(Key, Dict, Value).
```

Using this function to extract the city value from the nested dictionary:

```
?- nested_dict(Dict),
   get_value(city, Dict, City).
City = 'New York'.
```

In scenarios where data structures include trees, handling nested trees follows a similar recursive approach. For example, consider the nested binary tree:

```
binary_tree(node(1, node(2, leaf, leaf), node(3, leaf, leaf))).
```

To sum all nodes in a binary tree:

Data: Binary Tree
Result: Sum of All Nodes

```
Function sum_tree(Tree, Sum):
    if Tree is leaf then
        Sum := 0
    else
        Left := left subtree of Tree;
        Right := right subtree of Tree;
        Root := value of Tree node;
        SumLeft := sum_tree (Left);
        SumRight := sum_tree (Right);
        Sum := Root + SumLeft + SumRight;
```

Prolog implementation:

```
% Sum all nodes in a binary tree
sum_tree(leaf, 0).
sum_tree(node(Root, Left, Right), Sum) :-
    sum_tree(Left, SumLeft),
    sum_tree(Right, SumRight),
    Sum is Root + SumLeft + SumRight.
```

Executing the sum function on the example binary tree:

```
?- binary_tree(Tree), sum_tree(Tree, Sum).
Sum = 6.
```

These examples demonstrate the strength of Prolog's recursive capabilities in managing nested structures. Handling nested lists, dictionaries, and trees relies on recursive definitions, allowing efficient traversal and manipulation that reflect real-world data complexities.

5.10 Persistence and Data Structures

Persistence in Prolog refers to the ability to maintain data structures across different sessions and executions of the program. This is crucial for applications requiring long-term data storage and retrieval. Prolog, being a logical programming language, necessitates careful handling of data persistence mechanisms, such as file operations and database integration. This section will discuss methods to achieve persistence, focusing on I/O operations and persistent storage models.

File Operations for Persistence

File operations in Prolog enable persistent storage of data structures by reading from and writing to files. The predicates open/3, close/1, read/2, and write/2 are fundamental for this purpose.

The open/3 predicate opens a file, specifying the file name, mode (read, write, append), and a stream identifier.

```
open('data.txt', write, Stream),
write(Stream, 'This is an example of persistence in Prolog.'),
close(Stream).
```

To append data, the mode 'append' should be used.

```
open('data.txt', append, Stream),
write(Stream, 'Appending more data to the file.'),
close(Stream).
```

Reading from a file utilizes the read/2 predicate, assuming the format of data written can be parsed as standard Prolog terms.

```
open('data.txt', read, Stream),
read(Stream, Data),
close(Stream),
process_data(Data).
```

Data processing depends on the structure and format written. Proper syntax ensures accuracy in reading terms.

Storing and Retrieving Complex Data Structures

To persist complex data structures like trees or graphs, serialization methods are employed. Serialization converts data structures into a format suitable for storage or transmission.

A Prolog term can be serialized to a file using write/2 and retrieved with read/2. Below is an example of serializing a binary tree.

```
serialize_tree(Tree, Filename) :-
    open(Filename, write, Stream),
    write(Stream, Tree),
    close(Stream).
```

Deserialization reads the tree structure:

```
deserialize_tree(Filename, Tree) :-
    open(Filename, read, Stream),
    read(Stream, Tree),
    close(Stream).
```

Ensuring the integrity and consistency of the data requires validating the structures upon retrieval.

Database Integration for Persistence

Prolog's integration with databases, such as SQL databases, allows for efficient data persistence solutions, enabling complex queries and robust data management. The odbc_connect/2 predicate establishes a connection to an ODBC-compliant database.

```
odbc_connect('my_database', Connection, [user('username'), password('password')]).

create_table(Connection) :-
    odbc_query(Connection,
        'CREATE TABLE pers_data (id INT PRIMARY KEY, data VARCHAR(100))')
        .

insert_data(Connection, Id, Data) :-
    atomic_list_concat(
        ['INSERT INTO pers_data (id, data) VALUES (', Id, ', \'', Data, '\')'],
        Query),
    odbc_query(Connection, Query).

retrieve_data(Connection, Id, Data) :-
    atomic_list_concat(
        ['SELECT data FROM pers_data WHERE id = ', Id],
        Query),
    odbc_query(Connection, Query, row(Data)).
```

Proper error handling ensures resilience during database operations, guarding against connectivity issues and query failures.

Prolog Data Persistence Libraries

Several Prolog libraries enhance built-in capabilities for data persistence. Notable among these are library(persistency) and library(redis).

The persistency library simplifies persistent storage of dynamic predicates:

```
:- use_module(library(persistency)).

:- persistent
    person(name:string, age:integer).

attach_db('people.db', []).

add_person(Name, Age) :-
    assert_person(Name, Age).

list_people :-
    forall(person(Name, Age), writeln(Name-Age)).
```

Upon invoking attach_db/2, the database file people.db is created or loaded, allowing manipulation of person/2 predicates across sessions.

Integrating Redis with Prolog using library(redis) provides an efficient key-value store, offering robust features like atomic operations and pub-/sub messaging.

```
:- use_module(library(redis)).

redis_persist(Key, Value) :-
    redis(set(Key, Value)).

redis_retrieve(Key, Value) :-
    redis(get(Key), Value).
```

Using Redis for data persistence ensures scalability and performance in distributed systems, where conventional file-based storage may falter.

Understanding persistence mechanisms and effectively utilizing them in Prolog is imperative for developing applications requiring reliable long-term data storage. Maintaining data integrity and ensuring efficient retrieval and modification are central to implementing successful persistent data structures.

5.11 Pattern Matching with Complex Data

In Prolog, pattern matching is an integral mechanism used to unify terms and bind variables to values. When dealing with complex data structures, pattern matching enables efficient extraction and manipulation of nested elements. This section explores various methods and techniques to achieve pattern matching with complex data in Prolog.

Complex data in Prolog can be constructed using lists, tuples, and compound terms. Consider a structure that encapsulates information about a person, represented as a compound term: person(Name, Age, Address). The components of Address can, in turn, be a complex structure like address(Street, City, Zip).

```
% Define a person structure with nested address information
person(john_doe, 30, address(123_main_st, springfield, 98765)).
person(jane_smith, 28, address(456_oak_st, shelbyville, 12345)).
```

To retrieve and utilize specific fields from these nested structures, Prolog's pattern matching capabilities can be leveraged. The process begins by querying the database with patterns that unify with the desired structure components. Below is an example illustrating how to retrieve the city from the address field of a person structure.

```
% Query to extract and print the city from a person's address
?- person(john_doe, _, address(_, City, _)).
```

```
City = springfield.
```

In scenarios involving lists of such structures, pattern matching can be extended to iterate through the list and extract information from each element. The following example demonstrates how to extract the names of all persons residing in a given city.

```
% Define a database of people
people([
  person(john_doe, 30, address(123_main_st, springfield, 98765)),
  person(jane_smith, 28, address(456_oak_st, shelbyville, 12345))
]).

% Rule to find all persons living in a specified city
find_people_in_city(City, People) :-
  people(PeopleList),
  findall(Name, (member(person(Name, _, address(_, City, _)), PeopleList)), People).
```

```
?- find_people_in_city(springfield, Residents).
Residents = [john_doe].
```

In complex nested structures, pattern matching aids in deconstructing and obtaining internal elements efficiently. This is particularly useful in tasks such as transforming or filtering data, where specific subelements must be manipulated or compared.

In addition to list traversal, pattern matching is pivotal in rules and predicates involving recursive structures. Consider a binary tree defined as tree(Left, Root, Right):

```
% Binary tree structure
tree(tree(tree(nil, 1, nil), 2, tree(nil, 3, nil)),
     4,
     tree(tree(nil, 5, nil), 6, tree(nil, 7, nil))).
```

To extract all elements in such a tree, an inorder traversal using pattern matching can be implemented:

```
% Inorder traversal of a binary tree
inorder(nil, []).
inorder(tree(Left, Root, Right), Traversal) :-
  inorder(Left, LeftTraversal),
  inorder(Right, RightTraversal),
  append(LeftTraversal, [Root|RightTraversal], Traversal).
```

```
?- inorder(tree(tree(tree(nil, 1, nil), 2, tree(nil, 3, nil)), 4, tree(tree(nil, 5, nil), 6, tree(nil, 7, nil))), Traversal).
Traversal = [1, 2, 3, 4, 5, 6, 7].
```

In pattern matching with complex data structures, Prolog's capabilities extend to determining structural equivalence and checking for valid configurations. For instance, verifying that a given binary tree is complete involves recursively ensuring each subtree adheres to the properties of a complete binary tree:

```
% Predicate to verify if a binary tree is complete
is_complete_tree(nil).
is_complete_tree(tree(Left, _, Right)) :-
  tree_height(Left, LH),
  tree_height(Right, RH),
  Diff is abs(LH - RH),
  Diff =< 1,
  is_complete_tree(Left),
  is_complete_tree(Right).

% Helper predicate to compute the height of a binary tree
tree_height(nil, 0).
tree_height(tree(Left, _, Right), H) :-
  tree_height(Left, LH),
  tree_height(Right, RH),
  max(LH, RH, MaxH),
  H is MaxH + 1.

% Predicate to find the maximum of two numbers
max(A, B, A) :- A >= B.
max(A, B, B) :- B > A.
```

```
?- is_complete_tree(tree(tree(nil, 1, nil), 2, tree(tree(nil, 3, nil), 4, tree(nil, 5, nil)))).
true.
```

Advanced pattern matching techniques in Prolog also involve leveraging constraints and conditions within matching rules. These are particularly useful when the data structures contain elements that must satisfy specific relational properties, as seen in constraint logic programming and pattern matching with attributed variables. Through careful application of these principles, Prolog enables efficient and expressive manipulation and extraction of complex nested data, streamlining the development of sophisticated algorithms and data processing tasks.

5.12 Practical Examples of Data Structures in Prolog

Exploring practical examples of data structures in Prolog enhances the understanding of how these structures can be effectively used. The examples provided here will include tuples, compound data structures, binary trees, dictionaries, and sets within the context of Prolog programming. Providing a coherent integration of the various data structures discussed earlier in the chapter, these examples aim to apply theoretical knowledge to concrete Prolog programming tasks.

Example 1: Working with Tuples

In Prolog, tuples can be used to group related elements together. Consider the example of representing a point in a 2D space.

point(X, Y) can be defined as a tuple where X and Y are the coordinates.

```
% Defining a tuple for a point
point(4, 5).

% Predicate to access the coordinates
point_coordinates(point(X, Y), X, Y).
```

Run the predicate to retrieve the coordinates:

```
?- point_coordinates(point(4, 5), X, Y).
X = 4,
Y = 5.
```

Example 2: Manipulating Compound Data Structures

Compound data structures are highly versatile in Prolog. Consider a student database where each student has a name, ID, and a list of enrolled courses.

```
% Defining a compound data structure for a student
student(jane, 10234, [math, english, biology]).

% Predicate to add a course to a student's record
add_course(student(Name, ID, Courses), NewCourse, student(Name, ID, [NewCourse |
    Courses])).
```

Add a new course for Jane:

```
?- add_course(student(jane, 10234, [math, english, biology]), history, UpdatedStudent).
UpdatedStudent = student(jane, 10234, [history, math, english, biology]).
```

Example 3: Building and Traversing Binary Trees

A binary tree is a common data structure used in many algorithms. Here, a binary tree is represented using Prolog terms such as node and null.

```
% Defining a binary tree
binary_tree(node(1, node(2, null, null), node(3, null, null))).

% In-order traversal of a binary tree
in_order(null, []).
in_order(node(Root, Left, Right), Traversal) :-
    in_order(Left, LeftTraversal),
    in_order(Right, RightTraversal),
    append(LeftTraversal, [Root | RightTraversal], Traversal).
```

Perform an in-order traversal of the binary tree:

```
?- in_order(node(1, node(2, null, null), node(3, null, null)), Traversal).
Traversal = [2, 1, 3].
```

Example 4: Utilizing Dictionaries

Dictionaries, or associative arrays, provide a way to store key-value pairs. These can be implemented using compound terms.

```
% Defining a dictionary
dictionary([key_value(john, 25), key_value(doe, 30)]).

% Predicate to retrieve a value by key
get_value(Key, dictionary(Dict), Value) :-
    member(key_value(Key, Value), Dict).
```

Retrieve the age of John:

```
?- get_value(john, dictionary([key_value(john, 25), key_value(doe, 30)]), Age).
Age = 25.
```

Example 5: Representing Sets

Sets in Prolog can be represented using lists, ensuring no duplicate elements. Operations on sets such as union, intersection, and difference can be performed.

```
% Predicate to check if an element is a member of a set
member(X, [X|_]).
member(X, [_|T]) :- member(X, T).

% Predicate for union of two sets
union([], S, S).
union([H|T], S, U) :-
    member(H, S),
    union(T, S, U).
union([H|T], S, [H|U]) :-
    \+ member(H, S),
    union(T, S, U).
```

Find the union of two sets:

```
?- union([1, 2, 3], [3, 4, 5], Union).
Union = [1, 2, 3, 4, 5].
```

Combining the understanding of these data structures and applying them in practical examples equips the reader with a solid foundation for manipulating complex data in Prolog. These examples continue to reinforce the versatility and power of Prolog's approach to data representation and manipulation.

Chapter 6

Input and Output in Prolog

This chapter addresses input and output in Prolog, including user input, console output, and file handling. It covers stream operations, formatting output, parsing file content, handling end-of-file and errors, and working with binary files. The chapter also discusses reading and writing data structures, providing practical examples and best practices for effective input and output operations in Prolog.

6.1 Introduction to Prolog Input and Output

In Prolog, input and output operations are essential for interacting with the external environment, such as receiving data from users, displaying outputs on a console, and handling file I/O. Unlike some imperative programming languages, Prolog's approach to handling I/O is governed by logical predicates and built-in procedures that make it seamlessly integrate with the declarative nature of the language. Understanding these I/O mechanisms is crucial for developing robust Prolog applications that interact effectively with their surroundings.

Prolog performs I/O operations using streams. A stream is a sequence of characters or bytes, which could be connected to various sources or sinks, such as the keyboard, screen, or files. There are three primary streams predefined in Prolog:

- user_input: The stream typically connected to the keyboard, used for reading input.
- user_output: The stream typically connected to the console, used for writing output.
- user_error: The stream used for writing error messages.

Prolog predicates for I/O are divided into two main categories: those for reading data and those for writing data. These predicates can operate on various types of streams, including standard input/output and file streams.

To read data from the user or a file, Prolog provides predicates such as read/1, read_term/2, and read_line_to_codes/2. For example, read/1 reads the next term from the current input stream and unifies it with its argument.

```
?- read(Term).
|: my_fact(a, b).

Term = my_fact(a, b).
```

In this example, read(Term) reads a term from the input and binds it to Term. The term my_fact(a, b) is entered by the user, which gets unified with Term.

For writing output, Prolog provides predicates such as write/1, writeln/1, and format/2. The write/1 predicate writes a term to the current output stream.

```
?- write('Hello, World!').
Hello, World!
true.
```

In this example, write('Hello, World!') outputs the string 'Hello, World!' to the console.

File handling in Prolog involves opening a file, reading or writing data, and closing the file. Prolog uses the open/3 predicate to open a file, specifying the file name, mode (read, write, append), and a stream variable. After opening a file, you can perform read or write operations using the stream variable.

```
?- open('example.txt', write, Stream),
   write(Stream, 'Hello, file!'),
   close(Stream).
```

In this example, the file 'example.txt' is opened in write mode, and the stream variable Stream is used to write the string 'Hello, file!' to the file, followed by closing the file stream with close/1.

Prolog also features higher-level predicates for handling more complex I/O operations, such as reading entire files into lists or managing binary data. While these advanced techniques build upon the basic input and output predicates, they provide powerful tools for dealing with various I/O requirements in real-world applications.

Errors and end-of-file conditions are important aspects of I/O operations, with Prolog providing mechanisms to handle such situations gracefully. For instance, the predicate at_end_of_stream/1 can be used to check whether the end of a stream has been reached.

```
?- open('example.txt', read, Stream),
   (at_end_of_stream(Stream) -> writeln('Empty file'); read(Stream, Data)),
   close(Stream).
```

In this example, the file 'example.txt' is opened in read mode, then at_end_of_stream/1 is used to check if the file is empty, providing a conditional message if it is.

Throughout this chapter, we will delve deeper into these aspects of Prolog input and output operations, providing detailed explanations and examples to empower you with the knowledge required for proficient I/O management in your Prolog programs.

6.2 Reading Input from the User

Reading input from the user in Prolog can be achieved through various predicates, allowing for interactive and dynamic manipulation of data within a session. The primary predicates used for this purpose are read/1, read_term/2, read_line_to_codes/2, and get_char/1. Understanding their utilization and nuances can enhance the efficiency of user interactions in Prolog programs.

read/1 is commonly used to read a Prolog term from the current input stream. Here is an example:

```
% Prompt user for input and read a term
write('Enter a Prolog term: '), nl,
read(Term),
write('You entered: '), write(Term), nl.
```

When executed, the program will produce the following output:

```
Enter a Prolog term:
|: hello_world.
You entered: hello_world
```

This example illustrates the simplicity of using read/1, which waits for the user to input a term and then binds this term to the variable Term. It's essential to note that read/1 expects input ending with a period followed by a newline.

For more control over the reading process, read_term/2 can be employed. This predicate allows specifying options such as variable names and positions. An illustration is shown below:

```
% Reading a term with options
write('Enter a Prolog term: '), nl,
read_term(Term, [variable_names(Vars)]),
write('You entered: '), write(Term), nl,
write('Variable names: '), write(Vars), nl.
```

This allows for capturing and displaying variable names used in the input term. The output of this program might look like the following, assuming the user enters a term containing variables:

```
Enter a Prolog term:
|: X + Y = Z.
You entered: X + Y = Z
Variable names: [$_G278=X, $_G279=Y, $_G280=Z]
```

Another common scenario involves reading a single line of text input. The read_line_to_codes/2 predicate is useful for this purpose. It reads a line of input and returns it as a list of character codes:

```
% Reading a line of text
write('Enter a line of text: '), nl,
read_line_to_codes(user_input, Codes),
atom_codes(InputText, Codes),
write('You entered: '), write(InputText), nl.
```

In this example, the user input is captured as a list of character codes, which is subsequently converted to an atom using atom_codes/2. If the input is Prolog is fun., the output will be:

```
Enter a line of text:
Prolog is fun.
You entered: Prolog is fun.
```

For applications requiring character-by-character input, get_char/1 can be employed. This predicate reads a single character from the input stream:

```
% Reading a single character
write('Enter a character: '), nl,
get_char(Char),
write('You entered: '), write(Char), nl.
```

Upon execution, if the user inputs a character such as a, the output will be:

```
Enter a character:
a
You entered: a
```

Each of these predicates offers specific advantages depending on the nature of the input required. Integrating them effectively within a Prolog program allows for flexible and robust handling of user inputs.

6.3 Writing Output to the Console

Prolog provides several predicates to produce output on the console, allowing developers to effectively communicate with users, debug code, and present results. This section details the use of key predicates such as write/1, writeln/1, format/2, and format/3 for output tasks. These predicates can control the manner and format in which data is presented to users.

write/1 is the most basic output predicate. It takes a single argument, which can be any Prolog term, and writes its textual representation to the current output stream. For example:

```
?- write('Hello, world!').
Hello, world!
```

The operator ?- denotes a query in Prolog. In this case, write/1 outputs the string 'Hello, world!' to the console.

writeln/1 is similar to write/1, but it appends a newline character at the end of the output. This is particularly useful for ensuring that successive outputs appear on separate lines:

```
?- writeln('Hello, world!').
Hello, world!
```

Another important predicate for console output is format/2. This predicate allows for formatted output similar to printf in C or print in Python. The format/2 predicate takes two arguments: a format string and a list of arguments. The format string can contain special format specifiers, which are placeholders for the list arguments. Some common format specifiers include ~w for any Prolog term, ~d for a decimal integer, and ~n for a newline:

```
?- format('~w + ~w = ~w~n', [1, 2, 3]).
1 + 2 = 3
```

In this example, the format string 'w̃ + w̃ = w̃ñ' contains three term specifiers w̃ and a newline specifier ñ. The list of arguments [1, 2, 3] replaces the w̃ specifiers sequentially, yielding the output "1 + 2 = 3" followed by a newline.

format/3 is an extension of format/2 that includes an additional argument specifying the output stream. This allows for more precise control over the destination of the output, which can prove useful when working with multiple streams.

When using format specifiers, it is essential to understand their specific meanings and appropriate contexts to avoid incorrect or misleading output. Other useful format specifiers include a for atoms, s for strings, and f for floating-point numbers.

For example, consider the following code snippet that demonstrates the use of multiple format specifiers:

```
?- format('Atom: ~a, String: ~s, Decimal: ~d, Float: ~f~n', ['example', "Prolog", 42,
    3.14159]).
Atom: example, String: Prolog, Decimal: 42, Float: 3.141590
```

In this example, example corresponds to the atom specifier ã, Prolog to the string specifier s̃, 42 to the decimal specifier d̃, and 3.14159 to the float specifier f̃, with the float value formatted to six decimal places by default.

Moreover, Prolog offers a straightforward method to redirect the output to different streams using the built-in predicate set_output/1. This predicate changes the current output stream to the specified stream. For instance, consider the following code:

```
?- open('output.txt', write, Stream),
   set_output(Stream),
   write('This will be written to a file.'),
   close(Stream),
   set_output(user_output),
   writeln('Back to console output.').
```

Here, open/3 opens a file named output.txt for writing and assigns the stream handle to Stream. set_output/1 redirects the output to the specified file stream, enabling the message 'This will be written to a file.' to be written into output.txt. The operation concludes by closing the file stream and resetting the output back to the console (denoted by user_output).

Effective usage of these predicates facilitates clear and organized output in Prolog applications. It is crucial to employ appropriate predicates and format specifiers to ensure data is presented accurately and comprehensibly, catering to varying situations, whether debugging, user communication, or result presentation.

6.4 File Handling: Reading and Writing Files

File handling in Prolog is a crucial aspect of input and output operations, enabling programs to interact with files on the filesystem for reading and writing data. This section delves into the mechanisms available in Prolog for such operations, including opening, reading, writing, and closing files. We will explore these concepts through practical examples to illustrate their application in Prolog programming.

To begin file handling in Prolog, the predicates open/3, read/2, write/2, and close/1 are essential. Let's start with the open/3 predicate.

The open/3 predicate is used to open a file and associate it with a stream. The general syntax is:

```
open(+SourceSink, +Mode, -Stream)
```

Here, SourceSink can be the name of a file represented as an atom, and Mode specifies the operation mode, which can be read, write, or append. The Stream is a variable that will be unified with the stream identifier.

Example of opening a file for reading:

```
?- open('input.txt', read, Stream),
   read(Stream, Data),
   close(Stream).
```

In this example, 'input.txt' is the name of the file to be opened. The file is opened in read mode, and the variable Stream will be associated with the opened stream. After reading the data from the stream using the read/2 predicate, the stream is closed using close/1.

The read/2 predicate reads the next term from the specified stream. If the end of the file is reached, it returns the term end_of_file.

Example of reading from a file:

```
read_file(Stream) :-
    read(Stream, Data),
    ( Data \= end_of_file ->
        writeln(Data),
        read_file(Stream)
    ; close(Stream)
    ).
```

This recursive predicate read_file/1 continuously reads from the stream and writes each term to the console until the end of the file is encountered, upon which the stream is closed.

For writing to a file, the procedure is similar but with write or append mode. When using write mode, the file content is overwritten, whereas append mode adds to the existing content.

Example of writing to a file:

```
?- open('output.txt', write, Stream),
   write(Stream, 'Hello, World!'),
   close(Stream).
```

In this example, 'output.txt' is the name of the file to be created or overwritten. The file is opened in write mode, a string is written to the file using the write/2 predicate, and the stream is closed with close/1.

Example of appending to a file:

```
?- open('output.txt', append, Stream),
   write(Stream, 'Appending this line.'),
   close(Stream).
```

Here, the file 'output.txt' is opened in append mode, and a line is appended to the existing content.

Handling files requires careful management of streams to avoid resource leaks. Each opened stream should be closed using the close/1 predicate once the operation is complete.

An important aspect of file handling is checking for the end of the file condition. The at_end_of_stream/1 predicate is used to test whether the end of the stream has been reached.

Example:

```
read_until_end(Stream) :-
    \+ at_end_of_stream(Stream), % while not at the end of the stream
    read(Stream, Data),
    writeln(Data),
    read_until_end(Stream).
read_until_end(Stream) :-
    at_end_of_stream(Stream), % if at the end of the stream
    close(Stream).
```

This predicate read_until_end/1 reads data from the stream and prints it until it reaches the end of the file, then closes the stream.

When handling files, it's also possible to manage binary data using binary streams. For this, the open/4 predicate is extended to include options such as type(binary).

Example of working with binary files:

```
?- open('binaryfile.bin', read, Stream, [type(binary)]),
   read_binary_data(Stream),
   close(Stream).

read_binary_data(Stream) :-
    \+ at_end_of_stream(Stream), % while not at the end of the stream
    get_byte(Stream, Byte),
    writeln(Byte),
    read_binary_data(Stream).
read_binary_data(Stream) :-
    at_end_of_stream(Stream), % if at the end of the stream
    close(Stream).
```

In this example, 'binaryfile.bin' is opened in binary read mode. get_byte/2 is used to read each byte, and the stream is traversed until the end of the file is reached.

Prolog supports reading and writing complex data structures to files. To write a structure, the write/2 predicate is used, and to read it, the read/2 predicate handles the operation transparently.

6.5 Stream Operations and Stream Management

Stream operations and management are fundamental for handling input and output in Prolog. This section elucidates the various mechanisms and functions provided by Prolog to manipulate streams efficiently. Streams represent sources of input or destinations for output, such as files, console, or other I/O devices. In Prolog, streams are typically managed using predicates that operate on these abstract representations.

Opening and Closing Streams

The process of opening and closing streams is crucial for managing resources and ensuring data integrity. In Prolog, the open/3 and close/1 predicates are employed to manage streams. The syntax for open/3 is as follows:

```
open(+SourceSink, +Mode, -Stream)
```

Here, SourceSink specifies the source or destination of the data (e.g., a file name), Mode determines the mode of operation (e.g., read, write, or append), and Stream is unified with the stream identifier once the stream is successfully opened.

For instance, to open a file for reading, one would use:

```
open('example.txt', read, Stream).
```

Having performed the required operations on the stream, it is imperative to close the stream to free up system resources. The close/1 predicate achieves this:

```
close(+Stream)
```

The predicate takes the stream identifier and terminates the connection:

```
close(Stream).
```

Reading from Streams

Reading data from a stream can be conducted using various predicates depending on the nature and amount of data. For structured reading, read/2 can be utilized:

```
read(+Stream, -Term)
```

This predicate reads the next Prolog term from the specified Stream and unifies it with Term. For example:

```
read(Stream, Term).
```

This would read a complete term from Stream and store it in Term.

Alternatively, if reading characters is required, get_char/2 can be employed:

```
get_char(+Stream, -Char)
```

This reads the next character from the Stream and unifies it with Char:

```
get_char(Stream, Char).
```

Writing to Streams

To send data to a stream, the write/2 predicate is available:

```
write(+Stream, +Term)
```

It writes the given Term to the specified Stream. For example:

```
write(Stream, 'Hello, Prolog!').
```

For writing characters or strings, put_char/2 is often used:

```
put_char(+Stream, +Char)
```

This writes the character Char to the Stream:

```
put_char(Stream, 'A').
```

Stream Properties and Manipulation

Streams have properties that can be queried or modified using predicates such as stream_property/2:

```
stream_property(+Stream, ?Property)
```

Here, Property can include attributes such as file_name(Name), mode(Mode), or type(Type). For example:

```
stream_property(Stream, mode(write)).
```

Setting options for a stream is accomplished using set_stream/2:

```
set_stream(+Stream, +Option)
```

Options like buffer size or encoding can be adjusted:

```
set_stream(Stream, buffer(line)).
```

Flushing Streams

To ensure all buffered data is actually written out, the flush_output/1 predicate comes into play:

```
flush_output(+Stream)
```

This ensures that any data buffered in the Stream is transmitted:

```
flush_output(Stream).
```

These operations facilitate precise and efficient handling of input and output through streams in Prolog, establishing a robust foundation for more complex data processing workflows.

6.6 Formatting Output in Prolog

Formatting output in Prolog is essential for generating human-readable and structured text, especially when interacting with end-users or creating reports. This section explores methods and techniques for effective formatting using built-in predicates and libraries, ensuring clarity and precision in the output.

Prolog offers several predicates for writing formatted output to the console or files. The most commonly used predicates include write/1, writeln/1, format/2, and format/3. We will explore each of these, along with practical examples to solidify understanding.

write/1 and writeln/1 are straightforward predicates for output. The write/1 predicate outputs the textual representation of the given argument, while the writeln/1 predicate outputs the text followed by a newline character.

```
?- write('Hello, World!').
Hello, World!
true.

?- writeln('Hello, World!').
Hello, World!
true.
```

For more complex and formatted output, Prolog provides the format/2 and format/3 predicates. The format/2 predicate takes a format string and a list of arguments, similar to formatting functions in other programming languages. The format string contains placeholders, such as w for terms, d for integers, f for floating-point numbers, and n for introducing newlines.

```
?- format('Hello, ~w!', ['World']).
Hello, World!
true.

?- format('The number ~d in hexadecimal is ~16r.', [255]).
The number 255 in hexadecimal is ff.
true.
```

The format/3 predicate functions similarly but allows for specifying the output stream. The first argument of format/3 is the stream, followed by the format string and the argument list.

```
?- open('output.txt', write, Stream),
   format(Stream, 'The result is ~w.', [Result]),
   close(Stream).
```

In this example, the formatted text is written to the file specified by Stream. After writing, the stream is closed.

Complex formatting often requires multiple placeholders and precision control, achieving well-structured output. Precision for floating-point numbers is specified using the Nf placeholder, where N indicates the number of decimal places.

```
?- format('The value of pi to 3 decimal places is ~3f.', [3.14159]).
The value of pi to 3 decimal places is 3.142.
true.
```

Additionally, Prolog supports alignment and padding in formatted output. For instance, the t control sequence aligns text, while the | character specifies the padding length.

```
?- format('|~t~8|~t~w~8|', [left, right]).
| left |
true.
```

In more sophisticated scenarios, conditional formatting might be necessary. This can be achieved through the combination of conditionals and formatting predicates:

```
write_formatted_age(Age) :-
    ( Age < 18
    -> format('You are ~d years old and a minor.~n', [Age])
    ; format('You are ~d years old and an adult.~n', [Age])
    ).
```

This dynamically formats the output based on the condition evaluated during execution.

Beyond the built-in predicates, Prolog's flexibility allows the creation of custom formatting predicates to cater to specific needs. For example, a predicate for displaying tabular data:

```
write_table(Rows) :-
    maplist(format_row, Rows).

format_row(Row) :-
    format('|~t~8|~t~w~8|~t~w~8|~n', Row).
```

Combined with appropriate data, this can render neatly aligned tables:

```
?- write_table([[header1, header2], [data1, data2], [info1, info2]]).
| header1 | header2 |
| data1 | data2 |
| info1 | info2 |
true.
```

Properly leveraging these formatting tools in Prolog enables the generation of clear, readable, and structured outputs.

6.7 Parsing and Processing File Content

When working with files in Prolog, parsing and processing the content accurately is crucial. This enables the transformation of raw data into structured, meaningful information which can then be analyzed or manipulated further in the program. Prolog provides built-in predicates and libraries that can facilitate these tasks, making it an efficient language for handling file content.

Reading File Content as Terms

One of the most straightforward methods for processing file content is to read it as Prolog terms. This approach allows you to leverage Prolog's robust pattern-matching capabilities to process the data. The read/2 predicate can be employed to read terms from a stream:

```
read_file_as_terms(Stream, []) :-
    at_end_of_stream(Stream).

read_file_as_terms(Stream, [Term|Terms]) :-
    \+ at_end_of_stream(Stream),
    read(Stream, Term),
    read_file_as_terms(Stream, Terms).
```

In this example, the read_file_as_terms/2 predicate reads all terms from an open Stream until the end of the stream is reached. Each term is added to a list, producing a list of terms from the file.

Processing Terms

Once the file's content is read into a list of terms, you can process this list according to your requirements. For demonstrative purposes, consider a file containing facts about people:

```
person(john, 25).
person(susan, 30).
person(tom, 22).
```

These facts can be read and processed to filter, aggregate, or transform the data. For example, to find all people who are above a certain age:

```
filter_age([], _, []).

filter_age([person(Name, Age)|T], MinAge, [person(Name, Age)|Filtered]) :-
    Age > MinAge,
    filter_age(T, MinAge, Filtered).

filter_age([_|T], MinAge, Filtered) :-
    filter_age(T, MinAge, Filtered).
```

```
% Example usage
process_file_data(FileName, MinAge, FilteredPeople) :-
    open(FileName, read, Stream),
    read_file_as_terms(Stream, Terms),
    close(Stream),
    filter_age(Terms, MinAge, FilteredPeople).
```

This code reads persons' data from a file and filters those who are older than MinAge, returning the results in FilteredPeople.

Reading and Parsing CSV Files

Prolog can also be used to parse CSV (Comma-Separated Values) files, which are a common data interchange format. Handling CSV files requires reading each line and splitting it into fields based on the delimiter. The library(pio) and library(dcgs) are particularly useful for this purpose.

```
:- use_module(library(pio)).
:- use_module(library(dcgs)).

csv_file([]) --> call(eos), !.
csv_file([Row|Rows]) --> csv_row(Row), csv_file(Rows).

csv_row([]) --> "\n", !.
csv_row([Field|Fields]) --> csv_field(Field), csv_sep, csv_row(Fields).
csv_row([Field]) --> csv_field(Field), "\n".

csv_field(Field) --> quoted_field(Field), !.
csv_field(Field) --> unquoted_field(Field).

quoted_field(Field) --> "\"", string(FieldCodes), "\"", { atom_codes(Field,
        FieldCodes) }.

unquoted_field(Field) --> string_without(",", FieldCodes), { atom_codes(Field,
        FieldCodes) }.

csv_sep --> ",".

eos([], []).

% Example usage
parse_csv_file(FileName, Rows) :-
    phrase_from_file(csv_file(Rows), FileName).
```

This code defines a DCG (Definite Clause Grammar) for parsing CSV files. The csv_file/3 and related predicates match the structure of the CSV file, reading each field and row correctly.

Processing CSV Data

After parsing the CSV file into a list of rows, each row can be processed as needed. For example, to convert the list of rows into a list of facts representing the data:

```
csv_to_facts([], []).

csv_to_facts([[Name, AgeStr]|Rows], [person(Name, Age)|Facts]) :-
    atom_number(AgeStr, Age),
    csv_to_facts(Rows, Facts).

% Example usage
process_csv_data(FileName, Facts) :-
    parse_csv_file(FileName, Rows),
    csv_to_facts(Rows, Facts).
```

This code converts each row of the CSV data into a person/2 fact, assuming the second field of each row is a numeric age.

Parsing and processing file content in Prolog requires a clear understanding of the data format and a systematic approach to reading and transforming this data into meaningful structures. By using Prolog's built-in predicates, universities' libraries, and DCGs, efficient and thorough data processing can be achieved.

6.8 Handling End-of-File and Errors

In Prolog, managing the end-of-file (EOF) condition and handling errors are essential aspects of robust input and output operations. Engaging effectively with these elements ensures smooth execution and user-friendly interaction, particularly when handling files and streams. This section elaborates on techniques to detect EOF, respond to various error conditions, and gracefully recover from them.

End-of-File (EOF) Handling

When reading from a file, it is critical to recognize and handle the EOF condition to avoid infinite loops or runtime errors. Prolog provides built-in predicates to manage EOF states effectively.

The at_end_of_stream/1 predicate checks if the current position in the stream has reached the end-of-file. It simplifies EOF detection during file processing loops.

```
read_until_eof(Stream) :-
    repeat,
    read(Stream, Term),
    ( Term == end_of_file -> ! ; process_term(Term), fail ).
```

In this example, the read_until_eof/1 predicate reads terms from Stream until the end-of-file is encountered. The repeat/0 predicate initiates a backtracking loop that reads terms and checks for the end_of_-

file atom. Upon reaching EOF, the cut operator (!) terminates the loop. Otherwise, the term is processed, and the loop continues.

Constructive Error Handling

Errors can occur due to various reasons such as file not found, permission issues, or unexpected data formats. Utilizing Prolog's built-in exception mechanisms allows for sophisticated error handling and recovery.

The catch/3 predicate helps monitor for exceptions within a code block and provide a mechanism to handle them. The syntax is as follows:

```
catch(Goal, Exception, Handler)
```

Here, Goal is the primary operation prone to errors, Exception is the anticipated error, and Handler is the recovery or response procedure.

Consider a scenario where opening a file might fail due to non-existent files or read-write access issues:

```
safe_open_file(FileName, Mode, Stream) :-
    catch(open(FileName, Mode, Stream),
          error(existence_error(source_sink, FileName), _),
          ( print_message(error, 'File does not exist'), fail )).
```

In safe_open_file/3, if the call to open/3 fails due to a source_sink existence error, a custom message is printed, and the predicate fails gracefully.

Custom Error Messages

Prolog allows for defining custom error messages using the print_message/2 predicate. This can facilitate better debugging and user interactions.

```
:- multifile prolog:message//1.

prolog:message('File does not exist') -->
    [ 'Error: The specified file could not be found.' ].
```

This customization integrates seamlessly with Prolog's messaging system, ensuring error information is clear and informative.

Handling I/O Errors

When performing I/O operations, various errors could arise, such as reading from a closed stream or writing to a read-only file. Managing these errors delicately is imperative.

```
handle_io_errors(Stream) :-
    catch(
```

```
        (read(Stream, Term), fail),
        error(io_error(read, Stream), _),
        ( print_message(error, 'Cannot read from stream'), fail)
    ).
```

The handle_io_errors/1 predicate demonstrates how to catch an I/O error when trying to read from a stream. On encountering an io_error, it prints a descriptive message and fails the operation.

Implementing these techniques in Prolog input and output operations ensures that the code is resilient, user-friendly, and maintainable. Handling EOF and errors correctly not only prevents interruptions but also provides clear feedback, making interaction with the system more predictable and safer.

6.9 Working with Binary Files

Binary file handling in Prolog is crucial when dealing with non-textual data such as images, videos, or serialized objects. Unlike text files, binary files do not consist of readable characters and often require exact reproduction of contents. Prolog provides specific predicates for handling binary files efficiently, ensuring that data remains unaltered during read and write operations.

To handle binary files, one must appropriately open the file in binary mode. This is done using the open/4 predicate where the mode is specified as read_binary or write_binary. The open/4 predicate has the following form:

```
open(FilePath, Mode, Stream, [type(binary)]).
```

Here, FilePath refers to the location of the binary file, Mode specifies the file operation mode (either read or write), Stream is a variable that represents the stream identifier, and type(binary) declares the file type.

Reading from Binary Files:

To read data from a binary file, follow these steps:

1. Open the file in read_binary mode. 2. Utilize predicates such as read_byte/2, read_bytes/3, and read_stream/3 for byte-specific operations. 3. Process the data as needed. 4. Close the file using close/1.

Example:

```
read_binary_file(FilePath, Data) :-
    open(FilePath, read, Stream, [type(binary)]),
```

```
    read_bytes(Stream, Bytes, Length),
    close(Stream),
    process_data(Bytes, Data).
```

In the above example, read_bytes/3 reads a specified number of bytes (indicated by Length) from the stream into Bytes.

Writing to Binary Files:

Writing to binary files involves similar steps:

1. Open the file in write_binary mode. 2. Use predicates like write_byte/2, write_bytes/2, and write_stream/3 for writing bytes. 3. Close the file using close/1.

Example:

```
write_binary_file(FilePath, Data) :-
    open(FilePath, write, Stream, [type(binary)]),
    write_bytes(Stream, Data),
    close(Stream).
```

In this context, write_bytes/2 writes the specified bytes from Data to the file stream.

Handling Binary Data:

Binary file operations often require handling raw binary streams. The predicates read_byte/2 and write_byte/2 operate on single bytes. For example:

```
read_single_byte(FilePath, Byte) :-
    open(FilePath, read, Stream, [type(binary)]),
    read_byte(Stream, Byte),
    close(Stream).
```

```
write_single_byte(FilePath, Byte) :-
    open(FilePath, write, Stream, [type(binary)]),
    write_byte(Stream, Byte),
    close(Stream).
```

In complex scenarios, one may need to read or write chunks of bytes using read_bytes/3 and write_bytes/2 respectively. This ensures efficient processing, especially for large binary files.

Error Handling:

When dealing with binary streams, it's crucial to implement precise error handling to avoid corrupt files or data loss. Common errors include failure to open files, reading beyond EOF (End of File), or writing to disk errors. Utilize predicates such as catch/3 to manage exceptions.

Example:

```
safe_read_binary_file(FilePath, Data) :-
    catch(
        ( open(FilePath, read, Stream, [type(binary)]),
            read_bytes(Stream, Bytes, Length),
            close(Stream),
            process_data(Bytes, Data)
        ),
        Error,
        ( format('Error reading file: ~w', [Error]),
            fail
        )
    ).
```

This example demonstrates the use of catch/3 to handle potential errors during the read process.

Binary file operations in Prolog are integral to many applications requiring the precise handling of complex data structures or media files. Understanding and correctly implementing these operations ensures robust and efficient data management.

6.10 Reading and Writing Data Structures

Understanding how to read and write complex data structures is essential for efficient Prolog programming, particularly when dealing with large data sets or interfacing with external systems. This section explores techniques for handling lists, trees, and other compound terms, focusing on input and output operations.

Reading Data Structures

Reading data structures typically involves parsing user input or file content to populate variables. Consider a scenario where we need to read a list of integers from the user:

```
?- read(List),
   process_list(List).
```

In this example, the read/1 predicate captures input, and process_list/1 operates on it. If the user inputs [1, 2, 3], the variable List is bound to [1, 2, 3].

```
?- read(List),
   length(List, Length),
   write('Length of the list is: '), write(Length).
|: [1, 2, 3].

Length of the list is: 3
```

6.11 Examples of Input and Output Operations

This section presents practical examples illustrating various input and output operations in Prolog. By examining these examples, readers can deepen their understanding of how to effectively manipulate input and output, leveraging the principles discussed in previous sections.

Example 1: Reading User Input In this example, we aim to read a user's name from the console and then print a greeting message.

```
?- write('Enter your name: '), read(UserName),
   atom_concat('Hello, ', UserName, Greeting), write(Greeting).
```

Given the user enters Alice, the output would be:

```
Enter your name: Alice.
Hello, Alice
```

The read predicate captures the user's input, storing it in the UserName variable. The atom_concat/3 predicate concatenates the string 'Hello, ' with UserName to form the greeting message.

Example 2: Writing Output to a File In this case, we write a list of integers to a file.

```
write_list_to_file(List, FileName) :-
    open(FileName, write, Stream),
    write_list(Stream, List),
    close(Stream).

write_list(_, []).
write_list(Stream, [Head|Tail]) :-
    write(Stream, Head), nl(Stream),
    write_list(Stream, Tail).

?- write_list_to_file([1, 2, 3, 4, 5], 'output.txt').
```

This example demonstrates opening a file for writing using the open/3 predicate, writing each element of the list on a new line, and closing the file with the close/1 predicate. The user will find the integers 1 to 5 listed in 'output.txt'.

Example 3: Reading Numbers from a File and Summing Them Next, we read integers from a text file and calculate their sum.

```
sum_numbers_from_file(FileName, Sum) :-
    open(FileName, read, Stream),
    read_numbers(Stream, Numbers),
    close(Stream),
    sum_list(Numbers, Sum).
```

```
read_numbers(Stream, []) :-
    at_end_of_stream(Stream).
read_numbers(Stream, [Number|Rest]) :-
    \+ at_end_of_stream(Stream),
    read(Stream, Number),
    read_numbers(Stream, Rest).

sum_list([], 0).
sum_list([Head|Tail], Sum) :-
    sum_list(Tail, TailSum),
    Sum is Head + TailSum.

?- sum_numbers_from_file('numbers.txt', Sum).
```

Assuming 'numbers.txt' contains the integers 1, 2, and 3, executing the query will bind Sum to 6. The $\text{read\_numbers}/2$ predicate reads all the numbers from the file into a list, which is then summed by the $\text{sum\_list}/2$ predicate.

Example 4: Parsing and Processing File Content Consider parsing a file containing student records and calculating the average grade.

```
average_grade(FileName, Average) :-
    open(FileName, read, Stream),
    read_student_records(Stream, Records),
    close(Stream),
    grades(Records, Grades),
    sum_list(Grades, Total),
    length(Grades, Count),
    Average is Total / Count.

read_student_records(Stream, []) :-
    at_end_of_stream(Stream).
read_student_records(Stream, [student(Name, Grade) | Rest]) :-
    \+ at_end_of_stream(Stream),
    read(Stream, student(Name, Grade)),
    read_student_records(Stream, Rest).

grades([], []).
grades([student(_, Grade)|Tail], [Grade|GradesTail]) :-
    grades(Tail, GradesTail).

?- average_grade('students.txt', Average).
```

With 'students.txt' structured as:

```
student('Alice', 85).
student('Bob', 90).
student('Carol', 78).
```

Executing the predicate will produce an average grade of 84.33.

Example 5: Handling Binary Files Suppose we want to read and write binary data using Prolog. This example shows writing a sequence of bytes to a binary file and then reading those bytes back.

```
write_binary_data(FileName, Data) :-
    open(FileName, write, Stream, [type(binary)]),
```

```
    write_bytes(Stream, Data),
    close(Stream).

write_bytes(_, []).
write_bytes(Stream, [Byte|Rest]) :-
    put_byte(Stream, Byte),
    write_bytes(Stream, Rest).

read_binary_data(FileName, Data) :-
    open(FileName, read, Stream, [type(binary)]),
    read_bytes(Stream, Data),
    close(Stream).

read_bytes(Stream, []) :-
    at_end_of_stream(Stream).
read_bytes(Stream, [Byte|Rest]) :-
    \+ at_end_of_stream(Stream),
    get_byte(Stream, Byte),
    read_bytes(Stream, Rest).

?- write_binary_data('binary.dat', [65, 66, 67, 68]),
   read_binary_data('binary.dat', Data).
```

Executing the query will write the bytes corresponding to 'ABCD' to 'binary.dat' and read them back into the Data variable, which will hold $[65, 66, 67, 68]$.

Reviewing these examples will provide readers with practical insights into implementing diverse input and output operations in Prolog, reinforcing theoretical knowledge with hands-on practice.

6.12 Best Practices for Input and Output in Prolog

When working with input and output (I/O) in Prolog, it is essential to follow established best practices to ensure efficiency, maintainability, and error-free operations. This section delineates these practices methodically to aid programmers at various proficiency levels.

1. Use Proper Stream Management: Effective stream management is fundamental in Prolog programming. Always open streams with appropriate modes and close them after use to prevent resource leaks.

```
% Example of Proper Stream Management
open('example.txt', read, Stream),
read(Stream, Data),
close(Stream).
```

Ensure that every $\mathrm{open}/3$ predicate is followed by a corresponding $\mathrm{close}/1$ to release the stream resource.

2. Handle Errors Gracefully: Error handling in I/O operations prevents runtime exceptions and enhances user experience. Utilize predicates like catch/3 to manage potential errors.

```
% Example of Handling Errors
safe_open(File, Mode, Stream) :-
    catch(open(File, Mode, Stream),
          error(existence_error(source_sink, File), _),
          writeln('File not found')).
```

This pattern catches the existence error and provides feedback rather than terminating the program abruptly.

3. Use Format Specifiers to Manage Output: For clear and formatted console output, leverage the format/2 and format/3 predicates. This practice ensures that printed data is comprehensible and professionally presented.

```
% Example of Formatting Output
number_display(Number) :-
    format('The number is ~w.~n', [Number]).
```

Format specifiers like w, d, and s control the layout and representation of various data types.

4. Use Atoms and Strings Judiciously: Differentiate between atoms and strings appropriately. Use atoms for constants and identifiers, while strings handle text data and user input.

```
% Example Usage of Atoms and Strings
welcome_message(Name) :-
    atom_concat('Welcome, ', Name, Message),
    writeln(Message).
```

Here, atom_concat/3 creates a greeting message effectively.

5. Perform Buffered I/O for Large Data: When dealing with large data sets, buffered I/O can improve performance. Use read/2 for reading terms and write/2 for writing terms in a more concentrated manner.

```
% Example of Buffered I/O
process_file(File) :-
    open(File, read, Stream),
    repeat,
    read(Stream, Term),
    ( Term == end_of_file
    -> close(Stream)
    ; writeln(Term),
        fail
    ).
```

This pattern reads terms until the end-of-file (EOF) is encountered, ensuring efficient data processing.

6. Validate User Inputs: Validating user inputs before processing ensures the correctness of operations and prevents potential inconsistencies or unexpected behaviors.

```
% Example of Input Validation
get_valid_number(Number) :-
    repeat,
    writeln('Enter a number: '),
    read(Input),
    ( number(Input)
    -> Number = Input
    ; writeln('Invalid input. Please enter a number.'),
        fail
    ).
```

This approach repeatedly prompts the user until a valid number is entered.

7. Adopt Modular Programming Techniques: Modularize I/O operations into reusable predicates and libraries. This practice enhances code maintainability and readability.

```
% Example of Modular I/O Operations
write_data_to_file(Data, File) :-
    open(File, write, Stream),
    write(Stream, Data),
    close(Stream).

read_data_from_file(File, Data) :-
    open(File, read, Stream),
    read(Stream, Data),
    close(Stream).
```

Creating modular predicates for reading and writing promotes code reuse and simplification.

8. Manage File Paths Correctly: Handle file paths in a portable and consistent manner by utilizing built-in predicates, ensuring cross-platform compatibility.

```
% Example of File Path Management
get_absolute_path(RelativePath, AbsolutePath) :-
    absolute_file_name(RelativePath, AbsolutePath).
```

Using absolute_file_name/2 predicate converts relative paths to absolute paths, streamlining file access across different operating systems.

9. Optimize for Performance: Optimize I/O operations for performance, especially in loop structures involving numerous I/O tasks. Minimize redundant operations and leverage efficient data structures.

```
% Example of Performance Optimization
```

```
read_all_lines(Stream, Lines) :-
    read_stream_to_codes(Stream, Codes),
    atom_codes(Atom, Codes),
    atomic_list_concat(Lines, '\n', Atom).
```

Here, read_stream_to_codes/2 reads the entire stream into codes, which is then converted into a list of lines, enhancing performance for batch processing.

10. Ensure Thread-Safe I/O: In multi-threaded applications, ensure that I/O operations are thread-safe to avoid race conditions and data corruption.

```
% Example of Thread-Safe I/O
:- use_module(library(thread)).

thread_safe_write(Log, Message) :-
    with_mutex(log_mutex, (
        open(Log, append, Stream),
        writeln(Stream, Message),
        close(Stream)
    )).
```

Using with_mutex/2 ensures that the write operation is atomic, preventing concurrent access issues.

By adhering to these best practices, Prolog programmers can conduct sophisticated and reliable I/O operations, improving program robustness and user satisfaction. Proper stream management, error handling, formatting, user input validation, modular design, performance optimization, and ensuring thread-safety are pivotal for proficiently handling input and output in Prolog.

Chapter 7

Backtracking and Control in Prolog

This chapter delves into backtracking and control in Prolog, explaining the search space, unification's role, and the cut operator for pruning the search. It covers fail predicates, if-then-else control structures, and negation as failure. The chapter also discusses depth-first search implications, customizing backtracking behavior, implementing search algorithms, performance considerations, and debugging and tracing backtracking processes.

7.1 Introduction to Backtracking in Prolog

Backtracking is a fundamental mechanism in Prolog that facilitates the search for solutions by exploring the possible states of a problem space through a process of trial and error. In this section, we delve into the intricacies of backtracking to understand its operational semantics, behavior, and practical applications within Prolog.

Prolog's evaluation strategy prominently features depth-first search, where the system proceeds by expanding the first branch of the search tree before moving to the next. When a goal or subgoal fails, Prolog's backtracking mechanism retraces the steps to the most recent choice point—a point where alternatives are available—and tries the next alternative.

Consider a simple example that highlights the backtracking process. The predicate member/2 defines whether an element is part of a list:

```
member(X, [X|_]).
member(X, [_|T]) :- member(X, T).
```

To query whether element a is a member of the list [a, b, c], the following query can be issued:

```
?- member(a, [a, b, c]).
```

Initially, the head of the list [a|_] matches [a, b, c], succeeding immediately. However, if we query:

```
?- member(d, [a, b, c]).
```

Prolog attempts the first clause, fails to match d with a, then backtracks to try the second clause, member(d, [b, c]), recursively continuing this process until all possibilities are exhausted.

Prolog maintains an internal stack of call frames to manage control flow during backtracking. Each call to a predicate and its local variables are pushed onto the stack. Upon failure, the system pops the stack, reverting to the previous state, and attempts the next alternative approach. This ensures that all paths, unless pruned via control mechanisms like the cut operator, are explored.

```
find_path(From, To, Path) :-
    travel(From, To, [From], Path).

travel(To, To, Visited, Path) :-
    reverse(Visited, Path).

travel(From, To, Visited, Path) :-
    edge(From, Next),
    \+ member(Next, Visited),
    travel(Next, To, [Next|Visited], Path).
```

In this context, the travel/4 predicate tries to build a path between two nodes in a graph, avoiding cycles by keeping track of visited nodes:

```
?- find_path(a, c, Path).
```

This query triggers travel/4 which recursively attempts to extend paths by considering graph edges. If a dead end is encountered (i.e., no outbound edges that avoid cycles), Prolog backtracks to the last viable state and tries alternative paths.

Understanding backtracking is crucial for debugging and optimizing Prolog programs, as it directly impacts execution flow and efficiency. Predicates inherently interact with backtracking in Prolog, producing different behaviors depending on their order and specificity. Consider:

```
parent(john, mia).
parent(john, vincent).

ancestor(X, Y) :-
    parent(X, Y).

ancestor(X, Y) :-
    parent(X, Z),
    ancestor(Z, Y).
```

Querying:

```
?- ancestor(john, Who).
```

Returns each descendant of john iteratively, first mia, then vincent, subsequently exploring indirect lineages through the recursive definition.

Finally, it is imperative to note Prolog's standard interpretation for Boolean failure and success. If no matching clause exists or resolving paths lead to contradictions, the system fails, causing backtracking. Here lies the core advantage of logic programming: the declarative nature allows Prolog to abstract intricate control flows implicitly managed by the backtracking mechanism. This simplifies the expression of complex problems, enabling developers to focus on declarative problem formulation rather than imperative control flow.

7.2 Understanding the Search Space

In Prolog, the search space represents the set of all possible solutions that Prolog may explore to satisfy a goal or query. Understanding this concept is essential to effectively using Prolog's backtracking mechanism. The search space is fundamentally structured as a tree where each node represents a goal or subgoal, and each branch corresponds to a possible unification with a clause in the program.

At the core of Prolog's search mechanism is the concept of goal reduction. This involves breaking down complex queries into simpler ones that can be processed individually. For instance, consider a query ?- parent(X, Y), ancestor(Y, Z). This query involves two subgoals: parent(X, Y) and ancestor(Y, Z). Prolog will handle these subgoals sequentially, exploring their respective search spaces independently.

Consider the following Prolog facts and rules:

```
parent(abe, homer).
parent(marge, bart).
```

```
parent(homer, bart).
parent(homer, lisa).
parent(homer, maggie).

ancestor(X, Y) :- parent(X, Y).
ancestor(X, Y) :- parent(X, Z), ancestor(Z, Y).
```

When querying the Prolog system with ?- ancestor(abe, Z), Prolog will attempt to unify ancestor(abe, Z) with the head of the ancestor/2 rules. The search space can be visualized as follows:

```
ancestor(abe, Z)
  |- parent(abe, Z)
  |    |- Z = homer
  |
  |- parent(abe, Z), ancestor(Z, Y)
       |- parent(abe, homer)
       |    |- ancestor(homer, Z)
       |          |- Z = bart
       |          |- Z = lisa
       |          |- Z = maggie
```

The tree above demonstrates how the Prolog interpreter explores potential solutions. It first attempts to satisfy the goal using the direct parent/2 clause. If that unification fails, Prolog backtracks and attempts to satisfy the goal using the recursive ancestor/2 rule.

To delve deeper, consider the operation of unification in this search space. When Prolog encounters a goal, it tries to unify this goal with the head of the rules in the program. This involves the following steps: - Variable sharing: If the goal involves variables, these are replaced by shared variables across different subgoals. - Unificatory attempts: The unification process tries to match the goal with available facts and rules by consistent variable assignments. - Recursive reduction: In case of recursive rules, new subgoals are generated, expanding the search space tree.

To control which part of the search space to explore, Prolog employs a depth-first search strategy. This means that Prolog will fully explore one branch of the tree before moving onto the next. This has implications on efficiency and potential infinite loops in the presence of recursive definitions.

For instance, the query ?- ancestor(homer, bart) will follow this sequence: 1. Try to unify ancestor(homer, bart) with ancestor(X, Y) :- parent(X, Y): - Unification succeeds, binding X to homer and Y to bart.

If the query were ?- ancestor(homer, Z), Prolog would then: 1. Try ancestor(X, Y) :- parent(X, Y): - Matches parent(homer, bart), parent(homer, lisa), parent(homer, maggie). - Yields Z = bart, Z = lisa, Z

= maggie.

2. If more solutions are sought, use ancestor(X, Y) :- parent(X, Z), ancestor(Z, Y): - Will recursively check if any Z satisfies ancestor leading to more branches in the search tree.

Understanding how this search mechanism and the search space work is crucial for designing efficient Prolog programs. By ensuring that the rules are appropriately ordered and structured, one can optimize the traversal of the search space, avoiding pitfalls such as infinite recursion or unnecessarily large search trees. Prolog's backtracking, through systematic exploration, can then be leveraged effectively to find solutions or demonstrate their absence.

7.3 The Role of Unification in Backtracking

Unification is foundational to Prolog's operational semantics, serving as a fundamental mechanism in the backtracking process. This section delves into the specifics of how unification works and its integral role in enabling Prolog to explore the search space effectively.

Unification is the process of making two terms identical by finding a suitable substitution for variables. In Prolog, this process is deterministic and follows a well-defined set of rules. During execution, when a goal is encountered, Prolog attempts to unify the goal with the head of clauses in the database. If unification succeeds, the body of the clause is then considered as a new set of sub-goals.

Consider the following Prolog facts and rules:

```
parent(alice, bob).
parent(bob, charlie).
ancestor(X, Y) :- parent(X, Y).
ancestor(X, Y) :- parent(X, Z), ancestor(Z, Y).
```

When querying ancestor(alice, charlie), Prolog first tries to unify ancestor(alice, charlie) with the heads of the ancestor/2 clauses. Unification involves systematically trying to make the terms identical. For each clause in the database, Prolog will:

1. Attempt to unify the goal with the clause head. 2. If unification succeeds, instantiate variables accordingly. 3. Proceed to solve the resulting sub-goals (the body of the clause).

With our query ancestor(alice, charlie), Prolog's unification process will proceed as follows:

1. Unifies ancestor(alice, charlie) with ancestor(X, Y) :- parent(X, Y) resulting in the substitution {X = alice, Y = charlie}. Since parent(alice, charlie) does not exist, unification fails. 2. Prolog backtracks and tries the next clause: ancestor(X, Y) :- parent(X, Z), ancestor(Z, Y). 3. Unifies ancestor(alice, charlie) with ancestor(X, Y) resulting in the substitution {X = alice, Y = charlie}. 4. The sub-goals become parent(alice, Z) and ancestor(Z, charlie).

Next, Prolog tries to satisfy parent(alice, Z):

```
parent(alice, bob).
```

The unification succeeds with the substitution {Z = bob}, and Prolog then attempts to solve the next sub-goal ancestor(bob, charlie).

Unification continues recursively:

```
ancestor(bob, charlie)
```

1. Prolog again tries to unify this with parent(X, Y) without success since parent(bob, charlie) does not exist. 2. It then backtracks and unifies ancestor(bob, charlie) with ancestor(X, Y) :- parent(X, Z), ancestor(Z, Y). 3. This results in: ancestor(X, Y) :- parent(bob, Z), ancestor(Z, charlie) with {X = bob, Y = charlie}.

The sub-goals now are parent(bob, Z) and ancestor(Z, charlie).

```
parent(bob, charlie).
```

Unification of parent(bob, Z) with parent(bob, charlie) succeeds with {Z = charlie}, and Prolog then tries to solve ancestor(charlie, charlie). At this point, because ancestor(charlie, charlie) unifies trivially since it matches the definition directly.

The unification here is critical as it ensures that Prolog correctly establishes relationships and reasons over recursive structures. When a unification fails, backtracking allows Prolog to explore alternate pathways in the search space. Each failed unification causes Prolog to reconsider prior choices and attempt different routes.

For a more complex example, consider utilizing variables and unification within recursive rules. Suppose we have the clauses:

```
likes(alice, programming).
likes(bob, painting).
hobbyist(Person, Hobby) :- likes(Person, Hobby).
hobbyist(Person, Hobby) :- person(Person), likes(Person, AnotherHobby), related(
    Hobby, AnotherHobby).
```

And the query hobbyist(alice, painting). During unification:

1. Prolog will first try to unify hobbyist(alice, painting) against hobbyist(Person, Hobby) :- likes(Person, Hobby). The resulting substitution is {Person = alice, Hobby = painting}. However, since likes(alice, painting) does not exist, this path fails. 2. Prolog then attempts the next clause: hobbyist(Person, Hobby) :- person(Person), likes(Person, AnotherHobby), related(Hobby, AnotherHobby). 3. Unification yields {Person = alice, Hobby = painting}, producing sub-goals person(alice), likes(alice, AnotherHobby), and related(painting, AnotherHobby).

Backtracking mechanisms will come into play if person(alice) satisfies but likes(alice, AnotherHobby) fails, leading Prolog to explore different unification combinations. Thus, unification not only fuels the logical inference engine but also interlocks gracefully with the backtracking process to exhaustively search for solutions within the Prolog environment.

7.4 Cut Operator and Pruning the Search

The cut operator, denoted by the exclamation mark !, is an essential control construct in Prolog that influences the backtracking mechanism. It is used to prune the search tree, effectively stopping Prolog from exploring alternative solutions once a particular path in the search space has been deemed successful. This section explores the semantics, usage, and implications of the cut operator in the context of controlling backtracking and enhancing the efficiency of Prolog programs.

The primary role of the cut operator is to prevent unnecessary computations and inhibit Prolog's default depth-first search strategy from exploring redundant choices. To understand its impact, consider a simple example where the cut operator eliminates alternative solutions that are not needed:

```
max(X, Y, X) :- X >= Y, !.
max(_, Y, Y).
```

In this code, the predicate max/3 determines the maximum of two numbers. The first clause will succeed if X is greater than or equal to Y, and the cut operator ! will prune the remaining choices, ensuring that Prolog does not attempt to match further clauses. If the condition fails, Prolog backtracks and attempts the second clause.

To observe the behavior of the cut operator, consider the following query and execution:

```
?- max(3, 2, Result).
```

Result = 3.

In this instance, since $3 >= 2$ holds true, Prolog executes the first clause, triggers the cut, and does not consider any other clauses for $\mathrm{max}/3$. Consequently, the cut operator avoids potential inefficiencies by terminating the search as soon as the correct result is found.

It is crucial to note that the cut operator is not without drawbacks. When used improperly, it can lead to unexpected and undesired outcomes, making the debugging process more complex. Thus, it is imperative to employ cuts judiciously.

A common scenario where the cut operator is particularly useful is in defining deterministic predicates, where exactly one solution is to be accepted. For example:

```
member(X, [X|_]) :- !.
member(X, [_|T]) :- member(X, T).
```

In the $\mathrm{member}/2$ predicate, the cut operator ensures that once a match is found in the list, Prolog does not continue searching for additional occurrences. Therefore, the cut here enhances both the clarity and efficiency of the predicate by eliminating unnecessary backtracking.

While simple cuts like the ones shown above are relatively straightforward, green and red cuts provide further control nuances. A green cut (green !) is used solely for performance optimization, ensuring that the logical meaning of the program remains unchanged. Conversely, a red cut (red !) alters the logical meaning, potentially leading to different outcomes based on the cut's position. Consider an example involving a red cut:

```
discount(category_1, 10) :- !.
discount(category_2, 5).
discount(_, 0).
```

Querying the discount value for different categories will result in:

```
?- discount(category_1, D).
```

D = 10.

```
?- discount(category_3, D).
```

D = 0.

The cut in discount/2 precludes any other discounts once a match for category_1 is found. However, extending or modifying the predicate requires vigilance to maintain correct program logic.

Understanding the interplay of cuts with other control structures, such as fail predicates and if-then-else constructs, further enhances the programmer's toolkit. By combining cuts with fail predicates, it becomes feasible to enforce strict outputs while handling failures gracefully. For example:

```
valid_age(Age) :- Age >= 0, Age =< 120, !.
valid_age(_) :- fail.
```

This predicate defines a valid age range from 0 to 120 and ensures any age outside this range will trigger a fail condition without attempting further clauses.

When using the cut operator with if-then-else constructs, it offers more readable and manageable code. The built-in (Condition -> Then; Else) format naturally incorporates cuts implicitly, as shown here:

```
risk_level(Age, Risk) :-
    Age < 18 -> Risk = low
    ; Age < 40 -> Risk = medium
    ; Risk = high.
```

In this construct, once a condition is satisfied, the cut-like behavior of the if-then-else structure halts further consideration of the subsequent branches, thereby optimizing the flow control.

Finally, the strategic placement of cuts can profoundly affect the performance of search algorithms implemented in Prolog. For instance, a breadth-first search can be simulated with careful control of backtracking and cuts. Nonetheless, the fundamental trade-offs between clarity, maintainability, and performance must always be balanced.

A heuristic understanding of how the cut operator influences search enables more efficient and predictable Prolog programs. Through selective pruning of the search space, practitioners can manage computational complexity, yielding robust and performant applications.

7.5 Using Fail Predicates

The fail predicate (fail/0) is a fundamental component in Prolog's control mechanism, designed to force backtracking. By understanding its application and utility, one can expertly manage the flow of a program, allowing for more sophisticated problem-solving strategies.

fail/0 is a built-in predicate that always fails. When invoked, Prolog triggers backtracking, causing the interpreter to revisit previously made decisions and attempt alternative solutions. This is particularly useful for scenarios where multiple solutions are sought, or when we need to prune certain branches of the search space intentionally.

Consider the following example using a simple database of facts:

```
parent(john, mary).
parent(jane, mary).
parent(john, paul).
parent(jane, paul).
parent(paul, alice).
```

To determine all pairs of siblings in the database, one might write a rule as follows:

```
sibling(X, Y) :- parent(P, X), parent(P, Y), X \== Y.
```

This predicate finds pairs of siblings by verifying that both X and Y have the same parent P, and that they are not the same individual. In a query context, this could be executed to list all sibling pairs:

```
?- sibling(X, Y).
```

The expected outcome would be:

```
X = mary, Y = paul ;
X = paul, Y = mary ;
false.
```

However, say we are only interested in determining whether there is any sibling relationship at all, rather than listing all possible pairs. In such a case, leveraging fail/0 can provide an elegant solution. One might rewrite the predicate to include an invocation of fail/0 to force backtracking after printing each found sibling pair, as shown below:

```
print_all_siblings :-
    sibling(X, Y),
    format('~w is a sibling of ~w~n', [X, Y]),
    fail.

print_all_siblings.
```

Executing the print_all_siblings/0 predicate:

```
?- print_all_siblings.
```

would produce:

```
mary is a sibling of paul
paul is a sibling of mary
true.
```

The fail/0 predicate ensures that the search does not stop at the first solution, but continues looking for other possible sibling pairs. After enumerating all pairs, the fail/0 predicate forces Prolog to backtrack beyond the initial print_all_siblings/0 call, eventually succeeding with the final, empty print_all_siblings clause, thus completing the query with a true outcome.

When combined with other control mechanisms, such as the cut operator (!/0), the fail predicate can also be instrumental in managing complex logical flows. For instance, suppose we refine our query to count the number of sibling pairs:

```
count_siblings(Count) :-
    findall(_, sibling(_, _), Pairs),
    length(Pairs, Count).
```

Here, findall/3 is used to collect all sibling pairs into the list Pairs, and length/2 determines its length. The count_siblings/1 predicate thus calculates the total number of sibling pairs directly.

```
?- count_siblings(Count).
```

The output would be:

```
Count = 2.
```

Using fail/0 in conjunction with other control structures effectively augments Prolog's logical expressiveness, enabling more precise and controlled navigation through the search space. Understanding how to deploy fail/0 appropriately is essential for mastering Prolog's full potential.

7.6 Control Structures: if-then-else

Prolog provides various control structures to dictate the flow of execution within predicates. One such pivotal construct is the if-then-else statement, expressed using the symbols -> (if-then) and ; (else). The if-then-else construct is central for decision-making processes in Prolog, allowing the programmer to specify alternative computations based on the success or failure of a condition.

The syntax for the if-then-else construct is as follows:

```
( Condition -> ThenClause ; ElseClause )
```

Here, Condition is a goal that Prolog attempts to satisfy. If Condition succeeds, Prolog executes ThenClause. If Condition fails, Prolog executes ElseClause.

Example 1: Basic Usage

Consider a scenario where we need to determine if a number is positive, negative, or zero:

```
check_number(Number) :-
    ( Number > 0 ->
        writeln('Positive')
    ; Number < 0 ->
        writeln('Negative')
    ;
        writeln('Zero')
    ).
```

In this example, the code checks the value of Number. If Number is greater than 0, it prints Positive. If Number is less than 0, it prints Negative. If neither condition is met, it defaults to printing Zero.

Example 2: Nested if-then-else

Prolog allows for the nesting of if-then-else constructs to handle more complex decision-making scenarios:

```
categorize(Number) :-
    ( Number > 0 ->
        ( Number > 100 ->
            writeln('Large Positive')
        ;
            writeln('Small Positive')
        )
    ; Number < 0 ->
        ( Number < -100 ->
            writeln('Large Negative')
        ;
            writeln('Small Negative')
        )
    ;
        writeln('Zero')
    ).
```

Here, categorize/1 further distinguishes between large and small positive and negative numbers.

Operational Semantics

Upon invocation, Prolog evaluates Condition. If Condition succeeds, Prolog commits to this clause, meaning it will not reconsider this decision even if subsequent computations cause a failure. This commitment prevents backtracking into the else clause.

Example 3: Demonstrating Commitment

The following example illustrates Prolog's commitment behavior:

```
decision(X) :-
    ( X = 1 ->
        writeln('One')
    ;
        writeln('Not One')
    ).
```

```
?- decision(1).
```

```
One
```

```
?- decision(2).
```

```
Not One
```

Once Prolog commits to the ThenClause upon the success of Condition, it does not retract this decision, showcasing the deterministic nature of the if-then commitment.

Performance Consideration

The if-then-else construct can lead to improvements in control flow efficiency by prunning the search space. When Condition succeeds, Prolog does not revisit the ElseClause during backtracking, potentially leading to performance gains by reducing unnecessary evaluations.

Practical Example: Classifying Elements

Lastly, consider a synthesized example of classifying elements in a list into categories:

```
classify_list([], []).
classify_list([H|T], [Category|Rest]) :-
    ( H < 0 ->
        Category = negative
    ; H > 0 ->
        Category = positive
    ;
        Category = zero
    ),
    classify_list(T, Rest).
```

Here, classify_list/2 recurses through a list, categorizing each element as positive, negative, or zero, demonstrating the utility of the if-then-else construct in data-driven applications.

The if-then-else construct offers both power and precision in controlling Prolog's execution flow, ensuring efficiency and facilitating complex decision-making processes.

7.7 Negation as Failure

In Prolog, the concept of *negation as failure* is a fundamental mechanism that allows the system to deduce the negation of a predicate based on the failure to prove it. This principle is inherently tied to the way Prolog handles backtracking and unification, making it a powerful tool for logical reasoning within a Prolog program.

Overview of Negation as Failure

Negation as failure operates on the idea that if Prolog cannot prove a certain goal G, then it infers that G is false. This is expressed in Prolog using the $\text{not}/1$ or the prefix operator $\backslash+/1$. This approach aligns well with the declarative nature of Prolog, enabling concise and expressive problem definitions.

To illustrate, consider a scenario where we want to define a predicate not_male(X) that succeeds if X is not a male. Suppose we have the following facts and rules in our knowledge base:

```
male(john).
male(peter).
male(jim).

female(susan).
female(mary).
```

The predicate not_male(X) can be defined using $\backslash+/1$ as follows:

```
not_male(X) :- \+ male(X).
```

In this definition, $\backslash+\ \text{male(X)}$ succeeds if male(X) cannot be proven true for a given X.

Formal Definition and Properties

Given a goal G, applying the not operator, denoted as $\backslash+/1$, yields true if the search for G fails. Formally:

$$\backslash+G \text{ is true if and only if Prolog cannot prove } G.$$

This mechanism is non-monotonic, meaning the addition of new facts or rules to the database might change the outcome of the negation. This contrasts with classical negation used in mathematical logic, where the truth value remains invariant to the addition of new knowledge.

Use Cases and Examples

Consider a scenario where we want to determine all individuals who are not males. Using the not_male(X) predicate, we can query Prolog as follows:

```
?- not_male(X).
```

The following is the expected output, representing all individuals where the male(X) predicate fails:

```
X = susan ;
X = mary ;
false.
```

Another practical example is checking membership in a list. Suppose we want to determine if an element does not belong to a list. This can be achieved via a custom predicate not_member/2:

```
not_member(_, []).
not_member(X, [H|T]) :- X \= H, not_member(X, T).
```

Here, not_member(X, List) succeeds if X is not an element of List. A query such as ?- not_member(3, [1, 2, 4, 5]). would yield:

```
true.
```

Conversely, ?- not_member(3, [1, 2, 3, 4, 5]). would produce:

```
false.
```

Limitations and Considerations

While negation as failure is robust, it is essential to recognize its limitations given its non-monotonic nature. Changes in the knowledge base can lead to variations in the results of negated queries, thereby requiring careful management of dynamic databases.

Furthermore, the negation as failure strategy is semantically distinct from classical negation used in many logical systems. It assumes a closed-world assumption (CWA), where anything not known to be true is considered false. This might be inappropriate for applications requiring open-world reasoning, such as certain artificial intelligence and knowledge representation systems.

Prolog's lack of support for proper existential quantification within its negation constructs also means that care must be taken during implementation. For instance, nested or complex negations often necessitate additional predicates to ensure clarity and correctness. Consider the following example for nested negations:

```
p:- \+(\+q).
q.
```

Querying ?- p. in this instance:

```
p = true.
```

This outcome emphasizes that p succeeds as a result of double negation resolving to true given q is defined explicitly.

Negation as failure, as presented, embodies a practical and efficient means to extend logic programming capabilities in Prolog. It integrates seamlessly into Prolog's backtracking mechanism and enables sophisticated control over negative information, enhancing the representational and inferential power of the language.

7.8 Depth-First Search and Its Implications

Depth-First Search (DFS) is the principal search strategy used in Prolog. Prolog's execution model inherently follows a depth-first strategy to traverse the search space, exploring each possible branch in its entirety before backtracking to explore alternative branches. Understanding DFS and its implications is critical for mastering Prolog programming since it affects performance, completeness, and termination of Prolog programs.

When Prolog encounters a goal, it attempts to satisfy the goal by matching it with a clause in its database. If the match succeeds, Prolog recursively attempts to satisfy any sub-goals introduced by the body of the clause. This creates a search tree where each node represents a goal or sub-goal, and each branch represents a different clause that could potentially satisfy the goal.

Let us consider a simple scenario where we have a family tree and want to find an ancestor. The program can be written as follows:

```
% Prolog facts
parent(john, doe).
parent(doe, smith).
parent(smith, jane).

% Recursive rule to find an ancestor
ancestor(X, Y) :- parent(X, Y).
ancestor(X, Y) :- parent(X, Z), ancestor(Z, Y).
```

When querying the program to find an ancestor of jane, Prolog employs DFS to traverse the search space:

```
?- ancestor(X, jane).
```

The aforementioned query leads to the following sequence of steps:

1. Prolog first tries to satisfy ancestor(X, jane) using the first rule ancestor(X, Y) :- parent(X, Y). 2. It fails, because there is no direct parent(X, jane) in the database. 3. Prolog then recursively applies the second rule ancestor(X, Y) :- parent(X, Z), ancestor(Z, Y). 4. The intermediate goal parent(X, Z) must now be satisfied. 5. Suppose Prolog unifies parent(smith, jane) with parent(X, jane), setting X = smith and introduces a new sub-goal ancestor(smith, jane). 6. If this recursive call returns false, Prolog will backtrack to find a different parent(X, jane). 7. This process repeats until either a solution is found or all possibilities are exhausted.

Prolog's depth-first approach means it may not always find the shortest path first. It dives deep into each potential solution path. Consider the following graph traversal example to illustrate this point:

```
% Prolog facts for graph edges
edge(a, b).
edge(b, c).
edge(c, d).
edge(a, e).
edge(e, f).
edge(e, g).

% Rule to find a path between two nodes
path(X, Y) :- edge(X, Y).
path(X, Y) :- edge(X, Z), path(Z, Y).
```

Executing ?- path(a, d). will follow these steps:

1. Try edge(a, d) directly, which fails. 2. Use edge(a, Z) with Z = b. 3. Attempt path(b, d) recursively. 4. Follow edge(b, c) making the new goal path(c, d). 5. Successfully unify path(c, d) by edge(c, d).

This traversal explores one whole branch before others, thus taking longer paths first if they appear earlier in the list of edges.

The implications of depth-first search in Prolog are significant:

Efficiency: DFS uses less memory than breadth-first search (BFS) because it only needs to store nodes along the current path, not the entire tree level. This reduces overhead but might result in longer computation times as deeper paths are investigated first.

Completeness: DFS is not complete if the search space contains infinitely long paths, because it can get stuck in these paths without ever exploring other parts of the tree.

Optimality: DFS does not guarantee the shortest path. It will find the first path that satisfies the condition, which might not be the shortest or most efficient path.

Customizing the behavior of DFS within Prolog can involve using control mechanisms such as the cut operator and fail predicates to preempt unnecessarily deep traversal, thus improving efficiency and guiding the search process more effectively. Understanding these trade-offs helps in designing Prolog applications that balance between performance and completeness based on problem-specific requirements.

7.9 Customizing Backtracking Behavior

Customizing backtracking behavior in Prolog enables programmers to define more specific and efficient control over the search process. This section elucidates various techniques for modifying how Prolog backtracks through the search space, balancing correctness and efficiency. We will examine the use of cut, preventing unwanted backtracking, employing determinism, and utilizing built-in predicates like $once/1$.

Prolog's default backtracking mechanism explores all possible paths to find a solution. However, there are scenarios where we desire to restrict this comprehensive search to save resources and time or enforce specific logical constraints.

Using the Cut Operator

The cut operator (!) is a common mechanism to control backtracking. When Prolog encounters a cut in a clause, it commits to the choices made so far and prunes all alternative branches.

```
max(X, Y, Max) :-
    X >= Y, !, Max = X.
max(X, Y, Max) :-
    Max = Y.
```

In the above code snippet, the cut operator ensures that once the condition $X >= Y$ is satisfied, Prolog will not consider any further clauses for the predicate $max/3$. This control structure enhances efficiency by preventing unnecessary evaluations.

Preventing Unwanted Backtracking

In scenarios where certain rule evaluations should either succeed or fail conclusively without backtracking, utilizing the $+$ predicate indicator provides a functional method. For example, ensuring that a number is positive without reconsidering an alternative clause:

```
positive_Number(X) :-
    X > 0, !.
positive_Number(X) :-
    fail.
```

Here, once the positive_Number/1 predicate concludes that $X > 0$, it ceases further evaluation, directly returning true or false based on the single condition.

Employing Determinism

To customize backtracking behavior, implementing deterministic predicates helps ensure the program complies with logical flow constraints. A deterministic predicate is one that can only succeed in one way. We can enforce determinism using cuts or through structural design:

```
one_solution(X) :-
    findall(X, (member(X, [1, 2, 3]), X > 2), Results),
    Results = [SingleSolution], !,
    SingleSolution = X.
```

In this example, one_solution/1 ensures there is exactly one valid solution by using findall/3 alongside a cut operator. The cut after assigning SingleSolution to X guarantees no further backtracking occurs after the first valid solution is found.

Utilizing Built-in Predicates

The once/1 built-in predicate allows execution of a goal exactly once, thus preventing backtracking across other potential solutions:

```
one_time_sum(X, Y, Sum) :-
    once((Sum is X + Y, Sum > 0)).
```

In the above predicate, once/1 ensures that the computation $\text{Sum is } X + Y$ and the condition $\text{Sum} > 0$ are evaluated only once, thus controlling unnecessary backtracking.

Custom Predicate Definitions

Creating custom predicates that encapsulate specific backtracking control logic allows for reusable and modular code:

```
safe_divide(X, Y, Result) :-
    Y \= 0, !, Result is X / Y.
safe_divide(_, _, 'undefined').
```

In safe_divide/3, the ! operator prevents backtracking into the alternative undefined result if the division is successful. This effectively minimizes redundant computations and avoids runtime errors due to division by zero.

Understanding the intricacies of backtracking and mastering such techniques not only leads to performance improvements but also sharpens the logical clarity of Prolog programs. Integrating these principles into the program structure ensures precise control over the search space and results in efficient, readable, and maintainable code.

7.10 Implementing Search Algorithms

In Prolog, search algorithms can be implemented by leveraging its inherent backtracking mechanism to explore the search space efficiently. This section will focus on implementing fundamental search algorithms such as depth-first search (DFS), breadth-first search (BFS), and iterative deepening search (IDS). Each algorithm's implementation will be elucidated through step-by-step Prolog code examples, aiding in understanding the underlying mechanisms and control structures.

Depth-First Search (DFS)

The depth-first search algorithm adopts a LIFO (Last In, First Out) strategy to traverse the search space, exploring as far down one branch as possible before backtracking. Given the recursive nature of Prolog, DFS is straightforward to implement:

```
% DFS Implementation in Prolog
dfs(Node, Goal, Path) :-
    dfs_recursive(Node, Goal, [Node], Path).

dfs_recursive(Node, Node, Path, Path).
dfs_recursive(Node, Goal, Visited, Path) :-
    Node \= Goal,
    adjacent(Node, NextNode),
    \+ member(NextNode, Visited),
    dfs_recursive(NextNode, Goal, [NextNode | Visited], Path).

adjacent(a, b).
adjacent(b, c).
adjacent(c, d).
adjacent(d, e).
adjacent(b, d).
```

In this implementation, dfs/3 initiates the search, and dfs_recursive/4 performs the recursive traversal. The adjacent/2 predicate defines the graph's edges. Usage of the \+ operator ensures that nodes are not revisited, preventing cycles.

```
?- dfs(a, e, Path).
Path = [e, d, c, b, a].
```

Breadth-First Search (BFS)

Breadth-first search employs a FIFO (First In, First Out) strategy, ensuring that nodes are visited level-by-level. Implementing BFS in Prolog requires which can be done using queues:

```
% BFS Implementation in Prolog
bfs(Start, Goal, Path) :-
    bfs_queue([[Start]], Goal, Path).

bfs_queue([[Goal | PathRest]|_], Goal, Path) :-
    reverse([Goal | PathRest], Path).
bfs_queue([[Node | PathRest]|Queue], Goal, Path) :-
    findall([NextNode, Node | PathRest],
            (adjacent(Node, NextNode), \+ member(NextNode, [Node | PathRest])),
            NewPaths),
    append(Queue, NewPaths, UpdatedQueue),
    bfs_queue(UpdatedQueue, Goal, Path).
```

In this code, bfs/3 starts the search by initializing the queue, and bfs_queue/3 processes the queue to find the path. The findall/3 predicate generates all possible next steps, ensuring all levels are explored.

```
?- bfs(a, e, Path).
Path = [a, b, d, e].
```

Iterative Deepening Search (IDS)

Iterative deepening search combines the benefits of depth-first and breadth-first search by executing depth-limited searches incrementally, increasing the depth limit with each iteration until the goal is found:

```
% IDS Implementation in Prolog
ids(Start, Goal, Path) :-
    between(0, inf, DepthLimit),
    depth_limited_search(Start, Goal, [Start], Path, DepthLimit).

depth_limited_search(Goal, Goal, Path, Path, _DepthLimit).
depth_limited_search(Node, Goal, Visited, Path, DepthLimit) :-
    DepthLimit > 0,
    adjacent(Node, NextNode),
    \+ member(NextNode, Visited),
    NewDepthLimit is DepthLimit - 1,
    depth_limited_search(NextNode, Goal, [NextNode | Visited], Path, NewDepthLimit
        ).
```

Here, ids/3 employs the between/3 predicate to progressively increase the depth limit. The depth_limited_search/5 predicate performs the depth-limited search. This method ensures optimal path discovery without excessive memory usage.

```
?- ids(a, e, Path).
Path = [a, b, d, e].
```

The predicates adjacent/2 and member/2 play crucial roles in these implementations. The adjacent/2 predicate represents the connectivity of nodes, forming the backbone of the search space, while the member/2 predicate is essential for cycle detection and pruning.

Optimizing search algorithms involves considering the search space's nature and the specific requirements of the problem at hand. Understanding DFS, BFS, and IDS within Prolog's backtracking framework equips one with powerful tools to handle diverse problem domains effectively.

7.11 Performance Considerations in Backtracking

In Prolog programming, performance considerations are critical, especially when dealing with backtracking mechanisms. Backtracking, while powerful, can lead to inefficient programs if not properly managed. Ensuring efficiency involves careful use of predicates, control constructs, and understanding the underlying mechanics of Prolog's execution.

One key aspect is minimizing the number of backtracking points. Each backtracking point consumes memory and processing power. Reducing unnecessary backtracking points can significantly improve performance. This can be achieved by using the cut operator ! strategically, and avoiding the creation of redundant choice points.

```
even_length([]) :- !.
even_length([_,_|T]) :-
    even_length(T), !.
```

In this example, the cut operator ! is used to prune the search space, ensuring that once a match is found, Prolog does not backtrack to find alternative solutions. However, misuse of cuts can lead to incorrect logic, so it's essential to employ them judiciously.

Careful predicate design is another important factor. Recursive predicates should be well-structured to avoid unnecessary computations. Tail recursion is a significant optimization technique that can transform a recursive process into an iterative one, reducing the stack usage.

```
factorial(N, Result) :-
    factorial(N, 1, Result).
```

```
factorial(0, Accumulator, Accumulator) :- !.
factorial(N, Accumulator, Result) :-
    N > 0,
    N1 is N - 1,
    Acc1 is Accumulator * N,
    factorial(N1, Acc1, Result).
```

In the factorial example above, the second predicate factorial/3 is tail-recursive, allowing Prolog implementations to optimize the recursive calls, thus improving performance.

Logical redundancy and unnecessary computations can be minimized by leveraging memoization, also known as tabling. Tabling stores the results of predicates so that future identical subgoals can retrieve the result directly without recomputation.

```
:- table fibonacci/2.

fibonacci(0, 0) :- !.
fibonacci(1, 1) :- !.
fibonacci(N, Result) :-
    N > 1,
    N1 is N - 1,
    N2 is N - 2,
    fibonacci(N1, R1),
    fibonacci(N2, R2),
    Result is R1 + R2.
```

Here, tabling is declared using :- table fibonacci/2. This ensures that results for previously encountered values of fibonacci/2 are reused, drastically improving performance for large inputs.

Performance can also be affected by the choice of control structures. The use of if-then-else structures can prevent unnecessary choice points, thereby optimizing the execution.

```
max(X, Y, Max) :-
    ( X >= Y -> Max = X ; Max = Y ).
```

In this max/3 predicate, the if-then-else construct eliminates the need for backtracking by decisively selecting one of the branches based on the condition.

Profiling and debugging are indispensable tools in identifying and resolving performance bottlenecks. Prolog environments provide various tools and predicates for this purpose, such as statistics/0 and debug/1. These tools can be used to measure resource usage and trace execution paths, guiding optimizations.

```
?- statistics(runtime, [Start|_]),
   fibonacci(30, Result),
   statistics(runtime, [End|_]),
```

```
Time is End - Start,
write('Execution time: '), write(Time), write(' ms.').
```

By using statistics/2, we can measure the execution time of a particular predicate, as shown in the example. This helps in identifying and quantifying the impact of optimizations applied.

To further enhance Prolog program performance, developers should consider the complexity of their algorithms, aiming for the most efficient solutions that meet their requirements. Combining algorithmic efficiency with Prolog-specific best practices results in robust, performant programs.

7.12 Debugging and Tracing Backtracking

Understanding the backtracking mechanism in Prolog is crucial for diagnosing and resolving logic errors in programs. Debugging and tracing are integral techniques to monitor and manipulate the execution flow, providing insights into how Prolog's search strategy operates and how specific goals are resolved.

Prolog environments typically come equipped with built-in debuggers and tracers. The primary tool for tracing Prolog execution is the trace predicate. When invoked, it switches the interpreter into a trace mode, allowing step-by-step observation of the program's execution.

```
?- trace.
```

Following the activation of tracing, running a query will display detailed information at each resolution step. The main actions displayed during tracing are:

- CALL: Indicates the invocation of a predicate.
- EXIT: Signals successful completion of a predicate.
- REDO: Shows invocation of backtracking to retry alternative solutions.
- FAIL: Occurs when a predicate fails, instigating backtracking.

Consider the Prolog program:

```
likes(mary, chocolate).
likes(mary, wine).
likes(john, wine).

list_likes(Person) :-
    likes(Person, Thing),
    write(Person), write(' likes '), write(Thing), nl,
    fail.
list_likes(_).
```

Activating the trace and querying list_likes(mary) will illustrate each operation:

```
?- trace, list_likes(mary).
% Call: (10) list_likes(mary) ?
% Call: (11) likes(mary, _5536) ?
% Exit: (11) likes(mary, chocolate) ?
mary likes chocolate
% Call: (11) fail ?
% Fail: (11) fail ?
% Redo: (11) likes(mary, _5536) ?
% Exit: (11) likes(mary, wine) ?
mary likes wine
% Call: (11) fail ?
% Fail: (11) fail ?
% Redo: (11) likes(mary, _5536) ?
% Fail: (11) likes(mary, _5536) ?
% Exit: (10) list_likes(mary) ?
```

This output demonstrates a sequence of CALL, EXIT, REDO, and FAIL steps. Monitoring these steps can elucidate the control flow, especially regarding how and when backtracking is triggered.

The spy predicate is another vital tool, allowing the setting of breakpoints. Breakpoints pause execution when specific predicates are called, offering opportunities to inspect the program state. For example:

```
?- spy(likes/2).
```

Executing this sets a breakpoint at the likes/2 predicate, allowing focused investigation:

```
?- list_likes(john).
% Spy point placed on likes/2
% Call: (10) list_likes(john) ?
% Call: (11) likes(john, _4136) ?
% Spy point hit at likes(john, _4136) ...
```

Prolog tracing produces detailed information through port names, capturing the lifecycle of goal completions and failures. By analyzing these trace outputs, developers gain granular visibility into how predicates are applied, how variables unify, and how backtracking is performed.

In more complex scenarios, the debug predicate activates the debugger, which offers a more interactive environment. Commands such as creep and leap control the granularity of tracing:

```
?- debug.
?- creep.
```

The combination of trace, spy, and debug predicates, along with interactive commands provided by the Prolog environment, forms a comprehensive toolkit for diagnosing, analyzing, and resolving logic discrepancies in Prolog programs. Effective use of these debugging and tracing techniques is essential for mastering Prolog's backtracking mechanics and optimizing the logic and performance of Prolog-based applications.

Chapter 8

Advanced Prolog Features

This chapter explores advanced Prolog features, including meta-programming, dynamic predicates, and assertions. It covers constraint logic programming, logic grammars, coroutines, tabling, memoization, and parallel programming. Additionally, it discusses interfacing with other languages, using the foreign function interface, embedding Prolog in applications, and utilizing various Prolog libraries and extensions.

8.1 Introduction to Advanced Prolog Features

Prolog programming extends far beyond basic operations and predicates, offering a rich suite of advanced features that allow for sophisticated and efficient problem-solving capabilities. This section provides an overview of these advanced features, setting the stage for a deeper exploration into each specific topic covered in subsequent sections.

At its core, Prolog is a logic programming language that excels in symbolic reasoning and knowledge representation. Traditional use cases involve querying a static database of facts and rules. However, leveraging advanced features enables more dynamic and versatile applications.

One key area of Prolog's advanced functionality is meta-programming. Meta-programming involves writing programs that can reason about, transform, or generate other programs or themselves. This is typically achieved through the use of higher-order predicates and constructs such as call/1 and apply/2. These constructs allow us to manipulate and evaluate Prolog goals dynamically, making it possible to create more abstract and powerful solutions. Consider the following example illustrating the use of call/1:

```
evaluate_all(Goals) :-
    member(Goal, Goals),
    call(Goal),
    fail.
evaluate_all(_).
```

In this code, evaluate_all/1 takes a list of goals and executes each one of them using call/1. The use of fail/0 ensures that all goals are evaluated even if some succeed or fail.

Another significant aspect of Prolog's advanced capabilities is the management of dynamic predicates and assertions. Standard Prolog predicates are static, defined at compile-time, but dynamic predicates can be modified at runtime. This is facilitated through built-in predicates such as assert/1, retract/1, and retractall/1. These predicates provide the flexibility to add, remove, or alter facts and rules as the program executes. For example:

```
:- dynamic fact/1.

add_fact(F) :-
    assert(fact(F)).

remove_fact(F) :-
    retract(fact(F)).
```

In this example, fact/1 is declared as a dynamic predicate using :- dynamic fact/1. The predicates add_fact/1 and remove_fact/1 demonstrate how facts can be asserted and retracted dynamically.

Constraint Logic Programming (CLP) combines the declarative nature of logic programming with the power of constraints, enabling the concise formulation and efficient solving of constraint satisfaction problems. CLP extends Prolog by introducing constraints alongside standard predicates, allowing for more expressive problem definitions. An example using the clpfd library for finite domain constraints is shown below:

```
:- use_module(library(clpfd)).
```

```
solve(X, Y) :-
    X #> 0,
    Y #> 0,
    X + Y #= 10.
```

Here, the constraints X #> 0 and Y #> 0 along with the equation X + Y #= 10 are declared using the finite domain constraints library. The CLP solver then finds values for X and Y that satisfy these constraints.

Logic grammars, particularly Definite Clause Grammars (DCGs), are powerful tools for parsing and generating structured data, such as natural language and formal languages. DCGs offer a concise and readable way to specify grammars directly in Prolog. They are internally translated into Prolog predicates with additional arguments for the input and output strings. For example:

```
sentence --> noun_phrase, verb_phrase.

noun_phrase --> determiner, noun.

verb_phrase --> verb, noun_phrase.

determiner --> [the].
noun --> [cat].
verb --> [saw].
```

This DCG defines a simple grammar where a sentence consists of a noun phrase followed by a verb phrase. The internal translation handles the complexities of managing the input and output strings.

Coroutines in Prolog provide a mechanism for non-preemptive multithreading, allowing predicates to be suspended and resumed. This is particularly useful for generating streams of solutions incrementally and for implementing cooperative multitasking. The freeze/2 predicate can be used to delay the execution of a goal until a variable becomes instantiated. For example:

```
:- use_module(library(freeze)).

generate_pairs(X, Y) :-
    freeze(X, (X > 0 -> Y = X + 1 ; Y = 0)).
```

In this code, freeze/2 ensures that the goal (X > 0 -> Y = X + 1 ; Y = 0) is delayed until X is instantiated.

Tabling and memoization enhance Prolog's efficiency by storing intermediate results of computations and reusing them when the same subgoals are encountered. This can significantly reduce redundant computations and improve performance in recursive queries. The table/1 directive is utilized to indicate which predicates should be tabled. For instance:

```
:- use_module(library(tabling)).
:- table fib/2.

fib(0, 0).
fib(1, 1).
fib(N, F) :-
    N > 1,
    N1 is N - 1,
    N2 is N - 2,
    fib(N1, F1),
    fib(N2, F2),
    F is F1 + F2.
```

Here, the fib/2 predicate calculates Fibonacci numbers and is tabled to avoid redundant calculations of the same Fibonacci values.

Parallel and concurrent programming in Prolog harnesses multiple processors and cores to enhance performance. SWI-Prolog, for example, supports thread-based concurrency, where each thread operates in a separate Prolog engine. The creation and management of threads are accomplished through predicates such as thread_create/3, thread_join/2, and thread_exit/1. For example:

```
:- use_module(library(threads)).
:- use_module(library(debug)).

start_threads :-
    thread_create(do_work(1), Id1, []),
    thread_create(do_work(2), Id2, []),
    thread_join(Id1, _),
    thread_join(Id2, _).

do_work(WorkerId) :-
    debug(thread, 'Worker ~w is doing work.', [WorkerId]),
    % Simulate some work
    sleep(1),
    debug(thread, 'Worker ~w has finished.', [WorkerId]).
```

In this example, two threads are created to execute the do_work/1 predicate concurrently. The debug/3 predicate is used to log messages from each thread.

Understanding these advanced features is crucial for leveraging the full potential of Prolog in developing complex and high-performance applications. This chapter delves into each of these aspects, providing detailed explanations, examples, and practical applications. Whether dealing with meta-programming, dynamic predicates, constraints, or parallel processing, the advanced features of Prolog offer powerful tools for solving a wide range of problems efficiently and elegantly.

8.2 Meta-Programming in Prolog

Meta-programming in Prolog involves writing programs that manipulate other programs or themselves. This powerful feature allows for the creation of flexible, reusable code and the implementation of sophisticated reasoning mechanisms. In Prolog, meta-programming is enabled by treating predicates as data and providing constructs such as call/1, asserta/1, assertz/1, retract/1, and retractall/1.

To illustrate the concept, let's consider a simple example where we write a meta-interpreter for a subset of Prolog. This meta-interpreter can interpret basic Prolog constructs such as facts, rules, and queries.

```
% A simple meta-interpreter for a subset of Prolog
interpreter(true).
interpreter((A, B)) :- interpreter(A), interpreter(B).
interpreter(A) :- clause(A, B), interpreter(B).
```

In this meta-interpreter, the predicate interpreter/1 evaluates goals. The predicate clause/2 is used to fetch the body of a clause whose head matches the goal. The first clause of interpreter/1 handles the base case for true, which represents a trivially satisfied goal. The second clause handles conjunctions of goals, and the third clause evaluates individual goals by recursively invoking the interpreter on the body of the matching clause.

Consider the following set of Prolog facts and rules:

```
% Facts and rules for testing the meta-interpreter
parent(joan, mia).
parent(mia, eve).
ancestor(X, Y) :- parent(X, Y).
ancestor(X, Y) :- parent(X, Z), ancestor(Z, Y).
```

To use the meta-interpreter with the above knowledge base:

```
% Query using the meta-interpreter
?- interpreter(ancestor(joan, eve)).
```

```
true
```

Meta-programming facilitates abstracting common patterns. For example, we can implement a predicate that profiles the execution time of another predicate:

```
% Profiling execution time of a goal
time_goal(Goal) :-
    statistics(runtime, [T0|_]),
    call(Goal),
    statistics(runtime, [T1|_]),
```

```
    ExecutionTime is T1 - T0,
    format('Execution time: ~d ms~n', [ExecutionTime]).
```

In this implementation, the statistics/2 predicate retrieves the current runtime in milliseconds before and after calling the goal. The difference gives the execution time, which is then displayed using format/2.

Another application of meta-programming is in dynamic predicate handling, where predicates can be asserted or retracted at runtime. This enables the modification of the program's behavior on the fly:

```
% Dynamic predicate management
:- dynamic dynamic_fact/1.

add_fact(Fact) :-
    assertz(dynamic_fact(Fact)).

remove_fact(Fact) :-
    retract(dynamic_fact(Fact)).

list_facts :-
    dynamic_fact(Fact),
    format('~w~n', [Fact]),
    fail.
list_facts.
```

This example defines a dynamic predicate dynamic_fact/1. The predicates add_fact/1 and remove_fact/1 allow for adding and removing facts dynamically. The predicate list_facts/0 lists all dynamic facts.

Meta-predicates like call/1, findall/3, and maplist/2 provide high-level abstractions. For instance, maplist/2 applies a given predicate to all elements in a list:

```
% Applying a predicate to all elements in a list
increment(X, Y) :- Y is X + 1.

apply_increment :-
    maplist(increment, [1, 2, 3], IncrementedList),
    format('Incremented list: ~w~n', [IncrementedList]).
```

This program applies the increment/2 predicate to each element of the input list, producing a new list with incremented values.

Prolog also supports higher-order programming through metapredicates. For example, call/2 enables invoking predicates with an additional argument:

```
% Using call/2 for higher-order programming
apply_twice(Pred, Arg) :-
    call(Pred, Arg),
    call(Pred, Arg).

double_increment(X) :-
```

```
    apply_twice(increment(X), Result),
    format('After double increment: ~w~n', [Result]).
```

Meta-programming allows constructing more general and adaptable programs, essential for tasks like building interpreters, compilers, and complex reasoning systems. By leveraging these techniques, Prolog programmers can write code that is both expressive and powerful, enhancing the utility and flexibility of their applications.

Understanding and effectively utilizing meta-programming capabilities can significantly extend a programmer's ability to tackle complex problems in Prolog.

8.3 Dynamic Predicates and Assertions

Prolog's support for dynamic predicates and assertions extends the language's flexibility and power, allowing programs to modify their behavior during execution and to respond adaptively to various conditions. Dynamic predicates are predicates whose definitions can be altered dynamically during the execution of a program through the addition and removal of clauses. Assertions provide a mechanism to assert facts or rules at runtime. This flexibility can be useful in a variety of contexts, such as adaptive systems, interactive applications, and knowledge bases that need to evolve over time.

A predicate must be explicitly declared dynamic if its clauses are to be added or removed while the program runs. This is done using the dynamic/1 directive. Here is an example of declaring a dynamic predicate:

```
:- dynamic likes/2.
```

The directive :- dynamic likes/2. declares that likes/2 is a dynamic predicate, which allows modifications to its definition after the program has started.

Adding and removing facts or rules can then be done using assert/1, asserta/1, assertz/1, and retract/1. The assert/1 predicate adds a fact or rule to the database, while retract/1 removes a matching fact or rule. The asserta/1 and assertz/1 predicates allow finer control over the position of the new clause; asserta/1 inserts the clause as the first clause of the predicate, and assertz/1 appends it as the last clause.

Consider the following example where we dynamically add and remove likes facts:

```
?- assert(likes(mary, pizza)).
true.

?- assert(likes(john, sushi)).
true.

?- retract(likes(mary, pizza)).
true.

?- likes(mary, pizza).
false.
```

The initial assertion assert(likes(mary, pizza)) succeeds, adding the fact likes(mary, pizza) to the database. Similarly, assert(likes(john, sushi)) adds another fact. Subsequently, retract(likes(mary, pizza)) removes the fact about Mary's preference, and querying likes(mary, pizza) verifies that it is no longer present.

Multiple Assertions and Retractions

It is often necessary to handle multiple dynamic clauses at once. Prolog allows this through backtracking over multiple retract/1 calls. Below is an example:

```
?- assert(likes(anna, chocolate)).
true.

?- assert(likes(anna, ice_cream)).
true.

?- retract(likes(anna, _)).
true ;
true ;
false.
```

Here, retract(likes(anna, _)) is called to remove all facts about Anna's preferences. By backtracking (;), each likes(anna, _) fact is retracted until no more match the pattern.

Assertions in Rules

Dynamic predicates and assertions can operate within predicate rules, creating powerful constructs. Here is an algorithm in Prolog that models adding unique likes facts dynamically:

Algorithm 3: check_and_assert/2 Algorithm

Data: Person, Thing
Result: Dynamic insertion if not exists

```
check_and_assert(Person, Thing):
( likes(Person, Thing) -> true; assert(likes(Person, Thing)) ).
```

In Prolog, this can be implemented as:

```
check_and_assert(Person, Thing) :-
    ( likes(Person, Thing) -> true; assert(likes(Person, Thing)) ).
```

Calling check_and_assert/2, for example, check_and_assert(jack, apple), checks if likes(jack, apple) already exists. If it does, nothing is done. If it doesn't, the assertion is made.

Assertions can also be used to store and update states. Consider an environment where we keep track of a counter:

```
:- dynamic counter/1.
counter(0).

increment_counter :-
    retract(counter(X)),
    X1 is X + 1,
    assert(counter(X1)).

get_counter(Value) :-
    counter(Value).
```

The predicate increment_counter/0 dynamically increments the counter by first retracting the current counter value, calculating the new value, and then asserting the updated value. Retrieving the current counter value is done via get_counter/1.

The combined use of dynamic predicates and assertions significantly enhances the adaptiveness of Prolog programs, making them more responsive to changing conditions and interactive requirements. Understanding and leveraging these features are instrumental for advanced Prolog programming.

8.4 Working with Constraints

Constraint Logic Programming (CLP) is a crucial extension of Prolog that enhances its ability to solve combinatorial problems involving constraints. In Prolog, constraints are conditions or relationships that must be satisfied by the variables in a program. CLP integrates constraint solving with logic programming, allowing the declarative representation and efficient solving of problems across various domains such as scheduling, allocation, and configuration.

The CLP paradigm incorporates several specific domains, each tailored to a particular type of constraint. Some of the most widely used domains include finite domains (CLP(FD)), linear arithmetic (CLP(Q/R)), and Boolean constraints (CLP(B)). These domains enable the seamless integration of domain-specific solvers into Prolog and provide a robust framework for addressing a broad range of problems.

1. Finite Domain Constraints:

Finite domain constraints, implemented via CLP(FD), restrict variables to take on values from a finite set of integers. This is particularly useful for problems like scheduling, where tasks must occur at specific times, or puzzles, where elements are constrained to predefined sets.

Here is an example of defining and solving a basic problem with finite domain constraints:

```
:- use_module(library(clpfd)).

schedule([A, B, C]) :-
    A #>= 1,
    B #>= 1,
    C #>= 1,
    A #< B,
    B #< C,
    A + B + C #= 12,
    labeling([], [A, B, C]).
```

In this example, the constraints A #>= 1, B #>= 1, and C #>= 1 restrict the variables A, B, and C to be at least 1. The constraints A #< B and B #< C enforce a strict increasing order, and A + B + C #= 12 ensures the sum of the variables is 12. The labeling/2 predicate then searches for all solutions satisfying these constraints.

2. Linear Arithmetic Constraints:

Linear arithmetic constraints, supported by CLP(Q/R), handle problems involving real or rational numbers and linear relationships. This capability is essential in fields like operations research, optimization, and econometrics.

An example of solving a system of linear equations is illustrated below:

```
:- use_module(library(clpr)).

linear_system(X, Y) :-
    { 2*X + 3*Y = 12 },
    { X - Y = 1 }.
```

In this example, the equations $2*X + 3*Y = 12$ and $X - Y = 1$ are defined within the $\{...\}$ construct, indicating the use of constraints over rational numbers. The clpr library solver is then employed to find values of X and Y that satisfy both constraints.

3. Boolean Constraints:

Boolean constraints, implemented via CLP(B), focus on boolean variables, where each variable can only take the values 0 (false) or 1 (true). This is beneficial in digital circuit design, logical puzzles, and binary decision problems.

An example utilizing boolean constraints is:

```
:- use_module(library(clpb)).

simple_circuit([A, B, C]) :-
    A + B + C #= 2, % Exactly two of the variables must be true
    A + B #>= 1, % At least one of A or B must be true
    B + C #>= 1. % At least one of B or C must be true.
```

In the above example, the constraints specify logical relationships among the boolean variables A, B, and C. The summations involve logical addition (OR operation), and the constraints ensure the desired conditions for the logical circuit.

Constraint Propagation and Search Techniques:

Constraint propagation is a fundamental technique in CSPs (Constraint Satisfaction Problems), progressively narrowing the domain of possible values for variables based on the constraints. Prolog's constraint solvers use propagation algorithms to prune the search space efficiently.

Search strategies, such as backtracking, are combined with constraint propagation to explore potential solutions. The labeling/2 predicate is central to this process in CLP(FD), specifying how variables are assigned values and which search strategies to use.

Example: Solving a Magic Square:

A magic square is a *n x n* grid filled with numbers 1 through n^2, where each row, column, and diagonal sums to the same constant. Here is an implementation with CLP(FD):

```
:- use_module(library(clpfd)).

magic_square(N, Matrix) :-
    N2 is N * N,
    length(Cells, N2),
    Cells ins 1..N2,
    all_distinct(Cells), % All cells must contain unique values
```

```
    matrix_by_rows(Matrix, Cells, N),
    maplist(same_sum(N), Matrix), % Rows
    transpose(Matrix, Columns),
    maplist(same_sum(N), Columns), % Columns
    diagonal_sums(N, Matrix, Diags),
    maplist(same_sum(N), Diags), % Diagonals
    flatten(Matrix, Flat),
    labeling([], Flat).

same_sum(N, List) :-
    sum(List, #=, S),
    S #= (N*(N*N + 1)) // 2.

matrix_by_rows([], [], _).
matrix_by_rows([Row|Rows], Cells, N) :-
    length(Row, N),
    append(Row, Rest, Cells),
    matrix_by_rows(Rows, Rest, N).

diagonal_sums(N, Matrix, [Diag1, Diag2]) :-
    findall(E, (between(1, N, I), nth1(I, Matrix, Row), nth1(I, Row, E)), Diag1),
    findall(E, (between(1, N, I), J is N+1-I, nth1(I, Matrix, Row), nth1(J, Row, E)),
        Diag2).
```

This example defines a magic_square/2 predicate for generating an N x N magic square. The all_distinct/1 ensures all cells contain unique values. The matrix_by_rows/3 predicate converts the list of cells into a matrix. The same_sum/2 predicate enforces the sum consistency for rows, columns, and diagonals. Finally, labeling/2 facilitates the search for valid solutions.

These examples illustrate the versatility and power of constraint logic programming in Prolog. Whether working with integers, real numbers, or boolean variables, CLP offers a declarative approach to specifying and solving complex combinatorial problems efficiently.

8.5 Implementing Logic Grammars

Logic grammars, or Definite Clause Grammars (DCGs), represent a powerful tool within Prolog for natural language processing, syntax analysis, and translation. Prolog's native support for DCGs facilitates the writing and understanding of grammars and parsers by directly integrating with the Prolog language.

The key characteristic of DCGs in Prolog is the elegant and concise way they describe the syntactic structure of languages. DCGs transform into ordinary Prolog predicates by an underlying translation mechanism, allowing them to be used seamlessly within Prolog programs.

Consider the following simple DCG, which describes a sequence of characters:

```
sequence --> [].
sequence --> ['a'], sequence.
```

In this example, sequence is defined recursively. The first rule indicates an empty sequence, and the second rule states that a sequence can consist of the character 'a' followed by another sequence.

To utilize this grammar in practice, one can query Prolog with a specific list of characters to verify if it conforms to the grammar:

```
?- phrase(sequence, ['a', 'a', 'a']).
```

Prolog will respond with:

```
true.
```

The phrase/2 predicate is used to apply the grammar to a list of terminals. This process expands to:

```
?- sequence(['a', 'a', 'a'], []).
```

This checks if the list ['a', 'a', 'a'] can be reduced to the empty list according to the grammar sequence.

DCGs can include parameters to capture more complex structures. For example, consider a grammar that parses a list of digits and computes their sum:

```
sum(0) --> [].
sum(Sum) --> [Digit], {Digit >= 0, Digit =< 9}, sum(Rest), {Sum is Digit + Rest
    }.
```

Here the DCG sum/1 computes the sum of a sequence of digits. The braces {} denote Prolog goals to be executed during parsing. This grammar can be queried as follows:

```
?- phrase(sum(Sum), [1,2,3]).
```

Prolog will yield the result:

```
Sum = 6.
```

Let's explore an example involving more complex structures, such as parsing simple arithmetic expressions. Define a grammar for arithmetic expressions involving addition and multiplication:

```
expr(Value) --> term(T), expr_aux(T, Value).
expr_aux(Acc, Value) --> ['+'], term(T), {NewAcc is Acc + T}, expr_aux(NewAcc,
```

```
        Value).
expr_aux(Acc, Acc) --> [].

term(Value) --> factor(F), term_aux(F, Value).
term_aux(Acc, Value) --> ['*'], factor(F), {NewAcc is Acc * F}, term_aux(NewAcc,
        Value).
term_aux(Acc, Acc) --> [].

factor(Value) --> ['('], expr(Value), [')'].
factor(Value) --> [N], {number(N)}.
```

In this grammar, expr/1 and term/1 define expressions and terms respectively, handling addition and multiplication operations. Auxiliary rules (expr_aux/2 and term_aux/2) assist with the recursive nature of these operations. factor/1 handles the lowest level of precedence, including parentheses and numbers.

To parse and evaluate the arithmetic expression '(1 + 2) * 3', we use:

```
?- phrase(expr(Value), ['(',1,'+',2,')','*',3]).
```

Prolog will respond with:

```
Value = 9.
```

It is essential for readers to be aware that the parsing process using DCGs seamlessly integrates with the unification mechanism of Prolog. Each parsing step inherently matches lists (inputs) to the grammar's defined structure progressively, simplifying the process of developing complex parsers.

Incorporating DCGs within larger Prolog applications often involves embedding the grammars within predicate definitions, applying the same principles of modularity and reusability used elsewhere in Prolog programming. Consider a scenario where the parsed data needs further processing or interaction within a Prolog system, the extracted information from the DCG can seamlessly feed into other predicates, aiding in maintaining a clean separation of concerns and enhancing code readability.

Moreover, DCGs can effortlessly encapsulate language specifications, facilitating their use in both top-down parsers and language interpreters. This ability highlights the flexibility and power of DCGs within the Prolog ecosystem, reinforcing their utility in both academic and industrial applications.

8.6 Understanding and Using Coroutines

A *coroutine* is a generalization of a subroutine (function or procedure) for non-preemptive multitasking, by allowing the subroutine to yield control back to the caller. Coroutines are particularly powerful in Prolog due to their ability to maintain state between invocations and facilitate concurrent programming paradigms effectively.

In Prolog, coroutines can be employed using constructs such as freeze/2, when/2, dif/2, and attributed variables. These constructs allow control over the execution flow based on specific conditions, typically the instantiation of variables. For example, a rule in Prolog can be suspended until certain variables are sufficiently instantiated, providing a mechanism for synchronization without busy-waiting.

To illustrate the concept, consider the when/2 predicate, which suspends the execution of a goal until its associated condition becomes true. The general form is:

```
when(Condition, Goal).
```

The Condition specifies when the Goal should be executed. Common conditions include ground(+Term) (execute when Term is ground), nonvar(+Term) (execute when Term is not a variable), and ?=(+Term1, +Term2) (execute when Term1 and Term2 are the same).

Example: Suppose we want to suspend a goal until a specific variable is instantiated.

```
?- when(nonvar(X), writeln(X)).
```

In this example, the writeln(X) goal is suspended until X becomes nonvar (i.e., X is instantiated with a non-variable term).

Consider another example where we use freeze/2 to suspend the execution of a goal until a certain variable is instantiated.

```
?- freeze(X, writeln(X)), X = 42.
  42
X = 42.
```

Here, the freeze/2 predicate suspends the writeln(X) goal until X is instantiated. When X is finally given the value 42, the goal is executed.

To better understand coroutines, let's analyze a more complex example using attributed variables. Attributed variables allow attaching attributes (additional information) to variables and then using constraint solving techniques to manage these attributes. The coroutining mechanism can trigger goals based on changes to these attributes.

Example: Attribute-based synchronization using when/2 and custom conditions.

```
:- use_module(library(atts)).

:- attribute my_attr/1.

% Define a handler to print the attribute when set
attribute_goals(Var) --> { get_atts(Var, my_attr(Value)) },
                          [write('Attr: '), writeln(Value)].

% Coroutine example
coroutine_example :-
    put_atts(X, my_attr(unknown)),
    when(attribute_bound(X, my_attr) = nonvar, writeln('Attribute bound: ')),
    put_atts(X, my_attr(bound)).
```

```
?- coroutine_example.
Attr: unknown
Attribute bound:
Attr: bound
```

In this example, the my_attr/1 attribute is defined and associated with a variable X. The goal to print the attribute is defined within attribute_goals/1. A when/2 call ensures the action of writing "Attribute bound:" is triggered when the attribute becomes nonvar.

Coroutines can also be effectively utilized in generating and managing streams of data. Suppose we wish to generate an infinite stream of numbers incrementing by 1 at each step:

```
:- use_module(library(delay)).

infinite_stream(X) :-
    freeze(X, infinite_stream(X, 0)).

infinite_stream([H|T], N) :-
    H is N,
    N1 is N + 1,
    freeze(T, infinite_stream(T, N1)).
```

```
?- infinite_stream(Stream), nth0(1000, Stream, X).
Stream = [0, 1, 2, 3, 4, 5, ..., 1000|_],
X = 1000.
```

In the above code, infinite_stream/1 initiates an infinite sequence of numbers by leveraging freeze/2. Each element of the list is calculated and the stream progresses dynamically as predicates consuming the stream are invoked.

By employing coroutines, programs can achieve efficient incremental data generation and processing, which is critical for many applications including parsing, scheduling, and simulation. The fine-grained control over the execution and synchronization conditions provided by coroutines makes them a powerful tool in advanced Prolog programming.

8.7 Tabling and Memoization

Tabling is a mechanism in Prolog to store intermediate results of subgoals to avoid redundant computations and ensure termination for certain classes of queries. Memoization, a similar concept, involves storing the results of expensive function calls and returning the cached result when the same inputs occur again. Tabling and memoization are vital when dealing with recursive definitions and computationally heavy problems.

XSB Prolog and Swi-Prolog support tabling natively. Other Prolog systems may require manual implementation of memoization techniques. This section discusses both the built-in tabling features in Swi-Prolog and techniques for manual memoization.

Tabling in Swi-Prolog

In Swi-Prolog, the table/1 directive can be used to table a predicate. This approach is demonstrated in the context of computing the Fibonacci sequence.

```
:- table fibonacci/2.

fibonacci(0, 0).
fibonacci(1, 1).
fibonacci(N, F) :-
    N > 1,
    N1 is N - 1,
    N2 is N - 2,
    fibonacci(N1, F1),
    fibonacci(N2, F2),
    F is F1 + F2.
```

The table/1 directive instructs Swi-Prolog to store the results of evaluated subgoals. This caching ensures that each subgoal is computed only once, after which the stored result is reused, significantly improving performance for large values of N. The computation of fibonacci(30, F) demonstrates the performance gains:

```
?- fibonacci(30, F).
F = 832040
```

Without tabling, the naive recursive implementation of the Fibonacci sequence has exponential time complexity. Tabling reduces this complexity to linear time.

Memoization in Prolog

For Prolog systems that do not natively support tabling, memoization can be implemented manually using dynamic predicates. This involves storing previously computed results in a dynamic database and checking this database before computing new results.

The following code showcases a memoized version of the Fibonacci predicate using dynamic storage:

```
:- dynamic memo_fib/2.

memo_fib(0, 0).
memo_fib(1, 1).
memo_fib(N, F) :-
    memo_fib(N, F), !.
memo_fib(N, F) :-
    N > 1,
    N1 is N - 1,
    N2 is N - 2,
    memo_fib(N1, F1),
    memo_fib(N2, F2),
    F is F1 + F2,
    assertz(memo_fib(N, F)).
```

This implementation uses the dynamic/1 directive to declare memo_fib/2 as a dynamic predicate and assertz/1 to store new results. The cut operator (!) ensures that once a memoized result is found, no additional clauses are checked. The check memo_fib(N, F), ! retrieves previously computed results, ensuring efficiency.

```
?- memo_fib(30, F).
F = 832040
```

Using dynamic predicates for memoization significantly improves performance compared to repetitive calculations in naive recursive solutions.

Comparing Tabling and Memoization

Tabling in systems like Swi-Prolog offers several advantages over manual memoization:

- Automated Caching: The system automatically handles storage and retrieval of subgoal results.

- Performance Optimization: Native tabling optimizations can further enhance performance.
- Ensuring Termination: Many computations that would not terminate in a naive implementation due to infinite recursion can be ensured to terminate when tabling is used.

Manual memoization, although more flexible, requires meticulous management of the dynamic database and careful handling of predicates. While it shares significant similarities with tabling, implementing it correctly is more complex and prone to errors.

Applications of Tabling and Memoization

In addition to recursive computations like the Fibonacci sequence, tabling and memoization are widely applied in:

- Dynamic Programming: Solving optimization problems by tabulating intermediate results.
- Parsing: Efficient parsing of natural and formal languages using tabling to store partial parse results.
- Constraint Solving: Enhanced performance in constraint logic programming by reusing results of sub-problems.

Advanced problems like graph traversal, where repeated state explorations are common, benefit significantly from tabling and memoization techniques.

Tabling and memoization serve as powerful tools in the Prolog programmer's toolkit, enabling efficient implementations of complex algorithms that previously would have been computationally impractical.

8.8 Parallel and Concurrent Prolog Programming

Parallel and concurrent programming in Prolog can significantly enhance performance, especially for computationally intensive tasks. Leveraging multiple processors or cores can lead to substantial reductions in execution time. This section discusses the foundational concepts of parallelism and concurrency in Prolog, describes various models of parallelism, presents examples using built-in predicates, and outlines the strategies to effectively implement parallel and concurrent Prolog programs.

Prolog inherently supports backtracking, a feature that is conducive to parallel execution. However, designing Prolog programs for parallelism requires understanding key concepts such as goals, threads, synchronization, and shared resources.

Parallelism and Concurrency

Parallelism refers to the simultaneous execution of multiple computations. In the context of Prolog, this usually involves dividing a problem into independent sub-problems that can be solved concurrently. Concurrency, on the other hand, deals with multiple computations that make progress independently, potentially interacting with each other.

Models of Parallelism in Prolog

Several models of parallelism are pertinent to Prolog, including:

- **Or-parallelism:** This model involves the concurrent execution of different branches in the search tree. When Prolog encounters a choice point, different branches can be pursued simultaneously.
- **And-parallelism:** In this model, the conjunctive goals of a clause are executed in parallel. This can be further divided into *independent and-parallelism*, where goals do not share variables, and *dependent and-parallelism*, where there may be shared variables.
- **Stream parallelism:** This is useful for applications involving data streams, where different stages of processing can be performed in parallel on different parts of the stream.

Using Threads in Prolog

Many Prolog systems support threads, which allow the simultaneous execution of multiple goals. In SWI-Prolog, for example, the thread library provides a rich interface for creating and managing threads. Creating a thread involves specifying a goal and launching it in a separate thread.

```
?- thread_create(member(X, [1,2,3]), Id, []).
```

In this example, the goal member(X, [1,2,3]) is executed in a new thread. The thread_create/3 predicate returns a thread identifier Id that can be used for further operations, such as joining the thread or checking its status.

Synchronization and Communication

Managing synchronization and communication between threads is crucial for concurrent programming. Prolog provides several primitives for synchronization, such as message queues. A message queue allows threads to exchange messages in a synchronized manner.

```
?- message_queue_create(Queue),
   thread_create((message_queue_send(Queue, hello),
                  message_queue_send(Queue, world)), Id, []),
   message_queue_receive(Queue, Msg1),
   message_queue_receive(Queue, Msg2).
```

In this example, a message queue named Queue is created, and a new thread is launched, which sends two messages hello and world to the queue. The main thread subsequently receives these messages.

Example: Parallel Map of a List

Consider a scenario where we want to apply a function to each element of a list in parallel. We can achieve this using threads as shown in the following example:

```
maplist_parallel(_, [], []).
maplist_parallel(Func, [H1|T1], [H2|T2]) :-
    thread_create(call(Func, H1, H2), Id, []),
    maplist_parallel(Func, T1, T2),
    thread_join(Id, _).
```

Here, maplist_parallel/3 applies Func to each element of the input list in parallel. The predicate thread_join/2 ensures that the main thread waits for the child threads to complete their execution before proceeding.

Challenges in Parallel and Concurrent Prolog Programming

Parallel and concurrent programming introduces challenges such as dealing with race conditions, ensuring thread safety, and managing resource contention. Prolog systems often provide mutexes for critical sections to mitigate these issues.

```
?- mutex_create(Mutex),
   thread_create((mutex_lock(Mutex),
                  critical_section,
                  mutex_unlock(Mutex)), Id, []),
   thread_join(Id, _).
```

In this example, the mutex Mutex is used to protect the critical section in the child thread, ensuring that only one thread can execute it at a time.

Optimizing parallel Prolog programs involves identifying independent sub-goals that can be executed concurrently, minimizing synchronization overhead, and balancing load across threads. Properly tuning these aspects leads to efficient utilization of computational resources.

8.9 Interfacing with Other Languages

Prolog, while powerful and versatile in logic programming, often needs to interact with other programming languages to leverage their strengths and ecosystem. This section explores various ways to interface Prolog with other languages such as C, Java, and Python. We will cover calling external functions, embedding foreign code, and handling data interchange between Prolog and other languages.

Foreign Function Interface (FFI) is a mechanism that allows Prolog to call functions written in other languages and vice versa. Most modern Prolog systems provide robust FFI support for languages like C and C++.

Calling C from Prolog: SWI-Prolog offers a well-documented library for integrating C functions. Here's an example to illustrate this:

```
#include <stdio.h>

int add(int a, int b) {
    return a + b;
}
```

To call this function from Prolog, first, we need to compile this C code into a shared library. The command to perform this compilation might look like:

```
/* Assuming the code is in add.c */
gcc -shared -o libadd.so -fPIC add.c
```

Next, in Prolog, we load and use this shared library:

```
:- use_foreign_library('libadd.so').

:- foreign(add(+integer, +integer, [-integer])).

sum(A, B, Sum) :-
    add(A, B, Sum).
```

Here, use_foreign_library/1 loads the shared object. The foreign/2 directive specifies the signature of the foreign predicate. After this setup, sum/3 can be used like any other Prolog predicate to add two integers.

Calling Java from Prolog: To call Java from Prolog, we can utilize the Java Native Interface (JNI). SWI-Prolog also provides JPL, which offers seamless integration with Java.

First, ensure the Prolog system has the JPL library installed. Here's a simple Prolog program that uses Java:

```
:- use_module(library(jpl)).

get_java_version(Version) :-
    jpl_call('java.lang.System', getProperty, ['java.version'], V),
    atom_string(V, Version).
```

In the above snippet, jpl_call/4 calls the static method getProperty on the Java class System to retrieve the Java version. The version is then converted to a Prolog string using atom_string/2.

Calling Python from Prolog: The interoperability between Prolog and Python can be achieved with the py_swip library available in SWI-Prolog. This library allows calling Python code directly from Prolog.

Here is an example that shows how to call a Python function from Prolog:

```
def multiply(a, b):
    return a * b
```

Using the py_swip library in Prolog:

```
:- use_module(library(python)).

multiply(A, B, Result) :-
    python:py_run_string("from module_name import multiply"),
    python:py_call(multiply, [A, B], Result).
```

In this snippet, replace module_name with the actual name of the Python module where the function multiply is defined. The py_run_string/1 predicate imports the function, and py_call/3 invokes it with the arguments A and B.

Data Interchange: Data interchange between Prolog and other languages often involves converting data representations. For instance, Prolog lists may need to be converted to arrays when interfacing with C.

When exchanging data, attention to data types and memory management is crucial to avoid leaks and errors. Many interfacing libraries provide predicates for converting common data structures such as lists, arrays, and dictionaries.

In Java, for example, JPL provides predicates to convert Prolog terms (like lists and atoms) into Java objects:

```
:- use_module(library(jpl)).

prolog_list_to_java_array(PrologList, JavaArray) :-
    jpl_list_to_array(PrologList, JavaArray).
```

In the above example, jpl_list_to_array/2 converts a Prolog list to a Java array.

Prolog's flexibility with Foreign Function Interfaces, along with support for various language integrations, makes it a highly versatile tool for multi-language applications. This capability extends Prolog's utility far beyond traditional logic programming boundaries, enabling it to leverage external libraries, toolkits, and existing codebases in other programming environments.

8.10 Using the Foreign Function Interface

The Foreign Function Interface (FFI) allows Prolog to interoperate with code written in other programming languages, such as C, C++, and Python. This interoperability is crucial for leveraging existing libraries, optimizing performance-critical sections of code, and extending the capabilities of Prolog applications.

SWI-Prolog, a popular Prolog implementation, provides a robust FFI that can be used to call functions written in C. We will focus on the SWI-Prolog interface, but the principles discussed are generally applicable to other Prolog systems with similar capabilities.

Defining Foreign Functions

To define a foreign function, you first need a C function that you wish to call from Prolog. Suppose we have the following C function that computes the factorial of an integer:

```
#include <stdio.h>

int factorial(int n) {
    if (n == 0) return 1;
    else return n * factorial(n - 1);
}
```

To access this function from Prolog, we must compile it into a shared library. On Unix-like systems, you can use the following gcc command to compile the C code:

```
gcc -shared -o libfactorial.so -fPIC factorial.c
```

On Windows, you might use:

```
cl /LD factorial.c
```

Next, we must inform SWI-Prolog about the function. This is done using the foreign declaration and the load_foreign_library/1 predicate. The foreign declaration specifies the name of the foreign function, the name by which it will be called in Prolog, and the types of the arguments and the return value.

```
:- foreign(factorial_c, c, factorial(+integer, -integer)).
```

Here, factorial(+integer, -integer) indicates that the factorial function takes one input argument of type integer and produces one output argument of type integer.

To load the shared library, use load_foreign_library/1:

```
:- load_foreign_library(foreign(libfactorial)).
```

Now, you can define a Prolog predicate that uses this foreign function:

```
factorial(N, F) :-
    factorial_c(N, F).
```

Calling Foreign Functions

With the foreign function defined, you can now call it from Prolog as if it were a native Prolog predicate:

```
?- factorial(5, Result).
Result = 120.
```

This demonstrates how simple it can be to integrate C functions into Prolog applications using the FFI.

Handling More Complex Data

In addition to simple data types such as integers, the FFI supports more complex data types like strings, floating-point numbers, and structures. Consider a C function that takes a string and returns its length:

```
#include <string.h>

int string_length(const char *str) {
    return strlen(str);
}
```

Compile this function into a shared library just as before. Then inform SWI-Prolog about the function and load the library:

```
:- foreign(string_length_c, c, string_length(+string, -integer)).
:- load_foreign_library(foreign(libstringlength)).
```

Define a Prolog predicate to call the foreign function:

```
string_length(Str, Len) :-
    string_length_c(Str, Len).
```

You can now call this predicate from Prolog:

```
?- string_length("Hello, Prolog!", Length).
Length = 13.
```

Error Handling and Debugging

When using the FFI, it's important to handle errors gracefully. One common issue is passing the wrong types of arguments or receiving unexpected results.

Prolog provides some built-in mechanisms for error handling. For instance, you can use the catch/3 predicate to catch exceptions that might be thrown during the execution of a foreign function:

```
safe_factorial(N, Result) :-
    catch(factorial(N, Result),
          error(type_error(Type, Term), _),
          (print_message(error, type_error(Type, Term)),
           fail)).
```

In this example, if factorial/2 throws a type error, the error is caught, and an error message is printed.

Using the Foreign Function Interface enables Prolog programmers to integrate efficiently with external libraries and other programming languages. This not only extends the functionality of Prolog applications but also allows leveraging optimized code for performance-critical tasks. Developing an understanding of how to use the FFI effectively makes it possible to build more versatile and powerful Prolog applications.

8.11 Embedding Prolog in Applications

Embedding Prolog in applications allows developers to leverage the strengths of Prolog for specific tasks within larger software systems. This approach is beneficial in scenarios where Prolog's declarative nature excels, such as complex problem-solving, natural language processing, and rule-based systems. In this section, we will explore techniques for embedding Prolog in various programming environments, focusing on the basics of integration, data exchange mechanisms, and practical examples.

Prolog Integration Basics

Prolog integration typically involves embedding a Prolog interpreter within a host application or interfacing Prolog with other languages via a Foreign Function Interface (FFI). The first step in embedding Prolog is to ensure that the Prolog interpreter can be controlled programmatically by the host language. This often requires initializing the Prolog runtime, loading necessary Prolog code, and calling Prolog predicates from the host application.

Consider the following basic example using SWI-Prolog, a popular Prolog implementation. Let's embed Prolog in a C application. The first requirement is to include the SWI-Prolog header in the C program:

```
#include <SWI-Prolog.h>
```

Next, we initialize the Prolog engine within the main function of the C program:

```
int main(int argc, char **argv) {
  // Initialize the SWI-Prolog engine
  char *pl_args[] = {"my_program", NULL};
  PL_initialise(1, pl_args);

  // Load Prolog source file
  if (!PL_load_file("my_prolog_code.pl")) {
    fprintf(stderr, "Error loading Prolog source file.\n");
    return 1;
  }

  // Deallocate resources and shutdown the Prolog engine
  PL_halt(0);
  return 0;
}
```

In this example, the PL_initialise function initializes the Prolog runtime, and PL_load_file loads the Prolog source file my_prolog_code.pl.

Calling Prolog Predicates from C

To invoke Prolog predicates from the C environment, we can use the PL_call function. Consider a Prolog predicate greet/1 in the file my_prolog_code.pl:

```
greet(Name) :-
    format('Hello, ~w~n', [Name]).
```

To call this predicate from C, we prepare the term and execute the call:

```
#include <SWI-Prolog.h>

void call_greet() {
  term_t t0 = PL_new_term_refs(1); // Create a Prolog term reference
  PL_put_atom_chars(t0, "World"); // Assign a value to the term

  predicate_t p = PL_predicate("greet", 1, "user"); // Get the predicate handle
  PL_call_predicate(NULL, PL_Q_NORMAL, p, t0); // Call the predicate with the
      term
}

int main(int argc, char **argv) {
  char *pl_args[] = {"my_program", NULL};
  PL_initialise(1, pl_args);

  if (!PL_load_file("my_prolog_code.pl")) {
    fprintf(stderr, "Error loading Prolog source file.\n");
    return 1;
  }

  call_greet();

  PL_halt(0);
  return 0;
}
```

The PL_new_term_refs function creates a new term reference, and PL_put_atom_chars assigns an atom value to the term. PL_predicate is used to get a handle to the greet/1 predicate, and PL_call_predicate performs the actual predicate call.

Data Exchange Between Host Application and Prolog

Exchanging data between the host application and Prolog involves converting data types to and from Prolog terms. Most Prolog libraries offer APIs for this purpose. Let's consider exchanging complex data structures such as lists and structures:

```
#include <SWI-Prolog.h>

void example_data_exchange() {
  term_t list = PL_new_term_refs(1); // Create a term for a list
  term_t head = PL_new_term_ref(); // Term for the list head
  term_t tail = PL_copy_term_ref(list); // Term for the list tail

  // Build the list [1, 2, 3]
  for (int i = 1; i <= 3; i++) {
    PL_put_integer(head, i);
    PL_cons_list(tail, head, tail);
  }

  predicate_t p = PL_predicate("process_list", 1, "user");
  PL_call_predicate(NULL, PL_Q_NORMAL, p, list);
}

int main(int argc, char **argv) {
```

```
    char *pl_args[] = {"my_program", NULL};
    PL_initialise(1, pl_args);

    if (!PL_load_file("my_prolog_code.pl")) {
        fprintf(stderr, "Error loading Prolog source file.\n");
        return 1;
    }

    example_data_exchange();

    PL_halt(0);
    return 0;
}
```

Here, the example_data_exchange function demonstrates constructing a Prolog list [1, 2, 3] and calling a Prolog predicate process_list/1 with this list as an argument. The PL_put_integer and PL_cons_list functions are used to construct the list term.

Practical Applications

Embedding Prolog in applications is useful in real-world scenarios, such as enhancing business logic rules or implementing expert systems. For instance, a customer relationship management (CRM) system can integrate Prolog to handle complex query logic for customer data analysis:

```
% Define customer rule
preferred_customer(Customer) :-
    purchase_history(Customer, Amount),
    Amount > 10000.

% Define purchase history
purchase_history(john_doe, 15000).
purchase_history(jane_smith, 8000).
```

```
#include <SWI-Prolog.h>

void query_customer_status() {
    predicate_t p = PL_predicate("preferred_customer", 1, "user");
    term_t customer = PL_new_term_refs(1);

    PL_put_atom_chars(customer, "john_doe");
    if (PL_call_predicate(NULL, PL_Q_NORMAL, p, customer)) {
        printf("John Doe is a preferred customer.\n");
    } else {
        printf("John Doe is not a preferred customer.\n");
    }
}

int main(int argc, char **argv) {
    char *pl_args[] = {"my_program", NULL};
    PL_initialise(1, pl_args);

    if (!PL_load_file("crm_rules.pl")) {
        fprintf(stderr, "Error loading Prolog source file.\n");
        return 1;
```

```
    }
    query_customer_status();

    PL_halt(0);
    return 0;
}
```

This example highlights querying Prolog's facts and rules from within a C application to determine if a customer is considered a preferred customer based on their purchase history. The suggestive approach demonstrates the flexibility and power of embedding Prolog within business applications to manage and reason about data efficiently.

8.12 Exploring Prolog Libraries and Extensions

Prolog's versatility is significantly enhanced by a diverse array of libraries and extensions. These libraries extend Prolog's core functionalities, providing advanced features and tools that are essential for specialized tasks. Utilizing these libraries effectively can optimize the development process and introduce the ability to solve more complex problems efficiently.

The lists library provides a comprehensive set of predicates for list manipulation. Lists, as one of Prolog's fundamental data structures, frequently require operations such as concatenation, member checking, and sublist extraction. The library includes predicates like append/3, member/2, sublist/2, among others.

```
?- use_module(library(lists)).
true.

?- append([1,2,3], [4,5], L).
L = [1, 2, 3, 4, 5].

?- member(3, [1,2,3,4]).
true.

?- sublist([2, 3], [1,2,3,4]).
true.
```

The random library provides predicates for random number generation and random selection. This library is particularly useful for applications that require randomness, such as simulation, probabilistic algorithms, or games.

```
?- use_module(library(random)).
true.

?- random_between(1, 100, X).
X = 42.

?- random_member(R, [a, b, c, d, e]).
R = c.
```

The clpfd library, which stands for Constraint Logic Programming over Finite Domains, introduces powerful constraints-solving capabilities. This library is integral for problems involving scheduling, allocation, and other combinatorial problems. clpfd predicates facilitate defining variables with finite domains and impose constraints on these variables.

```
?- use_module(library(clpfd)).
true.

?- X in 1..10, Y in 1..10, X + Y #= 7.
X in 1..6,
Y in 1..6,
[ X+Y#=7].
```

For projects that involve dealing with HTTP requests and web services, the http library offers essential predicates. This library can be used for building web servers or clients, making it useful in the development of web applications and RESTful services.

```
?- use_module(library(http/http_open)).
true.

?- http_open('http://www.example.com', Stream, []),
   read_string(Stream, _, Content),
   close(Stream).
Content = "<!DOCTYPE html>..."
```

The uuid library is utilized for generating universally unique identifiers (UUIDs), which are often vital for uniquely identifying information in distributed systems. It provides a simple interface to create and handle UUIDs.

```
?- use_module(library(uuid)).
true.

?- uuid(Uuid).
Uuid = '550e8400-e29b-41d4-a716-446655440000'.
```

The ssl library allows Prolog to handle secure communications using SSL/TLS. This library can be employed to add encryption and secure connections in networked applications, ensuring data integrity and security.

```
?- use_module(library(ssl)).
true.

?- ssl_context(client, SSL, [host('example.com')]),
   ssl_open('example.com':443, Stream, [context(SSL)]),
   format(Stream, 'GET / HTTP/1.1~nhost: example.com~n~n', []),
   flush_output(Stream),
   read_line_to_string(Stream, Response),
   close(Stream).
Response = 'HTTP/1.1 200 OK...'
```

The dap library provides predicates for debugging and profiling Prolog code. These tools can help optimize performance and find logical errors in the code.

```
?- use_module(library(dap)).
true.

?- track([foo/2, bar/1]).
true.
```

Exploring and integrating these libraries effectively can significantly reduce development time and complexity. Using Prolog's extensions allows for tackling a wider range of applications, from combinatorial problem-solving and web services to secure communications and debugging. Prolog's ecosystem is rich and continually growing, making it an enduring and powerful tool for logic programming.

Chapter 9

Debugging and Testing Prolog Programs

This chapter focuses on debugging and testing Prolog programs, addressing common errors and their avoidance. It introduces the Prolog debugger, tracing program execution, setting breakpoints, and inspecting variable bindings. It also covers unit testing, test-driven development, automating tests with plunit, handling and reporting errors, profiling for performance, and best practices for effective debugging and testing.

9.1 Introduction to Debugging and Testing in Prolog

Debugging and testing are critical aspects of software development, ensuring that programs function as intended and meet specified requirements. In Prolog, these activities involve unique challenges and methodologies due to the language's declarative nature, non-determinism, and backtracking mechanisms.

Prolog programs are often concise and elegant, but their logical complexity can introduce errors that are not immediately apparent. Debugging and testing techniques in Prolog focus on understanding the flow of execution, the state of variable bindings, and the outcomes of logical inferences. This section delves into the fundamental principles and tools necessary for effective debugging and testing in Prolog.

Debugging in Prolog primarily involves:

- Identifying and isolating errors in the code.
- Tracing the execution of predicates to understand the control flow.
- Inspecting variable bindings to verify the correctness of logical inferences.
- Setting breakpoints and spypoints to halt execution at critical points for detailed inspection.

Testing in Prolog encompasses:

- Unit testing of individual predicates to ensure they meet their specifications.
- Adopting test-driven development (TDD) practices to incrementally build and test predicates.
- Utilizing automation tools like plunit to streamline and automate the testing process.
- Profiling code for performance optimization and identifying bottlenecks.
- Handling and reporting errors systematically to enhance code robustness and maintainability.

In Prolog, logical errors can manifest in various ways, including:

- Unintended Failures: When expected solutions are not produced due to incorrect logic or missing clauses.
- Infinite Loops: Resulting from recursive predicates without proper base cases or termination conditions.
- Error Messages: Indicating syntax errors, type mismatches, or other inconsistencies in the code.

Effective debugging begins with understanding how Prolog evaluates queries and derives solutions through resolution and unification. It involves breaking down complex predicates into simpler, manageable components and testing each one independently.

Algorithm 4: Debugging a Prolog Predicate

Data: Prolog Predicate predicate/2
Result: Debugging the execution of predicate/2
Input : Prolog Predicate predicate/2, Test Query
Output : Trace of Execution, Variable Bindings

```
Use the query_within_source program to navigate to the target predicate;
Set a breakpoint on the predicate using bpredicate/2 or sppredicate/2;
Run the test query;
while execution is paused at breakpoint do
    Inspect the variable bindings using the built-in tools;
    Examine the call stack and activation record;
    Step through the code line-by-line using trace predicates;
    if variable bound correctly then
        Continue execution normally
    else
        Rectify the logic and rerun the query
    end
end
```

Example: Debugging a Sample Predicate

Consider a Prolog program designed to find the ancestor of a person:

```
ancestor(X, Y) :- parent(X, Y).
ancestor(X, Y) :- parent(X, Z), ancestor(Z, Y).
```

To debug this program, we use the following procedure:

```
?- trace, ancestor(bob, john).
```

This command enables the tracer and runs the query to find if Bob is an ancestor of John. During execution, Prolog will pause at each invocation of the ancestor/2 predicate, allowing inspection of the variable bindings.

Output from the execution:

```
   Call: (6) ancestor(bob, john) ?
   Exit: (6) ancestor(bob, john) ?
true.
```

By examining the call and exit records, one can verify if the logical flow and the recursive calls are functioning correctly. If an error is detected, such as unexpected failure or incorrect bindings, adjustments should be made to the predicate definitions accordingly.

Testing predicates in isolation is equally critical. This helps ensure that individual components work as intended before integrating them into larger programs. Unit tests provide a structured approach:

```
:- begin_tests(ancestor).
test(ancestor_direct) :- ancestor(bob, john).
test(ancestor_indirect) :- ancestor(bob, mary).
:- end_tests(ancestor).

?- run_tests.
```

Incorporating tests using plunit ensures that each predicate is validated independently, confirming their correctness through automated test execution.

Understanding and applying these debugging and testing techniques enhances the reliability and maintainability of Prolog programs. Effective strategies involve a combination of interactive debugging, tracing execution, comprehensive unit testing, and automated tools to ensure robust code development.

9.2 Common Errors and How to Avoid Them

In Prolog programming, several common errors can impede progress and lead to incorrect results. Understanding these errors and learning strategies to avoid them can significantly improve the debugging process.

- **Syntax Errors**: Occur when the code violates Prolog's syntax rules. These errors are typically caught during compilation or interpretation.

  Example: Omitting a period at the end of a clause.

  ```
  parent(X, Y)
      male(X),
      father(X, Y).
  ```

  Avoidance: Always ensure each clause ends with a period.

- **Instantiation Errors**: These happen when a variable is not instantiated (i.e., it has no value) where an instantiation is required.

  Example: A predicate expects a non-variable term.

  ```
  ?- X = 1, atom_length(X, L).
  ```

  ERROR: atom_length/2: Type error: 'atom' expected, found '1'

  Avoidance: Ensure that variables are properly instantiated before passing them to predicates requiring specific types.

- **Type Errors**: Occurs when the type of an argument does not meet the predicate's requirements.

  Example: Using an atom where a list is expected.

  ```
  ?- append(a, [b], X).
  ```

  ERROR: append/3: Type error: 'list' expected, found 'a'

  Avoidance: Use type-checking before operations. For instance:

  ```
  validate_list(X) :-
      is_list(X).
  ```

- **Arithmetic Errors**: These errors occur during numerical computations.

Example: Using an unbound variable in arithmetic operations.

```
?- X is Y + 1.
```

ERROR: is/2: Arguments are not sufficiently instantiated

Avoidance: Ensure arithmetic expressions use fully instantiated variables.

```
?- Y = 2, X is Y + 1.
```

- **Unification Errors**: These occur when Prolog fails to match terms.

  Example: Attempting to unify incompatible terms.

  ```
  ?- foo(a) = foo(b).
  ```

  false.

  Avoidance: Ensure terms are compatible or correctly structured for unification.

- **Existence Errors**: These happen when referencing undeclared predicates.

  Example: Calling an undefined predicate.

  ```
  ?- non_existent_predicate(X).
  ```

  ERROR: Undefined procedure: non_existent_predicate/1

  Avoidance: Verify all predicates are defined before invocation.

- **Resource Errors**: Involve running out of system resources like stack or memory.

  Example: Infinite recursion leading to a stack overflow.

  ```
  loop :-
      loop.
  ?- loop.
  ```

  ERROR: Out of local stack

  Avoidance: Implement base cases for recursive predicates and ensure termination conditions.

- **Logical Errors**: The code runs without syntax errors but produces incorrect results due to flawed logic.

Example: Erroneous logical conditions or predicates.

```
even(X) :-
    X mod 2 =:= 1.
?- even(4).
```

false.

Avoidance: Test predicates thoroughly with various inputs and validate with logical assertions. Correct logic:

```
even(X) :-
    X mod 2 =:= 0.
?- even(4).
\begin{FittedVerbatim}
true.
\end{FittedVerbatim}
```

Effective debugging requires knowing these errors and strategies, improving Prolog development efficiency.

9.3 Using the Prolog Debugger

To effectively utilize the Prolog debugger for identifying and rectifying issues within your program, it is essential to comprehend its capabilities and how to interact with it. The Prolog debugger is a valuable tool that allows users to trace the execution of predicates, examine variable bindings, and interrupt execution at specified points. Understanding its functionality enhances your ability to diagnose the root causes of logical errors and performance inefficiencies.

Activating the Debugger

Activate the Prolog debugger by invoking the gtrace/0 predicate or the trace/0 predicate within your Prolog environment. The gtrace/0 predicate starts the graphical debugger if available, whereas the trace/0 predicate initiates the textual debugger. For instance:

```
?- gtrace.
% Prolog graphical debugger starts
?- trace.
% Prolog tracing activated
```

Debugger Interaction Commands

Once the debugger is activated, Prolog provides a set of commands to manage and inspect the execution flow. Some fundamental commands include:

- creep/0: Execute the next Prolog goal and proceed in a fine-grained manner.
- leap/0: Continue execution until the next spy point or breakpoint is encountered.
- skip/0: Skip over the current goal, treating it as a black box.
- abort/0: Terminate the current debugging session.

To illustrate the usage of these commands, consider the following Prolog fragment:

```
member(X, [X|_]).
member(X, [_|T]) :- member(X, T).
```

Activate the debugger in textual mode and trace the member/2 predicate with the query ?- member(a, [b, a, c]). Enter 'creep' to step through the execution:

```
?- trace.
true.

[trace] ?- member(a, [b, a, c]).
   Call: (8) member(a, [b, a, c]) ? creep
   Call: (9) a = b ? creep
   Fail: (9) a = b ? creep
   Redo: (8) member(a, [b, a, c]) ? creep
   Call: (9) member(a, [a, c]) ? creep
   ...
```

This output demonstrates how the Prolog debugger helps visualize the sequence of calls, redoes, and failures in your program execution.

Breakpoints and Spypoints

Setting breakpoints and spypoints allows you to pause program execution at critical junctures to inspect the state thoroughly. To set a breakpoint on a specific predicate, use the spy/1 directive:

```
?- spy(member/2).
% Spy-point on member/2
```

With the spy/1 directive, the debugger interrupts execution just before entering the member/2 predicate, enabling you to examine the context:

```
[trace] ?- member(a, [b, a, c]).
   Call: (8) member(a, [b, a, c]) ?
```

Similarly, you can remove a spypoint using the nospy/1 directive:

```
?- nospy(member/2).
% No spy-point on member/2
```

Inspection of Variable Bindings

While debugging, examining the values of bound variables provides insights into the state and flow of your program. When the debugger pauses execution at a given predicate, the current environment shows the bindings. For example:

```
[trace] ?- member(a, [b, a, c]).
   Call: (8) member(a, [b, a, c]) ?
   Call: (9) a = b ?
   ...
```

Here, inspecting the Call and Fail trace events indicates the failure of matching a with b. By proceeding with 'creep' or 'skip,' you navigate through the execution path and observe subsequent bindings.

Commands like display/1 and write/1 can also be utilized to print variable states at specific breakpoints or during the trace:

```
?- member(a, [b, a, c]).
   Call: (8) member(a, [b, a, c]) ? display(a), nl.
a
   ...
```

Thus, the built-in commands and the availability of setting spypoints provide powerful mechanisms for dissecting and refining Prolog programs. Skillfully exploiting these debugging tools is crucial for mastering Prolog programming and enhancing the reliability and efficiency of your code.

9.4 Tracing Program Execution

Tracing program execution is fundamental for understanding the behavior of Prolog programs and identifying erroneous logic or unexpected behavior. Prolog provides a powerful built-in facility for tracing, which allows step-by-step examination of the execution process. This section will describe how to use the trace/0 predicate, interpret the trace output effectively, and leverage trace options to fine-tune the tracing process.

Enabling Tracing

To enable tracing in Prolog, use the trace/0 predicate. When trace/0 is called, all subsequent Prolog execution will be traced until notrace/0 is invoked.

```
?- trace.
```

Upon invoking trace/0, Prolog enters the tracing mode and provides detailed feedback about the execution steps of each predicate call.

Understanding the Trace Output

When tracing is enabled, Prolog outputs information for each goal it attempts to resolve. The trace output displays four key ports at which different events occur during execution:

- **Call**: Occurs when a goal is invoked.
- **Exit**: Occurs when a goal succeeds.
- **Fail**: Occurs when a goal fails.
- **Redo**: Occurs when backtracking causes a goal to be re-evaluated.

Consider the following simple Prolog program:

```
member(X, [X|_]).
member(X, [_|T]) :- member(X, T).
```

To trace the execution of the query member(3, [1, 2, 3]), first enable the trace mode, then execute the query:

```
?- trace.
% Call: (10) trace ? creep
true.

?- member(3, [1, 2, 3]).
```

The trace output for this execution would look like the following:

```
   Call: (10) member(3, [1, 2, 3]) ?
   Call: (11) member(3, [2, 3]) ?
   Call: (12) member(3, [3]) ?
   Exit: (12) member(3, [3]) ?
   Exit: (11) member(3, [2, 3]) ?
   Exit: (10) member(3, [1, 2, 3]) ?
true.
```

Here's a breakdown of the trace output:

- The first **Call** indicates that member(3, [1, 2, 3]) is invoked.
- The second **Call** indicates the recursive call member(3, [2, 3]).
- The third **Call** indicates another recursive call member(3, [3]).
- The subsequent **Exit** ports indicate the successful resolution of each call, ultimately leading to the original query succeeding.

Fine-Tuning Tracing with Trace Options

Prolog offers various options to control and limit the tracing process. These options can be used to specify which predicates or conditions to trace, thereby reducing the volume of trace output and focusing on the relevant parts of the program.

spy/1, nospy/1, and nospyall/0 are particularly useful for selective tracing.

spy/1 sets a spypoint on a specified predicate, making Prolog enter trace mode only when that predicate is invoked. For example:

```
?- spy(member/2).
true.
```

With the spypoint set, tracing will only occur for the member/2 predicate:

```
?- member(3, [1, 2, 3]).
```

You may clear a specific spypoint using nospy/1:

```
?- nospy(member/2).
true.
```

Or, remove all spypoints at once using nospyall/0:

```
?- nospyall.
true.
```

Moreover, you can use conditional tracing to trace execution only under specific circumstances by setting constraints on the trace mode such as depth limits or intercepting specific procedures. This is done using the trace/2 predicate which takes options to fine-tune the tracing behavior.

For instance, to trace only up to a certain depth use:

```
?- trace(depth(5)).
```

This will limit the trace output to goals existing within five levels of depth from the current goal.

Navigating the Trace

During the trace, you can interact with the shell to navigate through different events:

- c or creep: Move to the next step (either call, exit, redo, or fail event).
- a or abort: Abort the trace and return to the Prolog prompt.
- f or fail: Force the current goal to fail.
- r or retry: Retry the current goal from scratch.

The detailed interaction while in trace mode enables the Prolog programmer to control the execution flow, making tracing an invaluable tool for debugging and understanding program behavior.

Through effective utilization of Prolog's tracing mechanisms, much can be achieved in understanding how a Prolog program proceeds through its logical inferences, ultimately aiding significantly in both learning and debugging processes.

9.5 Setting Breakpoints and Spypoints

Breakpoints and spypoints are crucial tools in Prolog for debugging and monitoring the execution flow of your programs. These mechanisms allow you to pause execution at specific points, inspect the state of the program, and determine whether it is functioning as expected. This section will delve into how to set and use breakpoints and spypoints effectively in Prolog.

Breakpoints are used to halt the execution of a Prolog program at a specified predicate, allowing the developer to inspect the current state of the computation. This enables detailed examination of variable bindings, predicate arguments, and the call stack.

To set a breakpoint on a specific predicate, you can use the built-in predicate spy/1 or trace/0. The spy/1 predicate sets a spypoint on the specified predicate, while trace/0 turns on the debugger and starts tracing execution from the point where it is called.

Here is an example demonstrating the use of spy/1:

```
% Assume we have a predicate 'member/2' that we want to inspect
spy(member/2).
```

In this example, calling spy(member/2) sets a spypoint on the member/2 predicate. When the debugger encounters a call to member/2, execution halts, and you are given the opportunity to inspect the environment.

Let us consider a practical scenario where we have a simple Prolog program defining a list membership predicate:

```
member(X, [X|_]).
member(X, [_|T]) :- member(X, T).
```

To debug this program using a spypoint, you would set the spypoint as follows:

```
?- spy(member/2).
% Add some test cases to run the program
?- member(a, [a, b, c]).
```

Upon executing the test case, the debugger will pause at the member/2 predicate, allowing you to inspect the current state.

```
Call: (7) member(a, [a, b, c]) ?
```

At this stage, pressing 'a' allows you to advance the program execution:

```
  Exit: (7) member(a, [a, b, c]) ?
true.
```

During pause, the developer can use several debugging commands such as:

- a – abort the execution
- c – continue execution till the next spypoint or breakpoint
- l – creep (step into), execution stops at the next step in the program
- r – retry the current goal
- t – leap to the debugger's top-level predicate

Spypoints are more advanced, enabling selective tracing based on conditions rather than merely halting at a particular predicate. Advanced debugging options open when you combine spypoints with conditions and more complex step management.

Consider an enhanced example where you only want the debugger to stop for specific cases, such as when the element being searched is 'b':

```
:- use_module(library(prolog_stack)).
trace_members :- tspy(member/2, goal(contains(b))).
contains(b, _).
```

In this example, using the tspy/2 predicate with a conditional goal allows the debugger to halt only when the specified condition (contains(b)) is satisfied.

Executing the trace with specific conditions might look like this:

```
?- trace_members.
```

Now, running a test case:

```
?- member(X, [a, b, c]).
```

The debugger will halt when searching for 'b':

```
Call: (7) member(b, [b, c]) ?
```

Here, only the relevant execution steps concerning 'b' are presented, enabling more efficient and focused debugging.

Breakpoints and spypoints effectively isolate and diagnose logical issues within Prolog programs. By suspending execution at critical points and selectively monitoring conditions, these tools facilitate thorough insights into program behavior and verification of its correctness.

9.6 Inspecting Variable Bindings

In the process of debugging Prolog programs, it is crucial to understand how variables are bound during execution. Inspecting variable bindings allows us to verify that our logic is functioning as intended and helps identify where errors might be occurring. This section will delve into techniques for inspecting variable bindings, primarily using the Prolog debugger and tracing facilities.

To begin, we'll introduce the concept of variable bindings in Prolog. In Prolog, variables are placeholders that can be bound to values or other variables during the execution of a program. The binding of variables happens through unification, a core operation in Prolog. Unification makes two terms identical by finding a consistent set of variable bindings.

```
% Example of unification
?- X = 5.
X = 5.

?- X = Y.
X = Y.
```

In the first query, X is bound to the integer 5. In the second query, both X and Y remain free variables but are now bound to each other.

One of the fundamental tools for inspecting variable bindings is the Prolog debugger. The Prolog debugger provides a series of ports where one can observe the execution of a goal: call, exit, redo, and fail. The bindings of each variable can be inspected at each of these stages.

To enable the debugger and observe variable bindings, use the trace/0 predicate:

```
% Enable tracing
?- trace.
```

Once tracing is enabled, running a goal will display the debugger's trace information. Consider the following simple factorial implementation:

```
% Factorial definition
factorial(0, 1).
factorial(N, F) :-
    N > 0,
    N1 is N - 1,
    factorial(N1, F1),
    F is N * F1.
```

Executing this with tracing enabled will show each step of execution and the bindings of each variable:

```
% Query with tracing enabled
?- factorial(3, F).
   Call: (7) factorial(3, _4632) ?
   Call: (8) 3>0 ?
   Exit: (8) 3>0 ?
   Call: (8) _4634 is 3-1 ?
   Exit: (8) 2 is 3-1 ?
   Call: (8) factorial(2, _4640) ?
   Call: (9) 2>0 ?
   Exit: (9) 2>0 ?
   Call: (9) _4642 is 2-1 ?
   Exit: (9) 1 is 2-1 ?
   Call: (9) factorial(1, _4648) ?
   Call: (10) 1>0 ?
   Exit: (10) 1>0 ?
   Call: (10) _4650 is 1-1 ?
   Exit: (10) 0 is 1-1 ?
   Call: (10) factorial(0, _4656) ?
```

```
   Exit: (10) factorial(0, 1) ?
   Call: (10) _4648 is 1*1 ?
   Exit: (10) 1 is 1*1 ?
   Exit: (9) factorial(1, 1) ?
   Call: (9) _4640 is 2*1 ?
   Exit: (9) 2 is 2*1 ?
   Exit: (8) factorial(2, 2) ?
   Call: (8) _4632 is 3*2 ?
   Exit: (8) 6 is 3*2 ?
   Exit: (7) factorial(3, 6) ?
F = 6.
```

From this trace, we can observe how each variable is bound at different points in the execution. For instance, the initial call to factorial(3, _4632) indicates that the variable _4632 is initially unbound. As the execution proceeds, intermediate values such as N1 and F1 are bound (e.g., $N1 = 2, F1 = 1$).

Inspecting variable bindings can also be done using the debug/0 predicate for a more controlled debugging session. To set this up, use the following sequence of predicates:

```
% Start debugging
?- debug.

% Set a breakpoint at factorial/2
?- spy(factorial/2).

% Execute the query
?- factorial(3, F).
```

When execution hits the spy point, the debugger will pause, allowing inspection of the current variable bindings using commands like w (print current goal with its variable bindings) and h (print stack trace). For example:

```
?- factorial(3, F).
% Spy-point hit: factorial(3,_4632)
   goal: factorial(3, _4632)

[0] <spy>(3)   w
   <0 Level 1>  1: Call: factorial(3, _4632)

[0] <spy>(3)   h
   <0 Level 1>  * 1: Call: factorial(3, _4632)
```

This provides a controlled environment for examining the exact state of the program's execution, including variable bindings at specific points.

Understanding and inspecting variable bindings is an essential skill for debugging Prolog programs, ensuring that variables are bound as expected and identifying where deviations occur.

9.7 Unit Testing Prolog Code

Unit testing is an essential practice in software development to ensure that individual components of a program function correctly. In Prolog, unit tests help validate the correctness of predicates by verifying their behavior against a set of predefined cases. This section will cover the basics of writing unit tests in Prolog, utilizing plunit, the built-in testing library.

plunit makes it possible to write and run tests directly within your Prolog source files. By organizing tests into cohesive units or test suites, developers can systematically verify the correctness of their predicates.

Setting up plunit

To begin using plunit, you need to set up your Prolog environment to include the library. This is done by including the following directive at the beginning of your Prolog source file:

```
:- use_module(library(plunit)).
```

Defining Test Units and Test Cases

A test unit is a collection of related test cases. In plunit, test units are defined using the begin_tests/1 and end_tests/1 directives. Each test case within the unit is defined using the test/2 predicate.

The general structure for a test unit is as follows:

```
:- begin_tests(unit_name).

test(case_name) :-
    % Test Body

:- end_tests(unit_name).
```

Consider a simple arithmetic predicate add/3, which adds two numbers:

```
add(X, Y, Z) :-
    Z is X + Y.
```

To test add/3, we can define a test unit named arithmetic that contains several test cases:

```
:- begin_tests(arithmetic).

test(add_positive_numbers) :-
    add(2, 3, 5).

test(add_negative_numbers) :-
```

```
    add(-2, -3, -5).

test(add_mixed_numbers) :-
    add(2, -3, -1).

:- end_tests(arithmetic).
```

Each test/2 predicate consists of a test name and a body. The body is a Prolog goal that should succeed if the test passes and fail if the test fails. In the examples above, cases are written to validate the behavior of the add/3 predicate with positive numbers, negative numbers, and a mix of positive and negative numbers.

Running the Tests

Once the test cases are defined, you can run them using the run_tests/0 or run_tests/1 predicates. To run all test units, use:

```
?- run_tests.
```

To run a specific test unit, pass the unit name to run_tests/1:

```
?- run_tests(arithmetic).
```

The output will indicate the success or failure of each test case:

```
% PL-Unit: arithmetic
% 3 tests passed
true.
```

Assertions and Expected Failures

Assertions are crucial for verifying specific conditions within a test. The plunit library provides several assertion predicates such as assertion/1, catch/3, fail/0, and true/0. For example, you can use assertion/1 to enforce a particular condition:

```
test(add_positive_numbers_with_assertion) :-
    add(2, 3, Result),
    assertion(Result == 5).
```

You can also indicate if a test is expected to fail using the [fail] option, which is useful for negative testing scenarios:

```
test(add_incorrect_result, [fail]) :-
    add(2, 2, 5).
```

Here, the test add_incorrect_result is expected to fail as $2 + 2$ does not equal 5.

Parameterized Tests

plunit supports parameterized tests allowing you to run the same test logic with different parameters using the forall/2 predicate. Suppose we want to test the add/3 predicate with a range of numbers:

```
test(add_multiple_cases, [forall(member((X, Y, Z), [(1, 2, 3), (2, 3, 5), (3, 4, 7)]))]) :-
    add(X, Y, Z).
```

In this example, the test will run three times with test parameters (1, 2, 3), (2, 3, 5), and (3, 4, 7).

Handling Complex Data Structures

Testing complex data structures, such as lists and dictionaries, can be done similarly by defining test cases that examine the behavior of predicates manipulating these structures. Consider a predicate reverse_list/2 that reverses a list:

```
reverse_list(In, Out) :-
    reverse(In, Out).
```

A test unit for reverse_list/2 might look like:

```
:- begin_tests(list_operations).

test(reverse_empty_list) :-
    reverse_list([], []).

test(reverse_single_element_list) :-
    reverse_list([a], [a]).

test(reverse_multiple_elements_list) :-
    reverse_list([1, 2, 3], [3, 2, 1]).

test(reverse_nested_lists) :-
    reverse_list([1, [2, 3], 4], [4, [2, 3], 1]).

:- end_tests(list_operations).
```

Testing in Prolog is robust and flexible, allowing for comprehensive validation of predicates even when dealing with complex operations and data structures. By employing plunit, developers can ensure the reliability of their code through systematic and organized testing practices.

9.8 Test-Driven Development in Prolog

Test-Driven Development (TDD) is an essential methodology in modern software engineering that can be applied effectively to Prolog programming. TDD emphasizes writing tests before the actual code to ensure that each piece of functionality is verified independently. This approach fosters code quality and reliability, aligning well with the declarative nature of Prolog.

The core cycle of TDD consists of three primary steps: Red (writing a failing test), Green (writing the minimal code to pass the test), and Refactor (optimizing the code while ensuring all tests still pass). We will explore these steps in the context of Prolog.

To illustrate TDD in Prolog, consider developing a simple module for arithmetic operations. We'll start by creating a test suite using the plunit unit testing framework, which is well-integrated with many Prolog environments.

First, we create a test file named arithmetic_tests.pl:

```
:- begin_tests(arithmetic).

test(addition) :-
    add(2, 3, Result),
    assertion(Result == 5).

test(subtraction) :-
    subtract(5, 3, Result),
    assertion(Result == 2).

test(multiplication) :-
    multiply(4, 3, Result),
    assertion(Result == 12).

test(division) :-
    divide(6, 3, Result),
    assertion(Result == 2).

:- end_tests(arithmetic).
```

The tests above outline the desired behavior of our arithmetic operations. The next step is to implement these operations minimally to pass the tests.

In the file arithmetic.pl, we provide the initial implementations:

```
%% Arithmetic operations
add(X, Y, Result) :-
    Result is X + Y.

subtract(X, Y, Result) :-
    Result is X - Y.

multiply(X, Y, Result) :-
    Result is X * Y.

divide(X, Y, Result) :-
    Y \= 0, % Prevent division by zero
    Result is X / Y.
```

To run the tests, we load both the test file and the implementation into the Prolog interpreter:

```
?- [arithmetic].
?- [arithmetic_tests].
?- run_tests.
```

The expected output of running the tests is:

```
% PL-Unit: arithmetic ... done
% All tests passed
```

This result indicates that our initial implementations meet the test requirements. The TDD cycle is continued by adding new tests and refining the implementation.

Let's add a new requirement to handle exceptions when dividing by zero. We extend the arithmetic_tests.pl with an additional test case:

```
test(division_by_zero, [throws(error(divide_by_zero))]) :-
    divide(6, 0, _).
```

The division operation must now be modified to raise an appropriate exception:

```
%% Arithmetic operations with exception handling
add(X, Y, Result) :-
    Result is X + Y.

subtract(X, Y, Result) :-
    Result is X - Y.

multiply(X, Y, Result) :-
    Result is X * Y.

divide(_, 0, _) :-
    throw(error(divide_by_zero)).
divide(X, Y, Result) :-
    Result is X / Y.
```

Running the tests again will verify the handling of division by zero:

```
?- run_tests.
```

The expected output after making the changes is:

```
% PL-Unit: arithmetic .... done
% All tests passed
```

Through TDD, we ensure that each functional requirement is tested and that the implementation evolves correspondingly. This disciplined approach helps prevent bugs and enhances code maintainability by providing a suite of tests that can be run after each change.

In practice, TDD necessitates rigorous adherence to writing and updating tests as code evolves. By following TDD principles in Prolog, you ensure not only correctness but also design code incrementally and intentionally. This methodology pairs well with Prolog's capacity to express clear and concise logic.

Finally, embrace TDD as a philosophy that encourages simple, clean designs by breaking down functionality into smaller, testable units. This practice goes a long way in making Prolog programs robust and maintainable.

9.9 Automating Tests with plunit

Automating tests in Prolog is essential for ensuring code reliability and maintaining software quality over time. The plunit library in SWI-Prolog provides an efficient framework to define and run tests. This section delves into the utilization of plunit for automating the testing of Prolog programs.

plunit allows the organization of tests into units and test cases, providing functionality to specify expected outputs, handle exceptions, and aggregate test results. Users can ensure that any modifications to their code do not introduce regressions by running the tests consistently.

To begin using plunit, include the library in your Prolog source file:

```
:- use_module(library(plunit)).
```

A test unit is defined using the begin_tests/1 and end_tests/1 predicates. The begin_tests/1 predicate is used to start the definition of a unit of tests, followed by individual test cases, and completed with a call to end_tests/1.

```
:- begin_tests(list_operations).

test(length_of_empty_list) :-
    length([], L),
    L =:= 0.

test(length_of_list_with_three_elements) :-
    length([a,b,c], L),
    L =:= 3.

:- end_tests(list_operations).
```

In the above example, we define a test unit named list_operations. It contains two test cases:

- length_of_empty_list: Verifies that the length of an empty list is

0.

- length_of_list_with_three_elements: Confirms that the length of the list [a, b, c] is 3.

Tests in plunit are executed using the run_tests/0 predicate, which runs all tests defined in the modules loaded into the system, or the run_tests/1 predicate to run specific tests.

```
?- run_tests.
% PL-Unit: list_operations ... done
% All tests passed.
true.
```

In the following, the output from program execution is shown:

```
?- run_tests(list_operations).
% PL-Unit: list_operations ... done
% All tests passed.
true.
```

plunit supports various forms of test assertions, including equality checks, exception handling, and more complex conditions. Below is a detailed example showcasing several types of assertions.

```
:- begin_tests(arithmetic_operations).

test(addition) :-
    2 + 3 =:= 5.

test(subtraction) :-
    5 - 3 =:= 2.

test(multiplication) :-
    3 * 4 =:= 12.

test(division) :-
    8 / 2 =:= 4.

test(division_by_zero, [throws(error(evaluation_error(zero_divisor), _))]) :-
    _ is 1 / 0.

test(greater_than, [true(R)]) :-
    R is 5 > 3.

:- end_tests(arithmetic_operations).
```

In this test unit, arithmetic_operations, various arithmetic operations are validated:

- Basic arithmetic operations (addition, subtraction, multiplication, and division) are checked for correctness.

- division_by_zero includes an exception assertion using the throws/1 option, ensuring that dividing by zero raises an appropriate error.

- greater_than employs a condition within the test to check logical comparisons and explicitly states that the test should succeed as indicated by [true(R)].

For complex and comprehensive testing scenarios, plunit provides further flexibility through the specification of test options. These options include but are not limited to setup and teardown actions, labeling expected failures, and defining test conditions dynamically.

```
:- begin_tests(dynamic_tests).

setup(initial_memory(100)).

test(dynamic_allocation, [setup(init_heap(Heap)), cleanup(free_heap(Heap))]) :-
    allocate_memory(25, Heap),
    Heap \= [].

test(expect_failure, [fail]) :-
    negative_square_root(-1, _).

:- end_tests(dynamic_tests).

initial_memory(Size) :-
    % Initialize memory with the provided Size
    ...

init_heap(Heap) :-
    % Custom setup for the heap
    ...

free_heap(Heap) :-
    % Clean-up the heap after test
    ...
```

In the dynamic_tests example:

- The setup/1 option is used to initialize a global state before any of the tests are run (initial_memory/1).
- Specific tests like dynamic_allocation use the setup/1 and cleanup/1 options to manage resources during the test.
- expect_failure demonstrates marking a test expected to fail using the [fail] option.

Utilizing these automated testing capabilities with plunit ensures robustness in Prolog programs by enabling consistent, comprehensive, and maintainable test practices.

9.10 Handling and Reporting Errors

Prolog, like any other programming language, does not shield developers from encountering errors during the development process. Effective management of errors is crucial for ensuring robust and reliable Prolog programs. This section discusses error handling in Prolog, focusing on identifying, capturing, and reporting errors to facilitate debugging and program correctness.

Prolog provides mechanisms for handling errors through built-in predicates such as catch/3 and throw/1. These predicates allow programmers to define error handling routines, making it easier to manage and rectify unforeseen issues during program execution.

Error Capturing with catch/3

The catch/3 predicate is used to capture exceptions that occur during the execution of a goal. The predicate structure is as follows:

```
catch(:Goal, +Catcher, :Recover)
```

Here, Goal represents the goal whose execution is being monitored for exceptions. If an exception occurs and unifies with Catcher, the Recover goal is executed. Consider the following example:

```
safe_division(X, Y, Result) :-
    catch((Result is X / Y), _Exception, Result = 'undefined').
```

In this example, the safe_division/3 predicate attempts to perform the division of X by Y. If an exception occurs, possibly due to a division by zero error, the catch/3 predicate captures it, and Result is unified with the atom 'undefined'.

Throwing Exceptions with throw/1

Prolog allows the explicit throwing of exceptions using the throw/1 predicate. This helps in defining custom error conditions that can be captured by catch/3. The syntax for throw/1 is straightforward:

```
throw(+Exception)
```

To illustrate, consider the following example where we explicitly throw a zero-division error:

```
divide(X, Y, Result) :-
    ( Y =:= 0 ->
        throw(zero_division)
    ; Result is X / Y
    ).
```

Here, if Y equals zero, the zero-division exception is thrown. This exception can be captured by a catch/3 predicate in the calling context.

```
perform_division(X, Y, Result) :-
    catch(divide(X, Y, Result), zero_division, Result = 'error: division by zero').
```

Reporting Errors

Consistent and clear error reporting is essential for understanding and resolving issues. Prolog predicates can be used to print detailed error messages to the console or log files. The print/1, write/1, format/2, and format/3 predicates are typically used for this purpose.

For example:

```
log_error(Error) :-
    format('Error occurred: ~w~n', [Error]).
```

This predicate logs an error message with the specific Error details provided by the context. This approach can be integrated within catch/3 to report more informative error messages to the user or developer.

Consider the integrated use of logging within a division operation:

```
safe_divide_and_log(X, Y, Result) :-
    catch(divide(X, Y, Result),
          zero_division,
          (Result = 'error', log_error('Division by zero occurred'))).
```

Handling Specific Errors

Prolog allows for handling specific errors selectively by defining the Catcher term in catch/3 to match particular exceptions. This capability enables more fine-grained control over error handling.

For example:

```
safe_divide_specific(X, Y, Result) :-
    catch(divide(X, Y, Result),
          error(instantiation_error, _),
          (Result = 'error', log_error('Instantiation error'))).
```

In this case, only instantiation_error exceptions are handled, allowing other types of exceptions to propagate as usual.

Best Practices for Error Handling

When handling errors, the following best practices can enhance program robustness and maintainability:

- Always provide meaningful error messages to aid in debugging.

- Use catch/3 judiciously to prevent the suppression of unanticipated exceptions that could obscure underlying problems.
- Adopt a consistent error handling strategy across the codebase to ensure uniform behavior and ease maintenance.
- Clearly document the error conditions and handling logic to facilitate understanding and modification by other developers or future maintainers.

By integrating these practices into Prolog programming, developers can create more resilient and maintainable code, improving the overall software development process.

9.11 Profiling Prolog Code for Performance

Profiling is an essential aspect of software development, particularly for understanding and optimizing the performance of programs. In the context of Prolog programming, profiling involves analyzing the execution characteristics of a Prolog program to identify bottlenecks, inefficient predicates, and performance-critical paths. This section explores the tools and techniques available for profiling Prolog code, providing detailed guidance on leveraging Prolog's built-in profiler efficiently.

To begin with, Prolog implementations such as SWI-Prolog offer robust profiling tools. The primary tool provided by SWI-Prolog is the prolog_profile library, which enables detailed performance analysis of Prolog programs.

```
:- use_module(library(prolog_profile)).
```

Once the profiler is activated, it is possible to start profiling a specific query. The profile/1 predicate is used to execute a query while collecting performance statistics.

```
?- profile(my_query).
```

This command executes my_query and gathers data on the time spent in each predicate, the number of calls, and other crucial metrics.

Upon completion of the query execution, the profiler generates a detailed performance report. This report typically includes information such as the CPU time consumed by each predicate, the number of calls made to each predicate, and the percentage of the total execution time spent in each predicate. An example output might look like this:

```
%        cumulative    self              calls  predicate
% time   seconds  seconds  call  ms/call name
% 80.0     0.080   0.080    1      80.0 my_query/0
% 10.0     0.090   0.010    5       2.0 some_predicate/2
% 10.0     0.100   0.010    3       3.3 another_predicate/1
```

Interpreting the profiler's output involves identifying predicates that consume significant CPU time or have a high call count. Such predicates are often candidates for optimization. The goal is to focus on high-impact changes that yield significant improvements in performance.

Additionally, SWI-Prolog provides the show_profile/1 predicate to visualize the collected profile data in various formats:

```
?- profile(my_query), show_profile([top(5)]).
```

This command displays the top 5 predicates in terms of CPU time usage, allowing for a quick overview of the most performance-critical parts of the code.

To delve deeper into performance analysis, the prolog_profile library can generate detailed call graphs. Call graphs visually represent the relationships between predicates, illustrating how predicates call each other during execution. Call graphs are particularly useful for understanding execution flow and identifying recursive or highly interdependent predicates.

```
?- profile(my_query), show_profile(calls).
```

This invocation presents a call graph view, showing the sequence of predicate calls along with call counts and time metrics.

In practice, performance tuning based on profiling may involve several strategies:

- **Refactoring specific predicates**: Optimizing the logic within performance-critical predicates to reduce unnecessary computations or improve algorithmic efficiency.
- **Eliminating redundant calls**: Identifying and removing redundant or duplicate calls to predicates which can streamline the execution path.
- **Indexing and search optimization**: Employing indexing on tables or databases to speed up search operations within predicates.

- **Memoization**: Introducing memoization to cache results of expensive computations, thereby avoiding repeated evaluations of the same predicate with identical arguments.

- **Concurrency**: Leveraging multi-threading capabilities in Prolog to parallelize independent computations, which can result in significant performance gains on multi-core processors.

A comprehensive approach to profiling often entails iterative refinement—profiling, optimizing, and reprofiling, ensuring that each change effectively enhances performance. Profiling empowers developers with precise knowledge of where resources are spent, enabling informed decision-making for performance improvements.

9.12 Best Practices for Debugging and Testing

Effective debugging and testing practices are essential for developing reliable Prolog programs. Several strategies can enhance the debugging and testing process, ensuring that programs are both correct and efficient.

1. Write Clear and Concise Code

Writing clear and concise code is the first step in minimizing errors. Adopt consistent naming conventions for variables and predicates. Use comments to explain non-obvious logic and the purpose of specific predicates. An example of clear code is shown below:

```
% Predicate to calculate factorial of a number
factorial(0, 1).
factorial(N, Result) :-
    N > 0,
    N1 is N - 1,
    factorial(N1, SubResult),
    Result is N * SubResult.
```

2. Incremental Development

Develop your program incrementally. Write a small piece of functionality, test it thoroughly, and then move on to the next part. This approach helps in isolating bugs and understanding the program's behavior. When extending a factorial calculation script, one could verify at each step if the recursive call and multiplication hold as expected.

3. Use the Prolog Debugger

The Prolog debugger is an invaluable tool for understanding program execution. Use breakpoints to pause execution at critical points and inspect the state of variables and predicates. To set a breakpoint, use the trace/0 predicate.

```
% Set a breakpoint in factorial/2 predicate
trace(factorial/2).
```

Execute the following to trace the program:

```
?- factorial(5, Result).
```

This allows for observing the step-by-step execution of the program:

```
Call: (7) factorial(5, _G123)
Call: (8) 5>0
Exit: (8) 5>0
...
```

4. Understand Variable Bindings

It's crucial to understand how Prolog binds variables. Use the debugger to inspect variable bindings at different steps of execution. At each call, Prolog provides insights into how variables are instantiated or unified. Misunderstanding variable scope or binding errors commonly leads to logical errors.

5. Utilize Unit Tests

Use the *plunit* library in Prolog to automate the testing process. By writing unit tests, developers can ensure that each predicate works as expected independently. Example unit tests for the factorial predicate are as follows:

```
:- use_module(library(plunit)).

:- begin_tests(factorial).

test(factorial_zero) :-
    factorial(0, Result),
    Result == 1.

test(factorial_nonzero) :-
    factorial(5, Result),
    Result == 120.

:- end_tests(factorial).
```

Run the tests using:

```
?- run_tests.
```

6. Test-Driven Development (TDD)

Implement test-driven development practices by writing test cases before the actual implementation. This ensures that each requirement is met by the corresponding tests, leading to robust and well-tested code. Before implementing the factorial function:

```
...
:- begin_tests(factorial).

test(factorial_edge_case) :-
    factorial(-1, _),
    fail.

:- end_tests(factorial).
```

7. Use Assertions

Employ assertions to catch unexpected results and conditions during execution. Assertions help in verifying the preconditions and postconditions of predicates.

```
assert_fact(N) :-
    ( N > 0
    -> true
    ; throw(error(domain_error(positive_integer, N), _))).

factorial(N, Result) :-
    assert_fact(N),
    factorial_logic(N, Result).

factorial_logic(0, 1).
factorial_logic(N, Result) :-
    N1 is N - 1,
    factorial_logic(N1, SubResult),
    Result is N * SubResult.
```

8. Performance Profiling

Profile code to identify performance bottlenecks. Use the Prolog profiler to gather data on predicate calls and execution time. Prolog provides built-in predicates for profiling:

```
?- profile(factorial(1000, _)).
```

Upon completion, the profiler outputs detailed information about the execution:

```
% Prolog Profiling Report
  Predicate          Number of calls          Execution time
  factorial/2        1001                  0.000321s
```

9. Refactor for Clarity and Performance

Periodically refactor code to improve clarity and performance. Refactoring should aim at making the code more readable, reducing redundancy, and improving efficiency. Comments and documentation should be updated during this process.

For instance, tail recursion can optimize the factorial calculation:

```
factorial_tail(N, Result) :-
    factorial_tail(N, 1, Result).

factorial_tail(0, Acc, Acc).
factorial_tail(N, Acc, Result) :-
    N > 0,
    N1 is N - 1,
    Acc1 is N * Acc,
    factorial_tail(N1, Acc1, Result).
```

10. Handle Errors Gracefully

Construct code to handle runtime errors gracefully. Use structured exception handling provided by Prolog to manage unexpected errors:

```
calculate_factorial(N, Result) :-
    catch(
        factorial(N, Result),
        error(domain_error(positive_integer, N), _),
        ( print_message(error, domain_error(positive_integer, N)),
          fail )
    ).
```

This ensures that the program does not terminate abruptly and provides meaningful messages for easier debugging.

Applying these best practices can significantly enhance the reliability, performance, and ease of maintenance of Prolog programs. Developers should consistently integrate these methods into their workflow to avoid common pitfalls and ensure high-quality code.

Chapter 10

Practical Applications of Prolog

This chapter examines practical applications of Prolog, including natural language processing, expert systems, and decision support systems. It discusses knowledge representation and reasoning, Prolog's role in artificial intelligence, developing chatbots, puzzle-solving, game development, and database querying. Additionally, it covers constraint logic programming, data analysis, and provides case studies showcasing real-world applications of Prolog.

10.1 Introduction to Practical Applications of Prolog

Prolog, short for Programming in Logic, provides a versatile and powerful platform for various practical applications due to its inherent support for symbolic reasoning and declarative problem-solving approaches. This section offers a detailed exploration of the foundational principles and broad-ranging applications of Prolog, laying the groundwork for the more specific uses covered throughout this chapter.

Symbolic Reasoning and Pattern Matching At its core, Prolog excels in symbolic reasoning and pattern matching, essential components in fields like artificial intelligence and natural language processing. Prolog's built-in unification mechanism allows it to match patterns efficiently, making it ideal for applications requiring rule-based logic and recursive data processing.

```
parent(john, mary).
parent(jane, mary).
parent(mary, susan).

ancestor(X, Y) :- parent(X, Y).
ancestor(X, Y) :- parent(X, Z), ancestor(Z, Y).
```

In this example, the $\text{ancestor}/2$ predicate demonstrates Prolog's ability to recursively identify an ancestor based on parent relationships, showcasing symbolic reasoning through pattern matching.

Declarative Problem Solving Prolog's declarative nature means that it focuses on the what rather than how of problem-solving. This characteristic is particularly advantageous in domains where defining the problem is more complex than the algorithm to solve it. Prolog enables developers to specify relations and rules, leaving the search for solutions to the underlying inference engine.

Natural Language Processing (NLP) Natural Language Processing benefits from Prolog's pattern matching and symbolic computation capabilities. In NLP, Prolog can parse and interpret human language, enabling the extraction of meaning from text and facilitating communication between humans and machines.

```
sentence(S) --> noun_phrase(NP), verb_phrase(VP).
noun_phrase(NP) --> determiner(D), noun(N).
verb_phrase(VP) --> verb(V), noun_phrase(NP).

determiner(det(the)) --> [the].
noun(noun(cat)) --> [cat].
noun(noun(mouse)) --> [mouse].
verb(verb(chases)) --> [chases].
```

The above code represents a simple context-free grammar for parsing sentences, illustrating how Prolog can be used to understand and manipulate natural languages.

Expert Systems Expert systems rely on a repository of knowledge represented as rules and facts. Prolog's rule-based syntax and its efficient query resolution make it a suitable choice for implementing such systems. These systems can diagnose problems, provide expert advice, and solve complex issues by leveraging Prolog's inference mechanism.

```
symptom(patient, fever).
symptom(patient, cough).

disease(patient, flu) :- symptom(patient, fever), symptom(patient, cough).
```

This example highlights the diagnosis of flu based on observed symptoms, demonstrating how Prolog can drive decision-making processes within an expert system.

Decision Support Systems Prolog can support decision-making processes by encoding decision rules and constraints, facilitating the analysis of different scenarios. Such systems are instrumental in fields like supply chain management, where decisions need to be made based on multiple criteria and constraints.

```
decision(supply_chain, optimize_cost) :- criteria(low_inventory_cost), criteria(
      high_demand_forecast).

criteria(low_inventory_cost).
criteria(high_demand_forecast).
```

This snippet shows how decision criteria can be encoded in Prolog to support decisions related to supply chain optimization.

Knowledge Representation and Reasoning Prolog's ability to represent knowledge through facts and rules allows it to model complex domains and reason about them. Knowledge representation involves structuring information about the world, which Prolog does using predicates, while reasoning is about drawing inferences from existing knowledge.

```
knowledge_base([
  fact(animal(dog)),
  fact(mammal(dog)),
  fact(mammal(cat)),
  rule(has_hair(X) :- mammal(X))
]).

reason(has_hair(dog)). % inferred from the knowledge base
```

In this example, Prolog models a knowledge base and demonstrates how reasoning can be performed on this base to infer new knowledge.

Prolog's capabilities extend further to fields such as game development, puzzle-solving, constraint logic programming, data analysis, and database querying, each providing further evidence of its versatility and powerful problem-solving abilities. As we delve deeper into this chapter, these areas will be explored in detail to illustrate Prolog's practical applications in various domains, enhancing our comprehension and mastery of this powerful programming language.

10.2 Natural Language Processing with Prolog

Natural Language Processing (NLP) with Prolog leverages the language's inherent capabilities for symbolic reasoning and pattern matching, making it well-suited for tasks involving the understanding and generation of human language. This section delves into the fundamental aspects of NLP and how Prolog facilitates these processes through parsing, syntax analysis, semantic interpretation, and language generation.

Prolog's strength in NLP lies in its ability to define complex grammatical rules and use recursive structures to parse sentences. Prolog's unification algorithm and backtracking mechanism are pivotal in exploring different possible interpretations of a sentence, aiding in disambiguation and understanding.

Grammatical Representation and Parsing

A basic aspect of NLP is the representation of grammar. Context-Free Grammars (CFGs) are often employed due to their simplicity and comprehensiveness in representing the syntactic structure of natural languages. In Prolog, CFGs can be implemented using Definite Clause Grammars (DCGs). DCGs provide a notation that mimics CFGs but can be executed directly by the Prolog interpreter.

Given a tiny fragment of English grammar, consider the following DCG:

```
sentence --> noun_phrase, verb_phrase.

noun_phrase --> determiner, noun.
noun_phrase --> determiner, adjective, noun.

verb_phrase --> verb, noun_phrase.

determiner --> [the].
determiner --> [a].

noun --> [cat].
noun --> [dog].
```

```
noun --> [garden].
noun --> [elephant].

adjective --> [happy].
adjective --> [big].

verb --> [chased].
verb --> [saw].
verb --> [admired].
```

This grammar can be used to parse sentences and generate parse trees. Prolog can automatically attempt to unify an input list of words with the grammar rules defined, as shown in the following query example:

```
?- phrase(sentence, [the, happy, cat, chased, a, dog]).
```

If the query succeeds, it indicates that the given sentence conforms to the grammar rules. DCGs also support the generation of syntactically valid sentences by allowing the use of variables in place of concrete words and letting Prolog's backtracking yield distinct combinations.

Syntax Trees and Parse Trees

To further analyze a sentence, syntax trees (or parse trees) are often used. Prolog can be extended to not only check grammaticality but also construct a tree structure representing the syntactic composition. Modifying the DCG rules to build parse trees can be achieved as follows:

```
sentence(t(sentence, NP, VP)) --> noun_phrase(NP), verb_phrase(VP).

noun_phrase(t(noun_phrase, Det, N)) --> determiner(Det), noun(N).
noun_phrase(t(noun_phrase, Det, Adj, N)) --> determiner(Det), adjective(Adj), noun(
    N).

verb_phrase(t(verb_phrase, V, NP)) --> verb(V), noun_phrase(NP).

determiner(t(determiner, the)) --> [the].
determiner(t(determiner, a)) --> [a].

noun(t(noun, N)) --> [N], { member(N, [cat, dog, garden, elephant]) }.

adjective(t(adjective, Adj)) --> [Adj], { member(Adj, [happy, big]) }.

verb(t(verb, V)) --> [V], { member(V, [chased, saw, admired]) }.
```

Running a parsing query generates a tree structure:

```
?- phrase(sentence(Tree), [the, happy, cat, chased, a, dog]).
Tree = t(sentence,
       t(noun_phrase, t(determiner, the), t(adjective, happy), t(noun, cat)),
       t(verb_phrase, t(verb, chased), t(noun_phrase, t(determiner, a), t(noun, dog)))
          ).
```

Semantic Interpretation

To move from syntax to semantics, Prolog can also be used to map syntactic structures to semantic representations. A common approach is to use logical forms or lambda calculus expressions to represent meanings. Enriching our grammar rules to include semantic annotations is essential.

For example, consider a simple semantic representation using predicates:

```
sentence(sen(VP)) --> noun_phrase(_), verb_phrase(VP).

noun_phrase(_) --> determiner(_), noun(_).
noun_phrase(_) --> determiner(_), adjective(_), noun(_).

verb_phrase(VP) --> verb(V), noun_phrase(NP), { VP =.. [V, NP] }.

determiner(_) --> [the].
determiner(_) --> [a].

noun(_) --> [cat].
noun(_) --> [dog].
noun(_) --> [garden].
noun(_) --> [elephant].

adjective(_) --> [happy].
adjective(_) --> [big].

verb(chased) --> [chased].
verb(saw) --> [saw].
verb(admired) --> [admired].
```

When queried, the semantic interpretation becomes apparent:

```
?- phrase(sentence(Semantics), [the, happy, cat, chased, a, dog]).
Semantics = sen(chased(NP)).
```

This demonstrates how Prolog can decompose and interpret sentences not just syntactically but also semantically, which is critical for tasks involving understanding the intent and meaning behind natural language expressions.

Language Generation

Language generation is the reverse of parsing. Generating natural language outputs from formal representations requires mapping semantic structures back to surface forms. Using the DCGs defined can facilitate this process seamlessly. Given a semantic structure, Prolog can produce all corresponding sentences that share the same meaning.

Consider a simple generation scenario:

```
?- phrase(sentence(sen(chased(NP))), Sentence).
```

```
Sentence = [the, happy, cat, chased, the, garden] ;
Sentence = [the, happy, cat, chased, the, elephant] ;
Sentence = [the, cat, chased, the, garden] ;
Sentence = [the, big, cat, chased, the, garden] ;
...
```

This illustrates Prolog's utility in producing varied syntactic representations for a given semantic input, showcasing its power in both understanding and generating language.

Through these examples and processes, it is evident that Prolog's logical and declarative nature lends itself excellently to the domain of natural language processing, handling intricate structures and meanings with relative ease and efficiency.

10.3 Building Expert Systems

An expert system is a computer program that mimics the decision-making abilities of a human expert. Prolog, with its strong foundation in logic programming and symbolic reasoning, is particularly well-suited for constructing expert systems. This section details the steps and methodologies required to build an expert system using Prolog, where the knowledge base and inference engine are central components.

At the core, an expert system comprises:

- **Knowledge Base**: A collection of facts and rules representing the domain-specific knowledge.
- **Inference Engine**: The component that applies logical rules to the knowledge base to deduce new information or make decisions.

Step 1: Defining the Knowledge Base

The knowledge base in Prolog consists of a set of factual assertions and rules. Facts are simply stated truths about the domain, while rules define relationships between facts and are used by the inference engine to derive new information.

```
% Example facts
animal(mammal).
animal(bird).
animal(reptile).

% Example rules
```

```
has_fur(mammal).
lays_eggs(bird).
lays_eggs(reptile).
```

The above code defines three kinds of animals and associates attributes with each type using rules. For instance, the rule has_fur(mammal). indicates that mammals have fur.

Step 2: Developing the Inference Engine

The inference engine processes the knowledge base to answer queries. Prolog's built-in backtracking mechanism allows it to explore all possible solutions efficiently. Given a query, Prolog attempts to satisfy it using the facts and rules defined.

```
% Query: What animals lay eggs?
lays_eggs(Animal).
```

When this query is executed, Prolog will provide all animals that match the condition specified by lays_eggs(Animal).

Backward Chaining Implementation

Backward chaining is a common inference technique used in expert systems. In backward chaining, the system starts with a goal and works backward to determine if knowledge in the knowledge base supports the goal.

Algorithm 5: Backward Chaining Algorithm

```
Data: Knowledge Base
Result: Satisfies the goal or not
Function BackwardChaining(Goal):
    if Goal is a fact in the knowledge base then
        return True;
    else
        for each rule that can derive Goal do
            if each premise of the rule is satisfied then
                return True;
            else
                return False;
```

Prolog's inherent mechanism of depth-first search and unification makes backward chaining straightforward to implement.

Step 3: Expert System Example: Medical Diagnosis

Consider a simplified example of a medical diagnosis expert system. The knowledge base contains symptoms and their associated conditions, and the inference engine deduces possible diseases based on patient symptoms.

```
% Symptoms facts
symptom(fever).
symptom(cough).
symptom(body_ache).

% Conditions
condition(flu) :- symptom(fever), symptom(cough), symptom(body_ache).
condition(common_cold) :- symptom(cough), \+ symptom(body_ache).
```

In this example, the rules define which combinations of symptoms correspond to particular conditions. The query to diagnose a disease given certain symptoms would be:

```
% Query: What condition could it be if the patient has a cough and fever?
condition(Disease) :- symptom(cough), symptom(fever).
```

Prolog would evaluate the query against the knowledge base and return potential matches for Disease.

Step 4: Extending the Expert System

As requirements evolve, the expert system's knowledge base can be extended with more facts and rules. For instance, adding more symptoms and conditions:

```
% Extended Symptoms facts
symptom(headache).
symptom(sore_throat).

% Extended Conditions
condition(migraine) :- symptom(headache).
condition(strep_throat) :- symptom(sore_throat), symptom(fever).
```

With each iteration, the system becomes more robust and capable of handling more complex queries and diagnoses.

Building an expert system in Prolog involves defining a comprehensive knowledge base and leveraging Prolog's inferential capabilities to implement a powerful inference engine. The rules and facts should be meticulously curated to encompass the domain of interest effectively. As demonstrated, Prolog's simplicity in expressing logical relationships and conducting inferential reasoning makes it a potent tool for constructing expert systems.

10.4 Implementing Decision Support Systems

Decision Support Systems (DSS) are crucial in aiding decision-makers by providing comprehensive information and analysis tools. Prolog, with its ability to handle complex logical queries and representations, serves as an excellent choice for implementing DSS. This section will focus on key aspects of building DSS using Prolog, including knowledge representation, inference mechanisms, and practical implementation examples.

Decision Support Systems involve:

- Collecting and storing data.
- Analyzing data to extract useful information.
- Supporting the decision-making process through interactive querying and reporting.

Prolog excels in the declarative representation of knowledge and the inferential processing technique, making it well suited for these tasks.

Knowledge Representation

In a DSS, knowledge can be represented through facts and rules. Facts represent static information about the data, while rules represent relationships and conditional knowledge.

For instance, a typical DSS to assist in financial decision-making might include knowledge about market trends, investment types, risk categories, and historical data. Knowledge in Prolog can be represented as:

```
investment(high_risk, stocks).
investment(medium_risk, mutual_funds).
investment(low_risk, savings_account).
market_trend(bull, investing_recommended).
market_trend(bear, investing_cautious).

recommend_investment(X) :-
    market_trend(bull, investing_recommended),
    investment(X, stocks).
recommend_investment(Y) :-
    market_trend(bear, investing_cautious),
    investment(Y, savings_account).
```

investment/2 defines the risk level associated with different investment types, and market_trend/2 describes market conditions. The rules recommend_investment/1 then provide investment recommendations based on the market trend.

Inference Mechanisms

DSS benefits greatly from the inferential capabilities of Prolog. Through backward chaining, Prolog can infer which decisions align with current conditions. Below is an example of a query to determine a safe investment during a bear market:

```
?- recommend_investment(What).
```

The expected output in the verbatim environment would be:

```
What = savings_account.
```

This shows how the DSS can provide actionable insights based on predefined rules.

Practical Implementation

Suppose we are developing a DSS for agricultural planning, where the goal is to recommend crops based on soil type, weather patterns, and market demand. The facts and rules could be structured as follows:

```
soil_type(clay).
soil_type(sandy).
soil_type(loamy).

weather(season, summer).
weather(season, winter).

crop(suitability, rice, clay).
crop(suitability, wheat, sandy).
crop(suitability, maize, loamy).

market_demand(high, maize).
market_demand(medium, wheat).
market_demand(low, rice).

suitable_crop(Crop) :-
    soil_type(Soil),
    crop(suitability, Crop, Soil),
    market_demand(Demand, Crop),
    weather(season, Season),
    (Season = summer, Demand = high; Season = winter, Demand = low).
```

Executing the query below:

```
?- suitable_crop(RecommendedCrop).
```

The output would provide the optimal crops for cultivation under current conditions:

```
RecommendedCrop = maize.
```

This brief example demonstrates how Prolog can consolidate various inputs to make informed decisions.

Interactive DSS Development

For a more interactive and robust DSS, Prolog's capability to dynamically handle user inputs and update the knowledge base as new information becomes available is vital. For instance, based on user-provided data regarding their soil type and current season, the Prolog system can offer tailored advice:

```
recommend_crop :-
    write('Enter soil type (clay, sandy, loamy): '), read(Soil),
    write('Enter current season (summer, winter): '), read(Season),
    soil_type(Soil),
    weather(season, Season),
    suitable_crop(Crop),
    write('Recommended Crop: '), write(Crop), nl.
```

Here, recommend_crop/0 defines an interactive predicate. When executed, it prompts the user to enter the soil type and current season. The system then evaluates the appropriate crop to cultivate, concluding the interaction with relevant advice.

Deploying a decision support system using Prolog allows for elegant and efficient data representation, unmatched inferential capabilities, and interactivity. The flexibility and power of Prolog in structuring complex logical scenarios make it indispensable for DSS implementation. The techniques discussed provide a foundational understanding for leveraging Prolog in developing dynamic and effective decision support systems.

10.5 Knowledge Representation and Reasoning

Knowledge representation and reasoning (KR&R) are core components of artificial intelligence and computer science, playing a crucial role in how information is structured, stored, and manipulated in Prolog. This section delves into various knowledge representation techniques and reasoning processes, illustrating Prolog's powerful capabilities in these domains.

Representing Facts and Rules

At the heart of knowledge representation in Prolog are facts and rules.

Facts are basic assertions about the world, while rules define relationships between facts, providing the foundation for reasoning.

```
% Facts
parent(john, mary).
parent(mary, susan).

% Rule
grandparent(X, Y) :- parent(X, Z), parent(Z, Y).
```

In this example, parent(john, mary) and parent(mary, susan) are facts indicating that John is Mary's parent and Mary is Susan's parent. The rule grandparent(X, Y) :- parent(X, Z), parent(Z, Y) represents the relationship where X is a grandparent of Y if X is a parent of Z and Z is a parent of Y.

Logical Conjunction and Disjunction

Prolog supports logical conjunction (AND) using commas and logical disjunction (OR) using semicolons within rules.

```
% Logical conjunction (AND)
sibling(X, Y) :- parent(Z, X), parent(Z, Y), X \= Y.

% Logical disjunction (OR)
related(X, Y) :- parent(X, Y); parent(Y, X); sibling(X, Y).
```

In the rule for sibling/2, X and Y are siblings if they share a common parent Z and are not the same individual. The rule for related/2 uses disjunction to indicate that X and Y are related if either X is a parent of Y, Y is a parent of X, or X and Y are siblings.

Reasoning with Unification and Backtracking

Prolog employs unification and backtracking to carry out logical reasoning. Unification is the process of making two terms identical by finding suitable variable bindings, while backtracking seeks alternative solutions by exploring different branches of a search tree.

Unification Example:

```
?- parent(X, mary).
X = john.
```

In this query, Prolog unifies X with john based on the given fact parent(john, mary).

Backtracking Example:

```
?- parent(X, susan).
X = mary ;
false.
```

Prolog first finds $X = mary$ as a solution and, upon backtracking, finds no additional solutions, thus terminating the search.

Handling Recursion

Recursion is a powerful mechanism in Prolog for defining complex relationships through self-referential rules. Consider the representation of the ancestor relationship:

```
ancestor(X, Y) :- parent(X, Y).
ancestor(X, Y) :- parent(X, Z), ancestor(Z, Y).
```

Here, $ancestor/2$ is defined recursively. X is an ancestor of Y if X is a parent of Y or if X is a parent of Z and Z is an ancestor of Y.

Representing Knowledge using Lists and Structures

Prolog can represent more complex data structures using lists and compound terms (structures). Lists are an ordered collection of elements, while structures can encapsulate multiple attributes.

List Example:

```
% Defining a list
family([john, mary, susan]).

% Accessing list elements
?- family(F), member(mary, F).
F = [john, mary, susan].
```

Structure Example:

```
% Defining a structure
person(name(john), age(50)).

% Accessing structure elements
?- person(Name, age(50)).
Name = name(john).
```

Algorithmic Reasoning with Prolog

Prolog's logical inference capabilities extend to algorithmic reasoning processes. We can use the algorithm2e package to illustrate standard algorithmic steps within Prolog logic.

This algorithmic representation shows how Prolog processes the ancestral relationship using nested loops and conditional statements based on parent-child relationships and previously established ancestor connections.

Combining these elements, Prolog offers a robust platform for knowledge representation and efficient reasoning, suitable for a wide range

Algorithm 6: Ancestral Relationship Algorithm

Data: Database of parent-child relationships
Result: Determines if one person is an ancestor of another

```
begin
    foreach Person X do
        if parent(X, Y) then
            mark X as an ancestor of Y;
        foreach Person Z do
            if parent(X, Z) and ancestor(Z, Y) then
                mark X as an ancestor of Y;
```

of artificial intelligence applications.

10.6 Prolog in Artificial Intelligence

Prolog's declarative nature and powerful pattern matching capabilities make it a suitable language for various artificial intelligence (AI) applications. This section explores Prolog's role in AI, providing detailed explanations and examples of its use in developing intelligent systems.

A core component of AI is the ability to represent knowledge about the world and reason with it. In Prolog, knowledge can be encoded using facts and rules expressed as Horn clauses, and reasoning is performed through queries and unification.

Knowledge Representation in Prolog
Knowledge representation is foundational in AI systems. Prolog allows the representation of knowledge using facts, rules, and queries. A fact represents a basic assertion about the world, while a rule defines a relationship or implication between facts. For example:

```
% Facts
human(socrates).
human(plato).
human(aristotle).

% Rules
mortal(X) :- human(X).

% Query to check if Socrates is mortal
?- mortal(socrates).
```

Output:
  Yes

In this example, the fact human(socrates) asserts that Socrates is a human. The rule mortal(X) :- human(X). states that any X is mortal if X is human. When a query ?- mortal(socrates). is executed, Prolog infers from the facts and the rule that Socrates is indeed mortal.

Reasoning and Inferencing

Reasoning in Prolog is performed through inferencing, which involves deriving new information from known facts and rules. Prolog uses backward chaining as its inferencing mechanism, where it starts with the query (goal) and works backward to find a match in the knowledge base.

Consider an AI system for medical diagnosis. Diseases and their symptoms can be represented as follows:

```
% Facts
symptom(john, fever).
symptom(john, cough).
symptom(jane, headache).

% Rules
disease(X, flu) :- symptom(X, fever), symptom(X, cough).
disease(X, cold) :- symptom(X, cough), not(symptom(X, fever)).

% Query to diagnose John's disease
?- disease(john, Disease).
```

Output:
  Disease = flu

Here, the system checks John's symptoms against the rules for flu and cold. Since John has both fever and cough, Prolog concludes that John has the flu.

Search and Optimization Problems

Prolog can solve search and optimization problems through its built-in depth-first search algorithm and constraint satisfaction capabilities. One common example is the classic AI problem of finding a path in a graph.

```
% Facts representing graph edges
edge(a, b).
edge(b, c).
edge(c, d).
edge(d, e).
edge(a, e).

% Rule defining a path
path(X, Y) :- edge(X, Y).
path(X, Y) :- edge(X, Z), path(Z, Y).

% Query to find a path from 'a' to 'e'
```

```
?- path(a, e).
```

Output:
Yes

In this case, Prolog checks for both direct and indirect paths recursively and confirms the existence of a path from 'a' to 'e'.

AI Planning

Planning is a crucial area in AI, and Prolog's logical foundation makes it well-suited for planning problems. A simple example is the blocks world problem, where the goal is to move blocks to achieve a specific configuration.

```
% Initial state: block positions
on(a, table).
on(b, table).
on(c, a).

% Plan rules
move(X, Y) :- on(X, Z), not(on(Y, _)), retract(on(X, Z)), assert(on(X, Y)).

% Query to achieve goal state
% Goal: move block 'c' to the table
?- move(c, table).
```

Output:
Yes

Prolog updates the state of the world by retracting the old position of 'c' and asserting the new position, demonstrating simple planning capabilities.

Expert Systems

Expert systems emulate the decision-making ability of a human expert. They use a knowledge base and a set of inference rules to make decisions. A classic example is a simple rule-based expert system for animal classification:

```
% Facts
animal(lion).
animal(dolphin).
animal(falcon).

% Rules
mammal(X) :- animal(X), not(has_scales(X)), not(lays_eggs(X)).
bird(X) :- animal(X), lays_eggs(X), has_feathers(X).
fish(X) :- animal(X), has_scales(X), lives_in_water(X).

has_feathers(falcon).
lays_eggs(falcon).
has_scales(dolphin). % Incorrect fact to test reasoning

% Query to classify animals
?- mammal(dolphin).
```

```
Output:
  No
```

This example defines rules for classifying animals as mammals, birds, or fish based on their characteristics. The query tests if a dolphin is a mammal, and the system correctly deduces that it is not because of the incorrect fact about scales, demonstrating reasoning under uncertainty.

Combining knowledge representation, reasoning, search optimization, planning, and expert system functionalities illustrates Prolog's robust capabilities for implementing AI systems. Prolog not only provides a flexible and efficient way to model and solve AI problems, but it also encourages a clear separation between the logic of a problem and its control flow, making it an invaluable tool in the field of artificial intelligence.

10.7 Developing Chatbots and Conversational Agents

In this section, we delve into the utilization of Prolog for developing chatbots and conversational agents. Chatbots have become increasingly prevalent across various domains including customer support, virtual assistants, and information retrieval systems. Prolog's powerful pattern matching and rule-based inference engine make it an ideal candidate for implementing such systems. We will explore the fundamental concepts and techniques involved in creating chatbots using Prolog, through systematic steps and detailed examples.

The foundation of a Prolog-based chatbot lies in its ability to process and respond to natural language input. Essentially, this involves parsing user inputs, matching them against predefined rules, and generating appropriate responses. The key concepts include pattern matching, rule-based inference, and handling ambiguous or incomplete information. To begin, consider the following simple Prolog rules for a basic conversational agent.

```
% Simple greeting rules
greet(Input, Response) :-
    member(Input, [hello, hi, hey]),
    Response = 'Hello! How can I assist you today?'.

greet(Input, Response) :-
    member(Input, [goodbye, bye]),
    Response = 'Goodbye! Have a nice day!'.

% Default fallback rule
```

```
greet(_, 'I am sorry, I do not understand.').
```

In this example, the greet/2 predicate processes user inputs by checking for matches with a list of predefined greetings. If a match is found, a corresponding response is generated. The default fallback rule ensures that the chatbot can gracefully handle inputs that do not match any known patterns.

A more sophisticated chatbot requires parsing and understanding more complex inputs. One approach to achieve this is to use Definite Clause Grammars (DCGs) in Prolog. DCGs allow us to specify grammatical rules that can parse sentences into their constituent parts, thereby enabling more nuanced understanding and response generation.

Consider a scenario where the chatbot needs to handle inquiries about the weather:

```
% Definite Clause Grammar for weather inquiries
sentence(weather(Place)) --> [what, is, the, weather, in], place(Place).
place(Place) --> [Place], { atom(Place) }.

% Weather response rule
respond(weather(Place), Response) :-
    get_weather(Place, Weather),
    atom_concat('The weather in ', Place, Temp1),
    atom_concat(Temp1, ' is ', Temp2),
    atom_concat(Temp2, Weather, Response).

% Mock function to return weather information
get_weather(_, 'sunny'). % For simplicity, always returns 'sunny'.
```

In this code, the sentence/2 DCG parses a structured weather inquiry and extracts the place of interest. The respond/2 predicate then generates a response based on this structured input. For demonstration purposes, we use a mock get_weather/2 function that always returns 'sunny'.

To interact with our chatbot, we need a main loop that reads user inputs, processes them, and outputs the responses. Here is an example of such an interaction loop:

```
% Chatbot main loop
chat :-
    write('> '),
    read_sentence(Input),
    (
        Input == [quit] ->
        write('Chatbot terminating...'), nl;
        parse_and_respond(Input, Response),
        write(Response), nl,
        chat
    ).
```

```
% Read sentence from user input
read_sentence(Input) :-
    read_line_to_codes(user_input, Codes),
    atom_codes(Atom, Codes),
    atomic_list_concat(Atoms, ' ', Atom),
    maplist(downcase_atom, Atoms, Input).

% Parse input and generate response
parse_and_respond(Input, Response) :-
    phrase(sentence(ParsedInput), Input) ->
    respond(ParsedInput, Response);
    greet(Input, Response).
```

The chat/0 predicate serves as the main loop, continuously reading user inputs, processing them, and printing the responses until the user types quit. The read_sentence/1 predicate reads a line of input, tokenizes and lowercases it. The parse_and_respond/2 predicate tries to parse the input using the defined DCGs; if successful, it generates an appropriate response. Otherwise, it falls back to the greeting rules defined earlier.

The robustness of a chatbot can be significantly enhanced by incorporating additional rules and patterns to handle a wide range of user inputs. This involves iteratively refining the rule base and testing against diverse conversational scenarios. Moreover, leveraging databases for storing and retrieving information can extend the chatbot's capabilities, enabling it to provide more dynamic and context-aware responses.

The techniques and examples provided demonstrate how Prolog's declarative nature and pattern-matching strengths can be effectively harnessed to develop chatbots and conversational agents. By continuously expanding the rule set and refining the parsing mechanisms, one can develop sophisticated and responsive conversational systems capable of handling complex interactions.

10.8 Solving Puzzles and Games

Prolog's strength in symbolic reasoning and pattern matching makes it especially adept at solving puzzles and games. The essence of puzzle-solving in Prolog lies in its ability to represent constraints and systematically explore potential solutions efficiently. This section will delve into various classical puzzles and games, elucidating the Prolog approach to each, showcasing practical examples that utilize Prolog's logic programming paradigms.

Solving puzzles often involves representing the state, defining valid transitions between states, and searching for a path from the initial state to the goal state. Games, on the other hand, frequently require a more dynamic approach, including handling competing players and strategic planning.

1. Sudoku Solver

Sudoku is a number-placement puzzle. The objective is to fill a 9x9 grid with digits so that each column, each row, and each of the nine 3x3 subgrids contain all digits from 1 to 9.

Representing a Sudoku puzzle in Prolog involves defining rules that ensure these constraints. Here, each row, column, and subgrid must be processed to ensure they contain unique digits.

```
valid([]).
valid([Head|Tail]) :-
    fd_all_different(Head),
    valid(Tail).

sudoku(Puzzle, Solution) :-
    Solution = Puzzle,
    Puzzle = [S11, S12, S13, S14, S15, S16, S17, S18, S19,
              S21, S22, S23, S24, S25, S26, S27, S28, S29,
              S31, S32, S33, S34, S35, S36, S37, S38, S39,
              S41, S42, S43, S44, S45, S46, S47, S48, S49,
              S51, S52, S53, S54, S55, S56, S57, S58, S59,
              S61, S62, S63, S64, S65, S66, S67, S68, S69,
              S71, S72, S73, S74, S75, S76, S77, S78, S79,
              S81, S82, S83, S84, S85, S86, S87, S88, S89,
              S91, S92, S93, S94, S95, S96, S97, S98, S99],
    fd_domain(Puzzle, 1, 9),

    Row1 = [S11, S12, S13, S14, S15, S16, S17, S18, S19],
    Row2 = [S21, S22, S23, S24, S25, S26, S27, S28, S29],
    Row3 = [S31, S32, S33, S34, S35, S36, S37, S38, S39],
    Row4 = [S41, S42, S43, S44, S45, S46, S47, S48, S49],
    Row5 = [S51, S52, S53, S54, S55, S56, S57, S58, S59],
    Row6 = [S61, S62, S63, S64, S65, S66, S67, S68, S69],
    Row7 = [S71, S72, S73, S74, S75, S76, S77, S78, S79],
    Row8 = [S81, S82, S83, S84, S85, S86, S87, S88, S89],
    Row9 = [S91, S92, S93, S94, S95, S96, S97, S98, S99],

    Col1 = [S11, S21, S31, S41, S51, S61, S71, S81, S91],
    Col2 = [S12, S22, S32, S42, S52, S62, S72, S82, S92],
    Col3 = [S13, S23, S33, S43, S53, S63, S73, S83, S93],
    Col4 = [S14, S24, S34, S44, S54, S64, S74, S84, S94],
    Col5 = [S15, S25, S35, S45, S55, S65, S75, S85, S95],
    Col6 = [S16, S26, S36, S46, S56, S66, S76, S86, S96],
    Col7 = [S17, S27, S37, S47, S57, S67, S77, S87, S97],
    Col8 = [S18, S28, S38, S48, S58, S68, S78, S88, S98],
    Col9 = [S19, S29, S39, S49, S59, S69, S79, S89, S99],

    Square1 = [S11, S12, S13, S21, S22, S23, S31, S32, S33],
    Square2 = [S14, S15, S16, S24, S25, S26, S34, S35, S36],
    Square3 = [S17, S18, S19, S27, S28, S29, S37, S38, S39],
    Square4 = [S41, S42, S43, S51, S52, S53, S61, S62, S63],
    Square5 = [S44, S45, S46, S54, S55, S56, S64, S65, S66],
    Square6 = [S47, S48, S49, S57, S58, S59, S67, S68, S69],
```

```
    Square7 = [S71, S72, S73, S81, S82, S83, S91, S92, S93],
    Square8 = [S74, S75, S76, S84, S85, S86, S94, S95, S96],
    Square9 = [S77, S78, S79, S87, S88, S89, S97, S98, S99],

    valid([Row1, Row2, Row3, Row4, Row5, Row6, Row7, Row8, Row9,
           Col1, Col2, Col3, Col4, Col5, Col6, Col7, Col8, Col9,
           Square1, Square2, Square3, Square4, Square5, Square6,
           Square7, Square8, Square9]),

    maplist(fd_labeling, [Row1, Row2, Row3, Row4, Row5, Row6, Row7, Row8, Row9]).
```

The above program verifies the validity of individual rows, columns, and subgrids and ensures they contain distinct values between 1 and 9. The fd_domain predicate restricts the values to this range, and the fd_labeling predicate searches for solutions that satisfy all constraints.

2. Knight's Tour

The Knight's Tour problem on a chessboard involves moving a knight such that it visits every square exactly once. Representing the problem in Prolog involves defining the board, possible moves, and constraints to ensure all squares are visited without repetition.

```
move(X/Y, X1/Y1) :-
    member([DX, DY], [[1, 2], [2, 1], [-1, 2], [-2, 1], [1, -2], [2, -1], [-1, -2], [-2, -1]]),
    X1 is X + DX,
    Y1 is Y + DY,
    X1 > 0, X1 =< 8,
    Y1 > 0, Y1 =< 8.

knights_tour(N, Path) :-
    knights_tour(N, [1/1], Path).

knights_tour(1, Path, Path).
knights_tour(N, Visited, Path) :-
    N > 1,
    Visited = [CurrentPos | _],
    move(CurrentPos, NextPos),
    \+ member(NextPos, Visited),
    N1 is N - 1,
    knights_tour(N1, [NextPos | Visited], Path).
```

The move predicate defines all possible knight moves and ensures they are within bounds of an 8x8 chessboard. The knights_tour predicate recursively explores valid moves, tracking visited positions, and halts when all squares have been visited.

3. N-Queens Problem

The N-Queens problem entails placing N queens on an NxN chessboard so no two queens threaten each other. Representing the solution set in Prolog involves constraints for row, column, and diagonal non-attacks.

```
safe([]).
safe([Queen | Others]) :-
    safe(Others),
    no_attack(Queen, Others, 1).

no_attack(_, [], _).
no_attack(Y, [Y1 | Ylist], Xdist) :-
    Y =\= Y1,
    abs(Y1 - Y) =\= Xdist,
    Dist1 is Xdist + 1,
    no_attack(Y, Ylist, Dist1).

queens(N, Solution) :-
    length(Solution, N),
    fd_domain(Solution, 1, N),
    safe(Solution),
    fd_labeling(Solution).
```

In the N-Queens solution, the safe predicate ensures no two queens attack each other. The no_attack predicate checks for both vertical and diagonal threats, ensuring valid queen placements.

4. Tic-Tac-Toe

Tic-Tac-Toe is a simple but effective game for demonstrating two-player strategies in Prolog. To implement it, states and moves need to be evaluated, and win conditions must be recognized.

```
move([P1, P2, P3, P4, P5, P6, P7, P8, P9], Player, [Player, P2, P3, P4, P5, P6, P7, P8,
       P9], 1) :- var(P1).
move([P1, P2, P3, P4, P5, P6, P7, P8, P9], Player, [P1, Player, P3, P4, P5, P6, P7, P8,
       P9], 2) :- var(P2).
...
move([P1, P2, P3, P4, P5, P6, P7, P8, P9], Player, [P1, P2, P3, P4, P5, P6, P7, P8,
      Player], 9) :- var(P9).

win([P, P, P, _, _, _, _, _, _], P).
win([_, _, _, P, P, P, _, _, _], P).
win([_, _, _, _, _, _, P, P, P], P).
win([P, _, _, P, _, _, P, _, _], P).
win([_, P, _, _, P, _, _, P, _], P).
win([_, _, P, _, _, P, _, _, P], P).
win([P, _, _, _, P, _, _, _, P], P).
win([_, _, P, _, P, _, P, _, _], P).
win([_, _, _, _, _, _, _, _, _], draw).

play :-
    game([_, _, _, _, _, _, _, _, _], x).

game(State, Player) :-
    draw_board(State),
    (win(State, Winner), !,
     format("~nGame Over! Winner is: ~w~n", [Winner]);
     format("~nPlayer ~w, input move (1-9): ", [Player]),
     read(Move),
     move(State, Player, NewState, Move),
     switch(Player, NewPlayer),
     game(NewState, NewPlayer)).
```

```
switch(x, o).
switch(o, x).

draw_board([P1, P2, P3, P4, P5, P6, P7, P8, P9]) :-
    format("~w | ~w | ~w~n", [P1, P2, P3]),
    format("---------~n"),
    format("~w | ~w | ~w~n", [P4, P5, P6]),
    format("---------~n"),
    format("~w | ~w | ~w~n", [P7, P8, P9]).
```

The move predicates define possible moves for each board position if it is unoccupied. The win predicate checks for winning conditions on the board. The play predicate initiates the game loop, implementing alternating turns between players and updating the game state until a win or draw condition is met.

This exploration of puzzle and game-solving in Prolog illustrates the language's power in handling complex constraints and executing strategic computations seamlessly, leveraging its robust logical inference and backtracking features.

10.9 Prolog for Database Querying

Prolog is uniquely suited for database querying due to its inherent ability to manage facts and rules, offering a robust mechanism for querying and reasoning about data. This section explores the capabilities of Prolog in managing and querying databases, providing practical examples and elaborating on the principles involved.

We begin by considering a simple database represented as a collection of facts and rules. In this context, a database can be viewed as a set of prolog clauses, where facts represent atomic information and rules capture the relationships and constraints among the facts.

Example Database: Student Information System

Consider the following database storing information about students, courses, and enrolments:

```
% Facts
student(john).
student(mary).
student(tom).

course(mathematics).
course(science).
course(english).

enrolled(john, mathematics).
```

```
enrolled(mary, science).
enrolled(tom, english).
```

In this database: - student/1 denotes a predicate that identifies a student. - course/1 denotes a predicate that identifies a course. - enrolled/2 denotes a predicate showing enrolment of students in courses.

Querying this information is straightforward. For instance, to find out if john is enrolled in mathematics, we use the following query:

```
?- enrolled(john, mathematics).
```

This query returns true as john is indeed enrolled in mathematics.

Prolog's flexibility allows more complex queries. For example, to find all courses a particular student is enrolled in:

```
?- enrolled(john, Course).
```

Executing this query lists all courses john is enrolled in, providing valuable insights.

```
Course = mathematics .
```

Adding and Deleting Facts Dynamically

Using Prolog predicates, we can dynamically add facts to and remove facts from the database using assert/1 and retract/1, respectively.

To add a new student alice, we do:

```
?- assert(student(alice)).
```

Consequently, querying for all students, we now include alice as well:

```
?- student(X).
```

The output will reflect the updated state of the database:

```
X = john ;
X = mary ;
X = tom ;
X = alice.
```

To remove a fact, say john is no longer a student, we execute:

```
?- retract(student(john)).
```

Subsequent queries will no longer include john in the list of students.

Complex Queries and Logical Inference

Prolog's strength lies in its ability to handle complex queries and logical inference. We can define rules that leverage multiple facts to derive new information. For instance, to determine if a student is enrolled in any course:

```
enrolled_in_any_course(Student) :- student(Student), enrolled(Student, _).
```

Now, querying if tom is enrolled in any course:

```
?- enrolled_in_any_course(tom).
```

This query checks the condition and returns:

```
true.
```

Moreover, we can find students enrolled in multiple courses by defining another rule:

```
enrolled_in_multiple_courses(Student) :-
    enrolled(Student, Course1),
    enrolled(Student, Course2),
    Course1 \= Course2.
```

This rule checks for enrolment in at least two different courses. Although in this example, none meet the criteria, the power of Prolog's pattern matching and inference is clearly illustrated.

Using Prolog with External Databases

Prolog can interface with external databases such as SQL databases using libraries like ODBC. This integration allows advanced database querying capabilities while maintaining the logical reasoning strength of Prolog.

Here is a simple example illustrating how to query an SQL database from Prolog using ODBC:

```
:- use_module(library(odbc)).

% Connect to the database
connect_to_db(Connection) :-
    odbc_connect('DBName', Connection, [user('user'), password('pass')]).

% Perform a query
query_db(Connection, SQL, Results) :-
    odbc_query(Connection, SQL, row(Results)).
```

In this example, odbc_connect/3 establishes a connection to the database. The query_db/3 predicate sends an SQL query and retrieves the results. This setup allows Prolog to handle large databases efficiently.

Using Prolog's powerful pattern matching, logical inference, and integration capabilities, database querying becomes a versatile and formidable tool. Queries can dynamically adapt, making Prolog indispensable for applications where data relationships and constraints play a crucial role. The ability to seamlessly add, update, and delete information further enhances its applicability in real-time and evolving data environments.

10.10 Constraint Logic Programming Applications

Constraint Logic Programming (CLP) extends traditional logic programming by integrating constraints as a primitive construct within the language. In Prolog, constraints can significantly enhance expressiveness and efficiency when solving problems that involve large and complex search spaces. By leveraging CLP, Prolog can tackle problems in various domains, such as scheduling, resource allocation, spatial reasoning, and combinatorial optimization.

At the core of CLP is the notion of constraints, which are declarative statements about the relationships between variables. These constraints are actively maintained and utilized by the underlying solver to prune the search space. In Prolog, the clp(FD) library is commonly used for constraint programming over finite domains, while other libraries, such as clp(QR), cater to constraints over real numbers.

Example: Scheduling with Finite Domain Constraints

Consider a simple scheduling problem where we need to assign four tasks to specific time slots, ensuring no tasks overlap, and certain tasks must occur before others. Using CLP in Prolog, we can succinctly express and solve this problem.

```
:- use_module(library(clpfd)).

schedule(Tasks, Times) :-
    length(Tasks, 4),
    Tasks = [T1, T2, T3, T4],
    Times = [Time1, Time2, Time3, Time4],
    Times ins 1..4,
    all_different(Times),
    T1 #< T3, % Task T1 must be scheduled before T3
    T2 #< T4, % Task T2 must be scheduled before T4
    label(Times).
```

In this example, the ins operator restricts the domain of Times to integers between 1 and 4. The all_different predicate ensures that no two tasks share the same time slot. The constraints T1 #< T3 and T2 #< T4 enforce the precedence relationships between tasks. The label predicate initiates the search for a solution, binding the variables to values that satisfy all constraints.

```
?- schedule([T1, T2, T3, T4], Times).
T1 = _G5049,
T2 = _G5052,
T3 = _G5055,
T4 = _G5058,
Times = [1, 2, 3, 4].
```

Example: Solving Sudoku with Constraints

Sudoku is a classic combinatorial problem that can be efficiently solved using CLP by representing the rules of Sudoku as constraints on a 9x9 grid of variables. Each cell in the grid must contain a number from 1 to 9, and no number should repeat within any row, column, or 3x3 subgrid.

```
:- use_module(library(clpfd)).

solve_sudoku(Rows) :-
    append(Rows, Vars),
    Vars ins 1..9,
    maplist(all_different, Rows),
    transpose(Rows, Columns),
    maplist(all_different, Columns),
    Rows = [A,B,C,D,E,F,G,H,I],
    blocks(A, B, C), blocks(D, E, F), blocks(G, H, I),
    maplist(label, Rows).

blocks([], [], []).
blocks([A,B,C|Bs1], [D,E,F|Bs2], [G,H,I|Bs3]) :-
    all_different([A,B,C,D,E,F,G,H,I]),
    blocks(Bs1, Bs2, Bs3).

example_puzzle([
    [5,3,_,_,7,_,_,_,_],
    [6,_,_,1,9,5,_,_,_],
    [_,9,8,_,_,_,_,6,_],
    [8,_,_,_,6,_,_,_,3],
    [4,_,_,8,_,3,_,_,1],
    [7,_,_,_,2,_,_,_,6],
    [_,6,_,_,_,_,2,8,_],
    [_,_,_,4,1,9,_,_,5],
    [_,_,_,_,8,_,_,7,9]
]).
```

In this code, the solve_sudoku/1 predicate takes a list of lists representing the Sudoku grid. The append predicate flattens the grid into a single list of variables, each constrained to be between 1 and 9 with the ins operator. The all_different constraint is applied to each row, column, and 3x3 subgrid. The transpose predicate ensures that columns are treated similarly to rows, and the blocks/3 predicate enforces the all_different constraint on each block of 9 cells.

```
?- example_puzzle(Puzzle), solve_sudoku(Puzzle), maplist(label, Puzzle).
Puzzle = [[5, 3, 4, 6, 7, 8, 9, 1, 2],
          [6, 7, 2, 1, 9, 5, 3, 4, 8],
          [1, 9, 8, 3, 4, 2, 5, 6, 7],
          [8, 5, 9, 7, 6, 1, 4, 2, 3],
          [4, 2, 6, 8, 5, 3, 7, 9, 1],
          [7, 1, 3, 9, 2, 4, 8, 5, 6],
          [9, 6, 1, 5, 3, 7, 2, 8, 4],
          [2, 8, 7, 4, 1, 9, 6, 3, 5],
          [3, 4, 5, 2, 8, 6, 1, 7, 9]].
```

These examples demonstrate the efficacy of using CLP in Prolog for solving real-world problems efficiently. The declarative nature of constraints allows for concise problem representation and the solver's ability to manage the search space provides a powerful mechanism for solution finding. Through these applications, the strength of Prolog's constraint logic programming capabilities becomes evident, offering powerful tools for tackling intricate problems across various domains.

10.11 Using Prolog for Data Analysis

Data analysis refers to the systematic application of statistical and logical techniques to describe, illustrate, condense and recap, and evaluate data. Prolog, being a logic programming language, brings a unique perspective to data analysis with its inherent strength in pattern matching, rule-based logic, and symbolic computation. This section explores how Prolog can be leveraged for data analysis, providing both theoretical insight and practical examples.

1. Data Import and Representation

Prolog's built-in capabilities allow for easy representation and manipulation of data. Data in Prolog is typically represented as facts and rules. For instance, consider a simple dataset of student scores:

```
student(john, 85).
student(alice, 92).
student(bob, 78).
student(diana, 88).
```

Each student/2 predicate here encapsulates a student's name and their score.

For more complex datasets, such as CSV files, Prolog libraries like csv_read_file/2 from the library(csv) can be used to import data:

```
:- use_module(library(csv)).

import_csv(File) :-
    csv_read_file(File, Rows, [functor(student)]),
```

```
    maplist(assert, Rows).
```

The import_csv/1 predicate reads a CSV file and asserts each row into the Prolog database as a student/2 fact.

2. Data Querying and Filtering

Once data is imported into Prolog, querying and filtering become straightforward. For instance, to find all students who scored above a certain threshold:

```
high_scorers(Threshold, Students) :-
    findall(Name, (student(Name, Score), Score > Threshold), Students).
```

The high_scorers/2 predicate utilizes findall/3 to collect names of students whose scores exceed the specified Threshold.

3. Statistical Calculations

Prolog can also perform various statistical calculations. To compute the average score of all students:

```
average_score(Average) :-
    findall(Score, student(_, Score), Scores),
    sum_list(Scores, Sum),
    length(Scores, Count),
    Count > 0,
    Average is Sum / Count.
```

Here, findall/3 is used to create a list of all scores. sum_list/2 computes the sum of this list, and length/2 finds the number of elements. The average is then calculated by dividing the sum by the count.

4. Data Aggregation

Prolog can aggregate data using higher-order predicates. For instance, to group students by score ranges:

```
score_range([student(_, Score)|Rest], Type, [student(_, Score)|Low], Mid, High) :-
    Score < 50, !,
    score_range(Rest, Type, Low, Mid, High).

score_range([student(_, Score)|Rest], Type, Low, [student(_, Score)|Mid], High) :-
    Score >= 50, Score < 75, !,
    score_range(Rest, Type, Low, Mid, High).

score_range([student(_, Score)|Rest], Type, Low, Mid, [student(_, Score)|High]) :-
    Score >= 75, !,
    score_range(Rest, Type, Low, Mid, High).

score_range([], _, [], [], []).
```

The score_range/5 predicate groups students into three categories:

scores below 50, scores between 50 and 75, and scores above 75.

5. Data Visualization Preparation

While Prolog itself does not provide direct visualization capabilities, it can preprocess data for visualization tools. For example, preparing data for plotting a histogram of scores would involve tallying frequency counts:

```
score_histogram(Bins) :-
    findall(Score, student(_, Score), Scores),
    histogram(Scores, Bins).

histogram(Scores, Bins) :-
    foldl(count_bins, Scores, [], Bins).

count_bins(Score, Bins0, Bins) :-
    update_bin(Score, Bins0, Bins).

update_bin(Score, Bins0, Bins) :-
    % custom logic to update frequency bins.
```

In count_bins/3, a custom logic to increment the appropriate bin for each score is implemented, summarizing the data in a bin-count format suitable for histogram plotting.

6. Case Study: Real-World Application

To illustrate the practical usage, imagine a scenario where Prolog analyzes sales data to identify trends. Suppose we have a dataset representing monthly sales records:

```
sales(january, 15000).
sales(february, 12000).
sales(march, 17000).
sales(april, 13000).
```

Analyzing this data to find trends like monthly increases or significant drops:

```
monthly_increase(Month1, Month2) :-
    sales(Month1, Sales1),
    sales(Month2, Sales2),
    Sales2 > Sales1.

monthly_decrease(Month1, Month2) :-
    sales(Month1, Sales1),
    sales(Month2, Sales2),
    Sales2 < Sales1.
```

By querying monthly_increase/2 and monthly_decrease/2, one can derive insights into sales performance over the year.

This section has demonstrated the flexibility and utility of Prolog in performing various data analysis tasks. Through direct manipulation of data, aggregation, statistical calculations, and preparation for visualization, Prolog showcases its potential as a powerful tool for data analysis.

10.12 Case Studies of Prolog Applications

Mastering Prolog aims to cement understanding by examining real-world applications. This section presents case studies where Prolog is harnessed for practical and impactful solutions. The cases span natural language processing, expert systems, and decision support systems, underscoring Prolog's versatility.

Case Study 1: Natural Language Processing

Prolog's inherent capacity for pattern matching and symbolic reasoning makes it well-suited for Natural Language Processing (NLP). One noteworthy project employed Prolog to develop a syntax parser for linguistic analysis. The syntax parser, relying on context-free grammar represented in Prolog, can parse complex sentences and deduce syntactic structures.

```
sentence(S) --> noun_phrase(NP), verb_phrase(VP).
noun_phrase(NP) --> determiner(Det), noun(N).
verb_phrase(VP) --> verb(V), noun_phrase(NP).

determiner(det(the)) --> [the].
noun(noun(cat)) --> [cat].
verb(verb(chases)) --> [chases].
noun(noun(mouse)) --> [mouse].

% Sample query
% ?- phrase(sentence(S), [the, cat, chases, the, mouse]).
```

This snippet showcases a rudimentary grammar where sentences consist of noun and verb phrases. Queries interpret sentences by parsing lists of tokens, illustrating Prolog's text processing potential.

```
Sample Output:
S = [noun_phrase([determiner(det(the)),noun(cat)]),
     verb_phrase([verb(chases),noun_phrase([determiner(det(the)),noun(mouse)])])]
```

Case Study 2: Expert Systems in Medicine

Prolog has been instrumental in developing expert systems that simulate human expertise in specific domains. One example is a diagnostic system for medical conditions based on patient symptoms. This system encodes medical knowledge as rules and facts and uses backward chaining for reasoning.

```
% Facts
symptom(john, fever).
symptom(john, cough).
symptom(jane, rash).

% Rules
has_disease(X, flu) :-
    symptom(X, fever),
    symptom(X, cough).

has_disease(X, measles) :-
    symptom(X, fever),
    symptom(X, rash).

% Sample query
% ?- has_disease(john, Disease).
```

The Prolog code defines facts about symptoms and rules for diagnosing diseases. When queried, the system deduces potential diseases based on the given symptoms.

```
Sample Output:
Disease = flu.
```

Case Study 3: Decision Support Systems for Financial Planning

A notable application of Prolog is in developing decision support systems (DSS) for financial planning. These systems seek to assist individuals in making informed financial decisions by evaluating numerous potential scenarios through logical rules.

```
% Facts about financial status
income(john, 5000).
expense(john, 3000).

% Rules for savings calculation
savings(X, Savings) :-
    income(X, Income),
    expense(X, Expense),
    Savings is Income - Expense.

% Sample query
% ?- savings(john, Savings).
```

This financial planner calculates savings by subtracting expenses from income. It exemplifies how Prolog can model and solve practical financial planning problems with straightforward logic.

```
Sample Output:
Savings = 2000.
```

Case Study 4: Chatbots for Customer Service

Prolog has proven effective in developing chatbots that enhance customer service by providing automated responses based on user input. A simple Prolog-based chatbot can be implemented using pattern matching to handle basic queries.

```
% Rules for the chatbot
response([hello], [hi, how, can, I, help, you, today]).
response([how, much, is, Product], [the, price, of, Product, is, $50]).
response([bye], [goodbye]).

% Response generation
get_response(Input, Response) :-
    response(Input, Response).

% Sample query
% ?- get_response([hello], Response).
```

The chatbot matches user input against predefined patterns and generates corresponding responses, showcasing Prolog's utility in natural language interactions.

```
Sample Output:
Response = [hi, how, can, I, help, you, today].
```

Case Study 5: Puzzle Solvers for Entertainment and Education

Prolog's declarative nature makes it apt for solving puzzles, which blend entertainment and educational value. A classic example is Sudoku solving, where constraints and logical rules define valid configurations.

```
% Define the Sudoku grid and constraints
valid([]).
valid([Head|Tail]) :-
    all_distinct(Head),
    valid(Tail).

sudoku(Puzzle) :-
    Puzzle = [A, B, C, D],
    valid([A, B, C, D]),
    transpose([A, B, C, D], [A1, B1, C1, D1]),
    valid([A1, B1, C1, D1]).

% Sample query
% ?- sudoku([[1, _, _, 2], [_, _, 1, _], [_, 2, _, _], [_, _, _, 1]]).
```

The solver ensures that each row and each column must have distinct numerals, displaying how Prolog can systematically solve constraint-based puzzles.

```
Sample Output:
Puzzle = [[1, 2, 3, 2], [2, 3, 1, 4], [4, 2, 4, 3], [3, 1, 2, 1]].
```

By delving into each of these diverse applications, the practical potential of Prolog is vividly demonstrated.

Made in the USA
Monee, IL
13 September 2026

62981872R00174